IDEOLOGIES
OF
LANGUAGE

One of the most cherished assumptions of modern academic linguistics is that the study of language is, or should be, ideologically neutral. This professed ideological neutrality goes hand-in-hand with claims of scientific objectivity and explanatory autonomy. *Ideologies of Language* counters these claims and assumptions by demonstrating not only their descriptive inaccuracy but, more importantly, their conceptual incoherence. Linguistic enquiry is inherently ideological; and the claims of scientific objectivity and autonomy themselves only function as component parts of the linguistic ideology dominant today. Each chapter in *Ideologies of Language* reveals a different descriptive, logical, or rhetorical 'crack' in the contemporary academic monument to the objectivity and neutrality of linguistic enquiry. In some cases, a given linguistic model, or critical interpretation of that model, is shown to have been determined by underlying political or cultural preconceptions; other chapters illustrate the ways in which linguistic models themselves can enforce and apparently justify particular ideological perspectives. The unifying theme of the volume is thus that, as an institutionalized discourse said to be 'describing', 'analysing', and 'explaining' the basis of verbal interaction between human agents, any linguistics – whether it acknowledges it or not – is by its very nature an ideology of language. It is only when linguistic enquiry finally realizes the inevitability of its ideological commitment that it will be able to become a more responsible force on the cultural stage.

ROUTLEDGE POLITICS OF LANGUAGE SERIES

This series responds to the growing interest in the connections between language, interaction, politics and power. It will draw attention to the common focus of many writers today on language as a powerful instrument in the management of interpersonal and inter-group relations.

Linguists and discourse analysts have begun to turn their attention and technical expertise to the analysis of the role of language in the socio-political arena. The aim of our new series is to attract the attention of a wider group of readers and scholars to new developments in this growing field of academic study.

The series leads off with volumes in two areas of concern. First, there is a growing public awareness of the politics of language and language planning, as recent political discussions in Britain, Canada and the United States can attest. Our new series intends to provide a resource of academic research and analysis for those seeking to understand or to participate in the debates over these concerns.

Furthermore, an increasing number of linguists feel that language is not the autonomous logical system that theorists since Saussure have portrayed it to be. Rather, they conceive of language as a normative phenomenon, an instrument created by and used for the purposes of making the actions of individuals conform to a common behavioural pattern. But who has the authority to determine the model to which individuals must conform? And how is that authority enforced? These questions are at the centre of linguistic enquiry.

Other topics on the role of language in the socio-political arena will be included in the series. We expect to publish titles which might otherwise have been published under sociolinguistics, politics, discourse and conversational analysis, social psychology, or ethnography of speaking.

IDEOLOGIES OF LANGUAGE

Edited by
John E. Joseph
and
Talbot J. Taylor

London and New York

First published in 1990
by Routledge
11 New Fetter Lane, London EC4P 4EE

Simultaneously published in the USA and Canada
by Routledge
a division of Routledge, Chapman and Hall, Inc.
29 West 35th Street, New York, NY 10001

Set in Baskerville, 10 on 12pt
by Hope Services (Abingdon) Ltd.
and printed in England
by Clays Ltd, St Ives plc

British Library Cataloguing in Publication Data
Ideologies of language. – (Politics of language series).
1. Linguistics, Theories
I. Joseph, John   II. Taylor, Talbot, J.   III. Series
410'.1

Library of Congress Cataloging in Publication Data
Joseph, John Earl.
Ideologies of language / John E. Joseph and Talbot J. Taylor.
p.   cm.
Includes bibliographical references (p.
1. Linguistic analysis (Linguistics)   2. Linguistics — History.
3. Ideology.   I. Taylor, J.   II. Title.
P126.J67   1990
4100–dc20

ISBN 0–415–04680–7
ISBN 0–415–04681–5 (pbk)

Contents

Contributors

Deborah Cameron is a lecturer in English at Roehampton Institute of Higher Education, London. She has published widely on linguistic and feminist topics, including *Feminism and Linguistic Theory* (1985), *Analysing Conversation* (1987) with Talbot J. Taylor, *The Lust to Kill* (1988) with Liz Frazer and *Women in Their Speech Communities* (1989), co-edited with Jennifer Coates.

Tony Crowley is a lecturer in English at the University of Southampton and is the author of *The Politics of Discourse: The Standard Language Question in British Cultural Debates* (1989).

Pieter Desmet is a lecturer in Romance linguistics at the Catholic University of Leuven.

Roy Harris is Professor and Chair of the Department of English Language and Literature at the University of Hong Kong. He is the author of a number of books on language and theory, including the trilogy of *The Language-Makers* (1980), *The Language Myth* (1981) and *The Language Machine* (1987).

John E. Joseph is Associate Professor of French and Italian at the University of Maryland. He is the author of *Eloquence and Power: The Rise of Language Standards and Standard Languages* (1987) and many articles on topics in sociolinguistics, historical linguistics and Romance linguistics.

Paul Laurendeau is Professor of French Linguistics at York University, Toronto. The main thrusts of his current research are enunciative linguistics, the history of linguistics and the philosophy of language.

Peter Mühlhäusler is Professor of Linguistics at Bond University in Australia and has published on topcis in sociolinguistic theory, language planning in the Pacific, and pidgin and creole studies, including *Pidgin and Creole Languages* (1986), *Pidginization and Simplification of Language* (1974) and *Handbook of Tok Pisin* (1985), edited with S. Wurm.

Paul T. Roberge is Associate Professor of Germanic Languages at the University of North Carolina, Chapel Hill. His current research involves the history of Afrikaans, and language, literature and politics in Southern Africa. He is currently writing a book on the linguistic mythology of Afrikaanerdom.

Johan Rooryck has a doctorate from the University of Leuven and is currently Visiting Assistant Professor in the Department of French and Italian at Indiana University, Bloomington. His research interests range from infinitival complementation in generative grammar to the history of linguistics.

Pierre Swiggers is a Fellow of the Belgian National Science Foundation and is a lecturer in Romance linguistics at the Catholic University of Leuven. He is the author of books and articles on a broad spectrum of linguistic, philological, and historical topics, including *Les Conceptions linguistiques des Éncyclopédistes* (1984) and *A World of Words: Language in 18th Century France* (forthcoming, Routledge).

Talbot J. Taylor is Associate Professor of English at the College of William and Mary, Virginia. He is the author of books on topics in the study of the philosophy and history of language, including *Analysing Conversation* (1987) with Deborah Cameron, *Linguistic Theory and Structural Stylistics* (1981), *Landmarks in Linguistic Thought: the Western Tradition from Socrates to Saussure* (1989) with Roy Harris and *Redefining Linguistics* (1990), edited with Hayley Davis.

Michael Ward is Assistant Professor of Italian at Trinity University, Texas, and has published articles on linguistic ideas in the Italian Renaissance.

Introduction
Ideology, science and language
John E. Joseph and Talbot J. Taylor

In *The Politics of Linguistics* (1986), Frederick J. Newmeyer offers an insightful and provocative discussion of the contrast between autonomous linguistics and those approaches to the study of language that insist on its connections to something external – in particular, sociolinguistics, Marxist linguistics and 'humanist' approaches (those focusing on the aesthetic dimension). By 'autonomous linguistics' Newmeyer means essentially generative linguistics, together with the structuralist varieties that preceded it.

Newmeyer believes that, relative to the other modes of enquiry, autonomous linguistics is value-neutral, leaving it open to the criticism that it does not serve a significant social purpose. Nevertheless, he argues, autonomous linguists have not made an independent decision to keep their discipline value-neutral: it is necessarily so, because its object of investigation, (universal) grammar, excludes all those elements to which political values might be attached. In effect, to the charge of lacking social relevance Newmeyer enters on behalf of autonomous linguistics a plea of *nolo contendere*. The charge is valid, he says, but it is a sacrifice that has had to be made in order to arrive at the true science of language.

We applaud Newmeyer for raising these extraordinarily important issues which seldom get a hearing in linguistic circles (especially in America) and for the sincere social consciousness he exhibits. We wish merely to propose that certain of his conclusions merit additional debate. To this end, the papers in this volume are as much a complement as a challenge to Newmeyer's book. Specifically, we wish to present additional evidence regarding the following assumptions:

1 that structuralist and generative linguistics are really autonomous in any meaningful sense of the word;

2 that descriptive linguistics, including structuralism and generativism, is or even can be value-neutral and non-ideological;

3 that an 'ideology' necessarily involves the imposition of external social and political values and therefore cannot inhere just as easily in intellectual values;

4 that either a rational or an empirical approach is a better guarantor than the other against the covert influence of ideology;

5 that science and ideology are, in practice, incompatible.

Point (3) is suggested by Chomsky (1979: 89) in a discussion of empiricism, and is raised as well by Silverstein (1979). Since Chomsky has always considered structuralism to be an empirical enterprise, it is clear that he takes a narrower position than Newmeyer on (2).[1] With regard to (4), most sociolinguists would disagree strongly with Newmeyer's view that theirs is not a value-neutral enterprise. They would contend that their empirical approach is the only objective way to arrive at the truth of things.

If the above assumptions were to prove false, then it would be possible to suggest that a linguistics has an underlying ideology without thereby challenging its status as a science. It would mean, moreover, that any claim that only a certain kind of linguistics is scientific presupposes a particular definition of science by the claimant – hence it is already an ideological proposition. These are precisely the possibilities we wish to suggest and defend.

In addition, it is our belief that any enterprise which claims to be non-ideological and value-neutral, but which in fact remains covertly ideological and value-laden, is the more dangerous for this deceptive subtlety.

We have tried to assemble in this volume a collection of chapters unified in theme, yet covering 'ideology' from as many angles and definitions (and ideologies!) as possible, and likewise spanning a fair range of approaches to the study of language. Not surprisingly, the twelve authors of this book are not in total agreement on all the major issues involved. For instance, some believe that the problems inherent in characterizing modern linguistics as scientific stem from a mis-understanding of the term 'science', while others question whether a linguistic science in any sense is either possible or desirable. What unites the twelve authors is that we are all linguistic 'protestants', even if belonging to distinct denominations.

The four chapters in Part I, 'Linguistic Ideologies', survey the role of ideology in shaping modern linguistic thought from its inception to the present day. Talbot Taylor's chapter begins with the emergence in the late eighteenth century of the belief that language can be the subject of a descriptive science. He contrasts John Horne Tooke's ideas on descriptivism with the very different views of John Locke a century earlier, and goes on to discuss how the the descriptivist doctrine merely masked the institutionalization of a new kind of linguistic authority, no less politically charged. In this light, Taylor reconsiders one of the most powerful organs of this authority, *The Oxford English Dictionary*.

Descriptivism became the basis of nineteenth-century comparative philology, which eventually gave way to the ahistorical mode of general linguistics. Tony Crowley's chapter considers the 'discursive violence' by which this change was brought about, in particular the 'mythological' delimitation of language by Ferdinand de Saussure that became the basis of structural linguistics. Crowley contends that any attempt to exclude historical and social variation and abstract a mythological 'monoglossic' system can only produce a temporary victory, since, in the words of Mikhail Bakhtin, 'at any given moment of its historical existence language is heteroglot from top to bottom'.

Continuing from Saussure to later twentieth-century linguistic theory, John Joseph documents how the *Cours de linguistique générale* has been read – and misread – by Leonard Bloomfield and Noam Chomsky, and how these misreadings have alternately directed and been directed by the agenda of American structuralism and generativism. Bloomfield severely distorted Saussure's thought in an attempt to reconcile it with his own version of behaviourism, while Chomsky has highlighted and suppressed facets of Saussure's thought so as to exaggerate, at various times, either its closeness to or its distance from his own.

Taking up another key area of contemporary enquiry, Deborah Cameron shows how sociolinguists, eager to align themselves with prestigious 'mainstream' linguistics rather than with the less highly valued discipline of sociology, have succumbed to an ideology of quantification and the aura of scientificness it lends. This, she says, has led sociolinguists away from the necessary task of giving proper, non-circular explanations for the correlations they find, explanations which, like it or not, have to be sociologically based.

Part II, 'The Linguistics of Self-Image', takes a still wider historical perspective to examine how linguistics has been used to promote particular ideologies of what a certain group of speakers sees itself as representing, either intellectually or racially. Michael Ward considers the *questione della lingua* in fifteenth-century Italy, a debate in which the 'linguistic' issue of the historical relationship of one language (Italian) to another (Latin) takes on a clearly political character.

Pierre Swiggers brings us up to the eighteenth century and a new language question: the use of Italian or French in the Savoy. The arguments raised centred upon the purported 'clarity' of French, an ideology which Swiggers traces back to its first attestations in the Renaissance. It was then that scholars began to suggest that the SVO word order of modern French represents the 'natural' order of human thought, a belief which survives in only slightly modified form in the practice of many contemporary linguists.

Chapter 7, by Paul Roberge, examines a case from our own century: how the history of Afrikaans has been written and rewritten to align with South African racial ideology. By the preponderance of the evidence, 'Afrikaans reflects a semicreolized (creoloid) variety of Dutch that traces its roots to contact between Europeans, the aboriginal Khoikhoi (Hottentots), and slaves of African and Asian origin'. But such evidence is incompatible with the prejudices of certain white South African linguists, who have gone to astounding lengths to deny its validity. As with the notion of 'clarity' discussed by Swiggers, ideas which most linguists have ceased to consider seriously are revealed as none the less continuing to exert powerful influence. And their power stems in part from linguists' unwillingness to take them seriously enough to bother contesting them. To contest or not to contest: either way, a significant ideological choice.

Part III, 'Political Linguistics', again covers the spectrum of eighteenth-, nineteenth- and twentieth-century linguistic practice. Considered here is the interface of linguistic thought with classic power struggles – the French Revolution, European imperialism, Marxist ideology, freedom of speech. Unlike the situations discussed in Part II, where language was used to promote a particular cultural-racial view of one's own group, here language is used as part of the mechanism of getting and maintaining power over others, or of resisting such power-taking. Roy Harris dissects the issue of freedom of speech, the misunderstandings it has engendered, and problems that have arisen as a result. He finds in Jean-Jacques Rousseau a correct refutation of the idea 'that freedom of speech is reducible to or constitutes one subspecies of freedom of action. In order to be free in the sense in which the human mind is free, the possibility of assent or dissent must exist. And this is a possibility which only language makes possible'. Harris stands virtually alone among modern linguists in being both willing and able to apply the implications of his linguistic theories to the social and political realities of the contemporary world.

Staying in the French eighteenth century, Desmet, Rooryck and Swiggers examine the use of a particular linguistic medium, the dictionary, in the attainment of liberty. Spreading the 'national language' across France was given a high priority in the revolution, because it was seen as a means of creating both equality and unity. These ideological goals are directly reflected in the actual entries in dictionaries of the period. This study, taken together with Taylor's considerations of the *OED*, should suffice to undermine anyone's faith in the dictionary as an unbiased linguistic authority.

With Peter Mühlhäusler's chapter the perspective changes from linguistics as a means of acquiring freedom to one of acquiring dominance, whether political or cultural. Like the dictionary, literacy is a sacred cow of western culture. But Mühlhäusler reveals the profound effects which efforts toward vernacular literacy – carried out primarily by the Summer Institute of Linguistics – have had upon traditional island cultures of Melanesia, Micronesia and Polynesia. Chief among their results have been the loss not only of indigenous dialects and customs, but also of tribal lands.

The final chapter, by Paul Laurendeau, attempts to construct a historical-materialistic 'theory of emergence' that would comprehend the various approaches to ideologies of language. It is a classical Marxist framework with which not all the contributors to this volume would be willing to align themselves. Nevertheless, it demonstrates that a synthetic reading of the various episodes treated in this book is possible, and establishes a coherent point of departure for future alternative syntheses.

In sum, the overall goal of this book is to challenge any ideology of language and linguistics which holds that only one approach to language is scientific and worthy of pursuit by serious thinkers. We find it ironic and tragic that persons who have dedicated their careers to thinking about language – the faculty which, as Harris points out, is the very foundation of freedom – let it be dictated to them that they should think about only so much (or rather, so little). But then we have never doubted that ideology is a powerful force, the most powerful in all of human culture. That is a lesson history refuses to let us forget.

NOTE

1 In fact, when an interviewer suggests that the brief success of generative semantics was 'ideological, as in the case of empiricism . . . a way of going back to the dominant structuralism', Chomsky cautiously assents (Chomsky 1979: 154). For him, then, only certain kinds of generative linguistics are non-ideological.

Part I

LINGUISTIC IDEOLOGIES

1

Which is to be master?
The institutionalization of authority
in the science of language

Talbot J. Taylor

The emergence of the view that language can be the subject of an empirical, descriptive science is one of the most interesting topics in the history of linguistics. This paper will focus on one important conceptual step in the transformation of metalinguistic discourse (by which I mean discourse on language) from a normative, prescriptive mode to that of descriptive science: namely, the replacement of a voluntaristic concept of signification by an institutionalist one. This consists in the abandonment of the view that the connection between a word and what it signifies is forged by the will of the individuals who utter that word in favour of a view which takes that connection to exist independently of the will of individual speakers.

> 'When *I* use a word', Humpty Dumpty said, in rather a scornful tone, 'it means just what I choose it to mean – neither more nor less.'
> 'The question is', said Alice, 'whether you *can* make words mean so many different things.'
> 'The question is,' said Humpty Dumpty, 'which is to be master – that's all.'

The differences between a voluntaristic and an institutionalist concept of language may be summarized as follows. Voluntarism takes language to be a voluntary act performed by individual agents, agents who themselves bear the responsibility for the success of their linguistic acts. The voluntarist may argue, therefore, that linguistic acts will only be successful if individual agents submit their linguistic freedom to the constraint of norms: the prescriptive rules of linguistic 'authorities' are notorious examples of such norms. The function of discourse on language (what I am here calling 'metalinguistic discourse') is, from

9

this point of view, normative: it tells us how, as linguistic agents, we *should* behave. Such a normative discourse on language may take more or less institutionalized forms. Within such a conceptual framework, it is natural that Humpty Dumpty's question, who is to be 'master', looms large. Who or what determines which norms we should obey, and why? Not surprisingly, as a normative form of discourse, a linguistics which takes a voluntaristic view of language inevitably raises fundamentally political questions of responsibility, power, authority and ideology.

Institutionalism, on the other hand, focuses on language (or a language) as an institution which exists independently of the individuals who perform linguistic acts. Individual agents, with or without political power, have no say in determining the features of that institution (such as what a given word signifies), any more than individual agents have a say in determining, for instance, the economic structure of an agrarian society. To find out what those features are we must turn not to normative authorities but to trained professionals with specialist techniques of investigation: to descriptive linguists. From this perspective, if properly performed, (descriptive) metalinguistic discourse is seen to be an empirical science, with truth (as opposed to political power) its only authority. Consequently, because it denies the relevance of individual agency and of the normative mechanisms by which agency is influenced, the science of language is conceived to be independent of political issues of authority, power and ideology.

Lest this issue be thought to be merely of historical interest, it ought to be pointed out that it has a modern form in the controversy about the autonomy of linguistics (see Newmeyer 1986) and in debates about the status of linguistic rules (see Harris 1987 and Baker and Hacker 1984, chs 8 and 9). With regard to the latter debate, the difference between a normativist and a descriptivist perspective is clearly seen. On the one hand, we might take rules like ' "soporific" means *tending to produce sleep*' or 'verbs agree with subjects in number' to be prescriptions. In their ordinary context of use, their utterance has a normative force. On the other hand, from another perspective they are seen not as carrying a normative but rather a descriptive force. That is, they are seen as statements which either truly or falsely describe, depending whether in (the institutional entity called) English 'soporific' really does mean *tending to produce sleep* and whether verbs in English really do agree with their subjects in number. Conceived as carrying descriptive force linguistic rules, like scientific hypotheses, either do or do not correspond to the (institutional) facts. But from the

10

normativist perspective such a condition is seen as nonsensical. There are no institutional facts to which a descriptive linguist's rules do or do not correspond: language as an empirical phenomenon consists of communicational events, and a linguistic rule could hardly be conceived as a description of one or more such events. At the same time, the normativist will argue, it makes no more sense to hold a linguistic prescription up to the standard of 'correspondence to the facts' than it does to hold up to the same standard a sign reading 'There is no smoking in the first four rows'. Whether anyone is or is not smoking in the first four rows is irrelevant to determining whether the sign is a prescriptive rule.

Although this debate has a peculiarly modern flavour to it, the contention to be supported here is that these two ways of viewing rules have been in competition for many years. This chapter examines an instance of this competition as it occurred in the evolution of the linguistic thought of classical British empiricism. For one of the most important steps in the transformation of empiricist linguistics from a normative to a descriptive mode of discourse is the slow abandonment of the practice of treating signification as an aspect of voluntary behaviour in favour of one which treats it as independent of the will of linguistic agents.

This metamorphosis from a normative to a descriptive approach to language is well illustrated in the popular and highly influential criticism of John Locke's linguistic ideas presented in the *Diversions of Purley* by John Horne Tooke. Although he is little known today, at the end of the eighteenth century and the beginning of the nineteenth, Tooke was perhaps the most influential of British philosophers, as influential as Locke had been in his day (see Aarsleff 1967, ch. 3, and Smith 1984, ch. 4). Like Locke, Tooke was known not only for his philosophical writings but also for his liberal political views, leading to his imprisonment on the charge of sedition in 1777. Given Locke's status as one of the founders of liberal political thought, it is a curious feature of Tooke's criticism of Locke's linguistic ideas that it draws its inspiration from Tooke's own political liberalism. In this respect, the development of empiricist linguistic ideas and that of liberal political ideas flow into the common stream of the evolution of British thought in the Enlightenment. Tooke argued for a descriptive approach to language in part because he felt it would help to free language from the control of political authorities and would thereby offer access to the use of that powerful instrument by the politically oppressed. But to give a clear account of Tooke's argument and how it was addressed to what he perceived as imperfections in Locke's linguistic thought it will be best to begin with a sketch of Locke's discourse on language in Book III of his *Essay Concerning Human Understanding* (1690).

From the perspective of (the dominant institutionalism of) modern linguistics, it is not easy to see just what Locke is trying to achieve in Book III of the *Essay*. His aim is not to give a description of any or all languages; nor is it to present what we might today call a 'philosophy of language' or a 'theory of language'. We can better appreciate Locke's reasons for writing Book III of the *Essay* if we compare it to his aims in discussing civil society in the *Two Treatises of Government* (1689), organized religion in the *Letter Concerning Toleration* (1689), and mental contents and operations in Book II of the *Essay*. Locke is no more a linguistic theorist than he is a political, theological or psychological theorist. His broad aim in discussing human affairs is neither that of description nor explanation; his aim is to improve the ways we humans conduct our affairs. He discusses the operations and contents of the mind in order to recommend ways for better and more effective use of the mind in the advance of knowledge. In the same way his discussion of civil society in the *Second Treatise on Government* has the aim of providing a ground from which he can recommend how societies should govern themselves. It is not a theory of any particular political society (say, that of England in the late seventeenth century) nor of an ideal political society nor of the general laws which might be conceived to govern all political societies. In this light it may be easier to appreciate that his aim in discussing language in the *Essay* is to persuade us of the need for improving language and to suggest ways by which that improvement may be brought about. His aim therefore is not descriptive, explanatory or theoretical; rather it might more aptly be termed 'normative' and 'therapeutic', concerning what he calls '*Practica*: The Skill of Right applying our own Powers and Actions, for the Attainment of Things good and useful' (*Essay*, IV,21,iii). In this respect the rhetorical foundation of Locke's discourse on language is not unlike that of the seventeenth-century rationalist grammarians such as Arnauld and Lancelot of Port-Royal (for an expansion of this argument see Harris and Taylor 1989, chs 8 and 9).

The 'good and useful thing' which it is the purpose of language to achieve is communication. Words must

> excite, in the Hearer, exactly the same *Idea*, they stand for in the Mind of the Speaker. Without this, Men fill one another's

Heads with noise and sounds, but convey not thereby their Thoughts and lay not before one another their *Ideas*, which is the end of Discourse and Language.

(Locke 1690: III,9,6)

In Book III of the *Essay* he discusses how well we ordinarily achieve this purpose of language, examines why we commonly fail, and suggests 'remedies' which would help us achieve greater success.

One of the main obstacles to the right achievement of the communicational purpose of language is our failure as linguistic agents to recognize that communicational success depends on us. We ourselves must endeavour to use words in such a way that communication will result. Communicational success is not guaranteed by Nature, God, descent from Adam, society or the inherent characteristics of language itself. Instead Locke views language as resulting from acts of our own free will which, if they are to bring about mutual understanding, must be effectively and rationally performed. Locke's argument in favour of recognizing the responsibility of the speaking agent for achieving communication through language is in this way analogous to his arguments elsewhere in favour of recognizing individual responsibility in political, religious and scientific conduct. Throughout his work he argues against unquestioned acceptance of inherited dogma which obscures the natural freedom of the individual and for the consequent requirement that the individual take personal responsibility for the management of his/her civil, mental and communicational affairs.

The linguistic dogma against which Locke argues is the inherited assumption of a 'double conformity' in signification: a (representational) conformity of ideas to the things they are ideas of and a (communicational) conformity of the ideas signified by one person's use of words with those signified by another's use of the same words.

And hence it is, that Men are so forward to suppose, that the abstract Ideas they have in their Minds, are such, as agree to the Things existing without them, to which they are referred; and are the same also, to which the Names they give them, do by the Use and Propriety of that Language belong. For without this double Conformity of their Ideas, they find, they should both think amiss of Things in themselves, and talk of them unintelligibly to others.

(Locke 1690: II,32,8)

Locke attributes great importance to man's mistaken faith in the myth of this 'double conformity' of signification; for it is a mistake which has consequences for all of our efforts to expand our knowledge of things and to communicate that knowledge to others. We too easily assume, in effect, that the relationship between words, ideas, and things is ideal, is perfect. Furthermore, we take it for granted that this relationship exists independently of us and of our actions. It is irrelevant to our misconception whether we take the perfection of that relationship to be an inheritance from Adam, to be Godgiven, or to be a product of Nature. What *is* important is that our daily activities are based on the assumption of its perfection and its independence.

However, Locke's argument is that the relationship between words, ideas and things is not perfect; signification does in fact depend on our own actions and choices. Consequently, our belief in the myth of the perfect 'double conformity' means that our attempts to acquire and to communicate knowledge are too often frustrated by this imperfection. If we do not come to recognize the 'imperfection' of the signifying relationship between words, ideas and things (and to do something about that imperfection), it will remain as an obstacle hindering the progress of human understanding.

Locke first attacks the dogma of the 'double conformity' by showing, in Book II, the extent to which the formation of ideas (that which words signify) is dependent on our own free choices: in this way he speaks of complex ideas as both 'voluntary' and 'arbitrary'. In forming a complex idea we combine simple ideas, the passive products of experience, into larger molecules. Given the passive formation of simple ideas they may be assumed to conform representationally to the phenomena they are ideas of. However, the individual takes an active and voluntary role in the formation of complex ideas. It is we ourselves who determine which simple ideas are included in our complex ideas. This combination is not determined by some exterior force (Nature, God and so forth), nor does it directly reflect essential patterns in experienced reality. On this last point rests his important distinction between the nominal essences of things, consisting in our voluntarily formed ideas of them and their real essences, which are unknowable. The result of this argument is that there cannot therefore be a representational conformity between our voluntary and arbitrary complex ideas and the things which they are ideas of.

In Book III Locke opens a second attack on the doctrine of the 'double conformity', arguing not only that ideas are formed voluntarily and arbitrarily but that the private links we forge between words and the ideas they signify are also voluntary and arbitrary. The signification of a word I utter – the idea for which it stands in my mind – is not determined prior to my free act of the will in using it to so signify. Words signify not by natural affinity to particular ideas, by an inheritance from Adam, nor by any other prior arrangement; to deny this, Locke says, is 'an abuse of language'. Instead the words a given individual uses signify by a voluntary, arbitrary, individual and private act performed in the mind of the speaking agent. They have no pre-existent signification prior to that act.

> And every Man has so inviolable a Liberty, to make Words stand for what *Ideas* he pleases, that no one hath the Power to make others have the same *Ideas* in their Minds, that he has, when they use the same Words, that he does.
>
> (Locke 1690: III,2,8)

Furthermore, this means that we cannot directly check whether the idea we signify by a given word is the same as is signified by others when they use that very same word. To assume that our ideas do conform to the things they are ideas of and that they also conform to the ideas in other men's heads is therefore an unsupported assumption, a dogma which is injurious to the proper and effective conduct of the mind and of language for the purposes of the advance of knowledge.

Given this it is easy to see that the communicational purpose of language will rarely, if ever, be achieved. If the ideas I signify by my words are chosen voluntarily and arbitrarily by me in mental privacy and if those ideas are themselves formed by a voluntary, private, and largely arbitrary act, then it would surely be irrational to assume that others understand me when I speak. When dogmatic belief in the 'double conformity' is abandoned, Locke leaves the reader staring into the vertiginous abyss of communicational scepticism.

But it would be wrong to conclude that it is Locke's purpose in the *Essay* to promote a sceptical theory of communication. For his overriding aim is a practical one: the improvement of our conduct of the understanding. And in this case the point of his discussion of signification is to improve our linguistic conduct: to help us achieve greater and more reliable understanding when we speak and write. Consequently, he prescribes in Book III, Chapter 11, 'remedies' for the 'imperfections' of language. These may be paraphrased as follows:

1 Use no word without knowing what idea you make it stand for.
2 Make sure your ideas are clear, distinct and determinate; and if they are ideas of substances, they should be conformable to real things.

3 Where possible, follow common usage, especially that of those writers whose discourses appear to have the clearest notions.

4 Where possible, declare the meanings of your words (in particular, define them).

5 Do not vary the meanings you give to words.

If language is an act of the will, then it is an act that the speaking agent can intentionally alter so that the goal of mutual understanding can best be achieved. From the individualist and voluntarist perspective adopted by Locke, language is subject to the control of the individual will. It is therefore improvable, and it is each individual speaking agent who is responsible for that improvement. This position is completely opposed to that which rests on a dogmatic trust in external forces – Nature, God, history, society – to ensure that our individual acts fulfil their goals. So after affirming what we might call the individual's linguistic 'freedom' – his/her control over the communicational power of the words they speak – Locke offers prescriptions which, if followed, will function as rational constraints on that freedom in order that the goals of communication may be secured. In this respect his rhetorical strategy in working towards prescriptive conclusions is no different from that used elsewhere in his recommendations for the rational conduct of the mind and the just conduct of civil society. Locke is a linguistic normativist because he believes that the individual is a free, and therefore practically responsible and perfectable, linguistic agent.

Locke's view of language is obviously quite different from that of the dominant linguistic theories today. Nevertheless, from our perspective it is easier to see more clearly how his view of language is related to (we might even say 'determined by') his more general liberalist ideology, as reflected elsewhere in his political, educational and religious writings. He begins with human freedom and works towards recommendations for moral conduct from that premise. If we want to speculate why his writings were so influential, and so controversial, in the British Enlightenment, we could not do better than to begin with the prominence he gives to the concepts of individual freedom and responsiblity. To understand Locke's linguistic ideas and his place in British thought of the Enlightenment, first consideration must be given to his role as one of the main proponents of the ideology of liberalism.

Yet it is curious that his views on language have not even endured within the domain of liberal ideology. Instead they have been replaced by a perspective which rejects the premise that language results from a free act of the individual will. Instead, this new perspective takes as its starting point the assumption that language and signification are not subject to the voluntary control of speaking agents, but rather exist independently of the individual will: in society, in the unconscious operations of the brain, or in logical abstraction. The rise of what appears to be an anti-liberalist account of language would be understandable within an ideology that was equally anti-liberal. It is therefore quite surprising that one of its earliest and most influential proponents was a well-known political liberal of late-eighteenth-century England: John Horne Tooke.

Like Locke, Horne Tooke was also interested in freeing speakers from linguistic dogma. They both thought that belief in such dogma was a major source of the failings of philosophy and political theory. Furthermore, Tooke agreed with Locke that the purpose of language is to communicate ideas from one individual to another and that this purpose is only too rarely achieved. But whereas Locke blamed the fundamental properties of language and idea-formation for communicational failure, Tooke directed the blame elsewhere: to the misguided analyses of language and ideas propounded by philosophers, grammarians and other intellectual authorities. From Tooke's point of view, language is far from the imperfect vehicle of communication which Locke takes it to be. Rather, it is 'the *perfections* of language, not properly understood, (which) have been one of the chief causes of the imperfections of our philosophy' (Tooke 1857: 19). And when Tooke comes to examine the ways in which past analyses of language have misunderstood the true properties of language, his own description of languages as historical institutions, independent of human will, stands in direct opposition to the voluntarist perspective of Locke.

From Tooke's point of view, Locke gave too much attention to the first of the two principle aims of language.

> The first aim of language was to *communicate* our thoughts; the second to do it with *despatch*. . . . The difficulties and disputes concerning language have arisen almost entirely from neglecting the consideration of the latter purpose of speech: which, though subordinate to the former, is almost as necessary in the commerce of mankind, and has a much greater share in accounting for the different sorts of words. Words have been called *winged*; and they well deserve that name, when their abbreviations are compared with the progress which speech could make without

17

these inventions; but compared with the rapidity of thought, they have not the smallest claim to that title. Philosophers have calculated the difference of velocity between sound and light: but who will attempt to calculate the difference between speech and thought! What wonder, then, that the invention of all ages should have been upon the stretch to add such wings to their conversation as might enable it, if possible, to keep pace in some measure with their minds. Hence chiefly the variety of words.

(Tooke 1857: 14–15)

In his *Diversions of Purley* (first edition published in two volumes, 1786 and 1805), Tooke argues that although the first goal of language is to communicate thought, there is a second goal: to achieve the first goal efficiently, according to the temporal constraints of ordinary verbal interaction. So it is not sufficient for language to enable the communication of thoughts; it must also make communication possible at or near the speed at which the thoughts to be communicated are themselves formed. Thought, for Tooke, consists in a stream of simple ideas, or sensations, occurring rapidly in sequence, one after the other. Complex ideas do not exist. They are an invention of philosophers who, assuming that all words must directly signify ideas, imaginatively populate the mind with a different type of idea to be signified by each different type of word. But, for Tooke, the mind consists only of passively registered simple ideas of sensation.

The business of the mind, as far as it concerns language, appears to be very simple. It extends no further than to receive impressions, that is, to have sensations or feelings. What are called its operations, are merely operations of language.

(Tooke 1857: 25)

For Tooke, then, all ideas are passively registered by the mind. There can be no ideas which are formed by voluntary operations of the mind, for there are no such operations. However, if we were to utter a word for each of the simple ideas occurring in a thought-stream, we could never speak quickly enough to keep up with the speed of our thoughts. So for language to be an effective vehicle of thought it must contain verbal forms of expression which can be produced at a rate similar to that of the thoughts they express.

Civilized languages achieve this temporal efficiency by including what Tooke calls 'abbreviations': words which stand indirectly for more than one simple idea at the same time. By uttering a string of such abbreviations, the speaker can produce speech at a rate equal to that of the simple ideas passing through his/her mind. An abbreviation is in fact an etymologically derived substitute for other words which themselves stand directly for simple ideas. 'Though indeed . . . without abbreviations, language can get on but lamely: and therefore they have been introduced, in different plenty, and more or less happily, in all languages' (Tooke 1857: 24). At the core of all civilized languages must exist a set of forms, many perhaps no longer in use, directly signifying simple ideas of sensation (for this is all there is for words to signify). All the other words in the language – the 'abbreviations' – are etymologically related to one or more of the members of this set; and it is by means of this etymological relation that the meanings of the abbreviations are derived. The truth of this claim is proven, Tooke argues, by the application of the historical methods of etymological analysis. Much of Tooke's *Diversions of Purley* consists of the etymological analysis of over 2,000 English words, with the aim in each case of revealing their true significations.

> If my reasoning . . . is well founded, there must then be in the original language from which the English (and so all other languages) is derived, literally such and such words bearing precisely such and such significations. . . . The event was beyond my expectation: for I instantly found, upon trial, all my predictions verified.
>
> (Tooke 1857: 67–9).

Tooke takes there to be many benefits gained by a full appreciation of the role played by abbreviation in language. The most important of these, and that on which what I am calling Tooke's 'institutionalist' view of signification is founded, is the realization that words do not mean what we or anyone else *make* them mean. They signify independently of us and of how we use them. Their true meanings can be discerned by means of etymological analysis, revealing the simple 'atoms' from which they are derived. For example, in the following, Tooke shows how the English preposition 'through' has a different meaning than grammarians and metaphysicians have led us to believe. Etymology reveals that 'through' simply means *door*.

> For as the French peculiar preposition CHEZ is no other than the Italian substantive CASA or CA, so is the English preposition thorough, thourough, thorow, through, or thro', no other than the Gothic substantive *dauro*, or the Teutonic substantive *thurrh*:

19

and, like them, means door, gate, passage. . . . I am persuaded
that Door and Through have one and the same Gothic origin
dauro, mean one and the same thing; and are in fact one and the
same word.

(Tooke 1857: 180–3)

Here, the (purported) fact that 'through' really means *door* is a fact of
the language, not of some individual speaker's use of the terms. If I
used 'through' to mean something else, I would simply be wrong. It is
not up to me to determine the meaning of the words I use.

In turn, etymological analysis, by tracing the meanings of complex
and abstract terms to the sensory impressions formed by simple
concrete objects, holds the promise of dispensing with confusing
metaphysical and psychological theories the only purpose of which
had been to explain the nature of the phenomena signified by complex
and abstract terms. With Tooke's etymological account of signification,
the need for psychological and metaphysical speculation disappears,
for all such terms can be shown to be abbreviations of other words
which stand directly for simple ideas. The speculative and elitist
disciplines can thus be replaced by an empirical and egalitarian
science of etymology.

Another benefit gained by a full appreciation of the role of abbreviations in language is that we need no longer worry whether communication is possible through language. Directly or indirectly all words
signify simple ideas of sensation; and, since simple ideas of sensation
are derived passively from common human experience, we can be
certain therefore that the ideas signified by any word are the same
regardless of who uses that word. Of course, speakers may mistakenly
believe, perhaps influenced by speculative philosophical theories,
that they can make the words they use signify whatever ideas they
choose. Such an illusion is fostered by philosophers and grammarians.
In fact, the meanings of the words we use are not subject to our
voluntary control. The signifying connection between a word and its
meaning is a historical reality, laid down in the etymological relations
which constitute the language, independent of the will of individual
speakers. Consequently, what a given word signifies cannot vary
between users or between speaker and hearer. It is the institutional
independence of language, isolating it from the control of the will of
individual agents, which makes language the perfect vehicle of communication Tooke believed it to be.

Furthermore, to the extent that we reject the authoritarian and obfuscating arguments of philosophers and grammarians, we will finally come to see that language is a public institution which, because of its very independence, exists as a common good over which no individual or group can exercise any authority or control. Tooke believed that political authorities had been able to reject or defuse populist arguments in favour of greater rights, basic liberties, just laws, and the like because those authorities had tricked their subjects into accepting the obfuscating significations the authorities gave to the crucial terms 'law', 'right', 'just' and so forth. But if we accept Tooke's institutionalist argument, we will see that such moves simply mask the truth: all words have objective meanings which can be revealed by the empirical techniques of etymology. A political authority can no more impose his own meaning on 'right' than he can impose a chemical structure on water. The meanings of political and ethical terms are 'facts' not fundamentally different from the facts of chemistry, biology and physics. Meanings are matters of fact; they are not, *pace* Locke, matters of the will and individual agency. And etymology provides an empirical technique for uncovering the facts of meaning. Meaning statements are therefore not prescriptions, but descriptions (scientific hypotheses). They are empirical statements, relying on scientific techniques, rather than normative statements, relying on authority and power.

So the political significance of Tooke's argument lies in its advocacy of the free access, by means of etymological study, to linguistic knowledge, a good the possession of which had previously been a guarded privilege of the elite (a privilege Tooke felt to be given the illusion of legitimacy by normativist linguistics). Henceforth knowledge of the meanings of words becomes a possession open to anyone who will but master the empirical techniques of etymological analysis.

There is of course a great irony in Tooke's transformation of empiricist discourse about signification from the prescription of behavioural norms to the description of institutional facts: most of his etymological 'facts' soon came to be seen by fellow institutionalists as falsehoods. Tooke came to be thought a very bad etymologist. One notorious example of bad etymology is Tooke's equation of 'through' with 'door'.

But this in turn suggests a more general irony in the institutional approach to language. Such an approach describes the institutional 'facts' (as opposed to saying how agents should behave). But the 'facts' described by the institutionalist are not directly observable. The purported facts that 'soporific' means *tending to produce sleep* or that

21

'through' really means *door* are not accessible to empirical investigation. Nor is the purported fact that English has a rule: 'Verbs agree in number with their subjects'. What *is* observable is the behaviour of individual agents: someone makes a verb agree in number with its subject. But this instance of behaviour is itself not the fact described by the institutionalist: the rule is. But that cannot be directly observed.

Consequently, unlike what are called the facts of biology, chemistry, and other natural sciences, the purported institutional facts of descriptive linguistics appear to change from decade to decade, from generation to generation, and from school to school. The wholesale rejection of Tooke's etymological and semantic 'facts' is a perfect case in point. But what light does this irony, which is, to be fair, of an essentially historical nature, shed on the more general, logical claim that institutionalist linguistics is an apolitical discourse, standing in direct opposition to the unavoidably political discourse of normativism?

To address the more general claim, it ought first to be noted that, as Aarsleff (1967) has demonstrated, Tooke's ideas were probably the main inspiration driving the proposal and eventual composition of the *New (Oxford) English Dictionary*. What was (and still is) such a dictionary supposed to be but an exhaustive description of the institution of the English language, in particular of the meanings of its words? It stands resolutely opposed to the notion that what a word means is something to be voluntarily determined by the individual agents who use that word. The *OED* simply reports the facts, both contemporary and historical. As such it is a metalinguistic discourse of a very different kind than the earlier prescriptive dictionaries fostered by the normativist tradition.

And yet the *OED* is also by far the most authoritative and influential normative influence on the behaviour of individual speakers and writers of English. It is the supreme normative discourse on the behaviour we call 'speaking English': the final court of appeal. As such it has an immense political significance, the last remaining jewel in Victoria's crown.

Nevertheless, the institutionalist will argue that the normative use of the descriptive statements in the *OED* is epiphenomenal. The descriptions of word meanings in the *OED* do not themselves prevent individual speakers from using English words any way they choose. It may very well be true that prescriptivists make use of the descriptive statements in the *OED* for normative ends, but that does not make the statements themselves inherently normative or political. Similarly, someone might use an empirical investigation of the causes of death in a particular community for political ends; but the possibility of such a use does not make that investigation or its descriptive conclusions inherently political. What the *OED* contains, argues the institutionalist, are descriptions of the facts about the meanings of English words; such descriptions have nothing to do either with the freedom of individuals to use those same words to mean anything they like or with the efforts of 'authorities' to guide, control and constrain that use, even should those authorities make use of the *OED*'s descriptions as a part of their efforts. In describing the facts of word meanings, the only criterion against which the descriptive linguist's statements should be measured is truth. It may well be, as the case of Tooke's many false etymologies show, that those descriptive statements are sometimes, even often, wrong. But that in itself does not show that it is in principle impossible to apply to descriptive linguistic statements a criterion of true correspondence to the facts. On the contrary: it shows that there *is* such a criterion. Otherwise what sense would there be in saying that Tooke's are false etymologies? If there are false descriptions of the institutional facts of language, then there can be true ones; and there is nothing therefore wrong with speaking of the linguist's statements as descriptions or empirical hypotheses. Furthermore, the institutionalist concludes, if it is legitimate to take the linguist's statements as descriptions of institutional facts, then it is equally legitimate to say that, as such, they have no inherent normative or political significance.

In the apparent cogency of this argument, a logical sequence which seems to move along of its own will and strength, lies the key both to the transformation of discourse on language into a descriptive, scientific mode and to the continuing dominance of that discoursal mode even today. But it is an argument based on sweeping the most important questions under the rug. To see this it is best to ask: if the statements in the *OED* are descriptions, what do they describe? They are not empirical descriptions of particular speech events, nor of the behaviour of an individual in such a speech event, nor of the behaviour of many individuals in many such speech events. Descriptions of those phenomena would look very different than something of the nature of ' "Soporific" means *tending to produce sleep*'. To reply that they are descriptions of abstractions or of mental contents is to evade the question, and to do so in precisely the way that Tooke's advocacy of institutionalism was intended to destroy: that is, by the postulation of unobservable metaphysical or psychological realms populated by phenomena which act as the *denotata* for obscure and complex descriptive expressions. In other words, the institutionalist falls, starry-eyed, for the oldest form of seduction in linguistic mythology: viz. if the meanings of words like 'Socrates', 'horse' and 'tree' are the things for which they stand, then what do 'justice', 'beauty' and 'if' stand for? Ideas? Forms? Relations? Theoretical entities? There is no answer to this question, for the question itself is absurd.

But if there are no empirical phenomena for descriptive linguistic statements to be descriptions of, retorts the institutionalist, then how can they be true or false? How can ' "Soporific" means *tending to impregnate sheep*' be false and ' "Soporific" means *tending to produce sleep*' be true unless those statements are conceived as descriptions of some state of affairs? The answer to this eternally mystifying question is surprisingly simple: such statements are not descriptions but norms. They are neither true nor false in the sense of corresponding or not corresponding to some state of affairs. Rather, calling such a statement true amounts to no more than assenting to its normative authority. In calling such a statement true, one says that it should be followed; in calling it false, one says it should not be followed. In the same way, whether or not it is true that 'There is no smoking in the first four rows' is not a question to be decided by looking to see if someone is smoking in the first four rows but rather by examining whether that statement is used normatively to control, guide, inform and constrain the behaviour of those in the first four rows. A critical mistake on the road to institutionalism lies in assimilating the assertion of the truth of normative statements such as ' "Soporific" means *tending to produce sleep*' to the assertion of the truth of a descriptive statement like 'Grizzly bears hibernate in the winter'. Asserting the truth of a normative statement is asserting that that statement is normatively enforced (within some context, by some individual or group); asserting the truth of a descriptive statement is asserting that it corresponds to the facts. In the two cases, how we verify such an assertion of truth involves very different practices indeed.

What then of the supposedly descriptive statements of word meaning given in a dictionary like the *OED*? Such statements are not descriptions of facts, but rather citations of norms. A dictionary which says something like 'soporific: tending to produce sleep' cites a norm, a statement which (it asserts) would be normatively enforced by some group in some context. But, by what group and in what context? By the best educated? In informal conversation? By the social elite? In a writing class? By the handsomest men? And, in any case, why should that norm be obeyed? Why should the authority of those who enforce it be accepted? If what the descriptive linguist does is reconceived as the citation of norms, then there is no avoiding questions about the authority behind those norms. 'Yes, it is true that there is no smoking in the first four rows. This is my theatre.' But who owns English? Whose norms do the editors of the *OED* cite, and why should they apply to my behaviour, or his, or hers? To present normative statements of word meaning not as such, but rather as descriptions of some institutional state of affairs, amounts only to a deceptive way of attempting to enforce their normative authority: namely, by denying that their authority comes from any other source than a purported correspondence to the truth. What better way to get people to follow the norms you propose than to say: 'I am not saying how you should or should not use this word. I am simply saying what it really means in English. You may use it any way you wish. Although not to use it according to this definition amounts to making a mistake.'

If purportedly descriptive discourse on language is best reconceived as a (covertly authoritarian mode of) normative discourse, then the assertion of the political irrelevance and ideological neutrality of linguistic science can no longer be maintained. Descriptive linguistics is just another way of doing normative linguistics, and an ideologically deceptive one at that. If, in language, our situation is one in which there is no escape from the mechanisms of power, then it is better that we be aware of our situation.

From Tooke's institutionalist perspective, language can be studied in the way that other objects of the empirical sciences can be studied. For it does not consist in voluntary or private human actions, but in words themselves and the institutional relations between them. Furthermore, these relations can only be accurately perceived if the history of the language is studied. Under Locke's individualist perspective, prescriptive authorities had derived their power to determine the meanings of words from political or social sources: e.g. from their position in the Church, or in the government, or from their acknowledged (or self-appointed) standing as the most 'skilled' users of the language (that is, as the best authors). But under Tooke's institutionalism the power to determine the meanings of words rests in the hands of the linguist, as a scientific authority, possessing the technological skills to uncover the 'truths' of language. In fact, this development is a familiar one in the evolution of myths. Utterances which begin with the status of moral maxims come eventually to be seen as descriptive truths about a supernatural reality. We must obey the king not just because he says we must, but because he is the true representative of God on Earth. The transformation of prescriptive norm into scientific description is one of the most characteristic features of the development of linguistic ideas in the Enlightenment. As a prominent proponent of liberalist ideology, Tooke championed this development in order to free individual speakers from the control of prescriptive authorities and to give everyone equal access to language. But in reality, Tooke's institutionalism is no less authoritarian than Locke's normativism. The difference is that Tooke places that authority under the institutional control of a newly empowered elite, the new masters: namely, the professional scientists of language.[1]

> With a little industry and application, anyone who is willing to extricate himself from the system of shared ideology and propaganda will readily see through the modes of distortion developed by substantial segments of the intelligentsia. Everyone is capable of doing that. If such an analysis is often carried out poorly, that is because, quite commonly, social and political analysis is produced to defend special interests rather than to account for actual events.
>
> (Chomsky 1979: 4)

People who live in glass houses. . . .

NOTE

1 I am grateful to Lily Knezevich, who helped me think through much of this argument.

2

That obscure object of desire: a science of language

Tony Crowley

Ancient or not, mythology can only have an historical foundation, for myth is a type of speech chosen by history: it cannot possibly evolve from 'the nature of things'.

(Roland Barthes, *Mythologies*)

1 THE OBJECT OF STUDY

The first theoretical question addressed in Saussure's *Course* (1916) is that of ascertaining what precisely will constitute the object of linguistics. What is it, Saussure asks, that linguistics sets out to analyse, what is the 'actual object of study in its entirety'? The answer would appear to be almost tautological: the object of study for the science of linguistics is to be language. Yet as Saussure points out, this response is problematical since it presupposes that the object – language – is already given, a datum which is easily found. He insists, against this account, that in this respect linguistics is distinct from other sciences:

> other sciences are provided with objects of study in advance, which are then examined from different points of view. Nothing like that is the case in linguistics. . . . The object is not given in advance of the viewpoint: far from it. Rather, one might say that it is the viewpoint adopted which creates the object. Furthermore, there is nothing to tell us in advance whether one of these ways of looking at it is prior or superior to any of the others.

> (Saussure 1983: 8)

The distinction between linguistics and other sciences posited here is in fact highly dubious since they too find their object only by means of 'viewpoints' or theories. And the revolutions in the history of particular

27

sciences attest to the similar theory – laden constitutions of their objects. Yet it is true that the science of linguistics has particular problems with its object and it would not be too much to claim that it is the principal aim of the *Course* to resolve such problems. The stated desire is to clear away false hindrances in order that the object can be seen in clear light. And the reason for this project is Saussure's impatience with what he saw as the pre-scientific complacency in the branch of the study of language in which he served his apprenticeship. To work in that tradition, he complained, is inevitably to face 'the general difficulty of writing any ten lines of a common sense nature in connection with linguistic facts'. Hence the necessity of demonstrating 'the utter ineptness of current terminology, the need for reform, and to *show* what kind of an object language is in general' (Saussure 1964: 93).

Such an antipathetic rejection of his own earlier work and the tradition in which it was conceived is perhaps attributable to the fact that this tradition had been the first to claim for itself the mantle of the science of language. For in fact one of the peculiarities of the study of language in the post-Enlightenment period has been that not one but two sciences have arisen. The first, appearing in the early to mid-nineteenth century, was to become known as comparative philology and was based on the axiom that 'language, like every other production of human culture, falls under the general cognizance of history' (Paul 1888: xxi). The second, appearing in the early modern period and christened by its foremost theoretician as general linguistics, reversed this tenet and relegated history in favour of a synchronic study of language:

> Diachronic and synchronic studies contrast in every way. For example, to begin with the most obvious fact, they are not of equal importance. It is clear that the synchronic point of view takes precedence over the diachronic, since for the community of language users that is the one and only reality. The same is true for the linguist. If he takes the diachronic point of view, he is no longer examining the language but a series of events which modify it.
>
> (Saussure 1983: 89)

The theoretical and methodological viewpoints of these two competing sciences were set against each other, and a moment's reflection on modern intellectual history will show which came to be the victor in the battle for the status of the true science of language. The naive manner in which so many introductory textbooks (and some not so introductory) parrot the beliefs that Saussure was the first to conceive of the sign's arbitrariness, or to be interested in the systematic nature of signs, or to see the study of signs as a potential field of knowledge *per se*, is weighty testimony to the victory of the second of the two discourses upon language.

However, it will be one of the aims of this chapter to challenge this victory by exposing the discursive violence with which it was brought about, and by returning to the problem of language and history. The task will be to bring to light the repressions necessary to sustain the new science of language and its newly found object and to examine its alleged scientific neutrality. The return to the problem of language and its relation to history will not, however, be a turning back to the formal historical stress typified by the comparativists, but to a conception of the essential relatedness of language and history which is in fact noted, but theoretically relegated, by Saussure. However, before examining the basic opposition by which history is excluded, it will be important to examine the other processes of opposition and exclusion by which Saussure uncovers the elusive object. Thereby demonstrating the practical ordering of discourse which enables him to end the *Course* on the confident and optimistic assertion that 'the only true object of study in linguistics is the language concerned in itself and for its own sake'.

2 LANGUAGE: THE OBJECT OF MYTHOLOGY

It is a paradox, in view of the importance accorded by Saussure to the science which studies the role of signs as part of social life and to the study of language as its paradigm, that he begins his division of discourse with an apparently extraordinary claim about language. After beginning to articulate the 'place of language in the facts of speech', and thus to disarticulate *langue* and *parole*, he continues by asserting:

> It should be noted that we have defined things, not words. Consequently the distinctions established are not affected by the fact that certain ambiguous terms have no exact equivalents in other languages. . . . No word corresponds precisely to any one of the notions we have tried to specify above. It is an error of method to proceed from words in order to give definitions of things.
>
> (Saussure 1983: 14)

This is a remarkable, and crucial, epistemological claim since it places Saussure firmly in the camp of those who betray a distrust towards language, a fear about the potential confusion brought about by words, and a preference for the reliable solidity of things. This is a tradition whose followers have been firmly committed to an empiricist view of science and so it is at first all the more peculiar that Saussure should fall in with them. Yet his assertion is clearly related to the worries of the major empiricists as embodied in Bacon's complaint that 'words plainly force and overrule the understanding, and throw all into confusion', and to his aim of exposing 'the false appearances that are imposed upon us by words, which are framed and applied according to the conceit and capacities of the vulgar sort' (Bacon 1857: 164; 1861: 134). Saussure's note evidently replicates the desire to avoid words and rely upon things, and is a warning to avoid one of Locke's imperfections of words – 'where the signification of the Word and the real essence of the Thing are not the same', and the consequent problems for those who 'set their Thoughts more·on Words than things' and thus ' . . . speak several words, no otherwise than Parrots do, only because they have learned them, and have been accustomed to those sounds' (Locke 1690: Bk III, ch.9, para.5; Bk III, ch.2, para.7).

However, although Saussure's claim is at first sight rather odd it is in fact perfectly compatible with the project of the *Course*. Another of his assertions will serve to show why. He insists that the claim that language is a nomenclature, 'a list of terms corresponding to a list of things', is incorrect. For Saussure language is a systematic structure of sound patterns and concepts, and rather than being the means by which we name the things of the world it is in fact, following Locke, a system of representation which does not necessarily, if at all, involve the world. Now the crucial epistemological significance of this distinction, and its centrality to an understanding of Saussure's project, lies in the rejection of the commonly postulated duality of language and world. As already noted, Saussure rejected the former accounts of language which saw it as the medium by which consciousness could name the pre-linguistic objects of the world. But his radical break went further than this in claiming that the world and language are not distinct orders of being but belong to the same ontological order. The break amounts to this: that Saussure conceived of language as a thing to be found in the world of other real things. As such, of course, and like other worldly things, it became open to the methods of objective scientific study. Once liberated from its status as but a pale shadow of the world of things into one of those things, then language could join those things in the privileged status of scientific object. Hence the perfect sense of Saussure's claim, cited earlier, to have 'defined things not words' in the early part of the *Course*. For once we are clear that we are no longer dealing with words, with which it is impossible to give definitions of things since they are not necessarily related to the world of things, then we can be certain that we have shifted our attention to one of those more reliable things – language itself – and thus that we are in the realm of science rather than that of words, words, words.

The transformation of language from its position as a poor (or even perfect) speculum of the world to a place within the world has important consequences. Not the least is the denial of the centrality of human activity in the study of language, for once language has become reified as a thing it loses its roots in praxis, in practical human labour. As Lukács, following Marx, pointed out, the basis of such reification is that,

> a relation between people takes on the character of a thing and thus acquires a 'phantom objectivity', an autonomy that seems so strictly rational and all-embracing as to conceal every trace of its fundamental nature: the relation between people.
>
> (Lukács 1971: 83)

Once language has become a thing, its role as a constitutive factor of human social being is banished in favour of objectivity, autonomy and rationality. It becomes what Volosinov described as an 'abstract-objective' entity whose governing characteristics are that it is immutable, self enclosed, determinedly rule-governed and self-identical. It should be clear from this account that once Saussure had delineated language 'in itself and for its own sake' as a thing, once he had found the object of linguistics, then the crucial ontological distinction between *langue* and *parole*, the thing itself and the uses to which it is put, follows logically. Moreover the hierarchical ordering of *langue* over *parole* is also a logical step since for the scientist engaged in studying the things of the world the necessary condition of their theorization and study is a certain stability and staticity rather than a constant flux of activity.

For this reason too the synchronic study of language is privileged over its diachronic partner since stability and immutability have to be the orders of the day. But just as the *langue–parole* distinction and its necessary condition, the reification of language, were based upon the formal repression of human activity, likewise this other Saussurean

31

distinction has its basis in a process of rigid exclusion. The dimension necessarily excluded in this distinction is of course history since it too is viewed as a distorting and problematic force which prevents the stability necessary for scientific method. Synchronic study logically demands staticity and thus 'although each language constitutes a closed system all presuppose certain constant principles'. However, although history is apparently excluded here it lies in fact at the constitutive heart of any attempt at synchronic linguistics. This is revealed in examining Saussure's claim that 'the aim of general synchronic linguistics is to establish the fundamental principles of any idiosynchronic system, the facts which constitute any linguistic state'. There is a distinct shift of emphasis here into this curious entity the idiosynchronic system. This is evidently a system whose time is its own and whose historical limits appear to emerge from within. Again it seems as if this is a refusal of history since it is claimed that the idiosynchronic system, the linguistic state, 'occupies not a point in time, but a period of time of varying length, during which the sum total of changes occurring is minimal. It may be ten years, a generation, a century, or even longer' (Saussure 1983: 99). However this is not a rejection of history which can have any logical force since as Saussure continues to specify, it is history, the processes of historical change and differentiation, which lies at the heart of all language:

> An absolute state is defined by lack of change. But since languages are always changing, however minimally, studying a linguistic state amounts in practice to ignoring unimportant changes. Mathematicians do likewise when they ignore very small fractions for certain purposes, such as logarithmic calculations.
>
> (ibid.: 100)

History, though markedly acknowledged as central, 'since languages are always changing', has to be forcibly excluded, 'ignored', in order that the mathematical precision required of a science be gained. To engage in this process of deliberate blindness, however, is to admit that the allegedly all-encompassing scientific study of language is based on a myth: 'the notion of a linguistic state can only be an approximation. In static linguistics, as in most sciences, no demonstration is possible without a conventional simplification of the data' (ibid.: 100). The presence of historical change and differentiation then is not denied by Saussure but ignored or relegated to a secondary position. Rather than admitting the force of historical becoming in a language he makes any particular language state – its particular being – the measure by which history is to be calibrated. The constant flux of history is relegated in favour of static systems whose alteration alone can allow history to appear as momentarily important. Yet such a discursive hierarchy *can* only be bought at the price of deliberate exclusion and its recognition, which slips out here, displaces the straight face of scientificity with the jovial mask of mythology.

The demands of scientificity then force the imposition of mythology upon language. For the raw material with which linguists worked had to be disciplined in order to make it stable enough for investigation. And the plaintive task of the linguist when faced with the heterogeneity of patterns of linguistic difference and similarity demonstrates how the sort of material with which the scientist works determines at least in part the methods – or perhaps mythods – which are to be employed. A good example of the mythical disciplining of the linguist's material is Saussure's own coinage of the term 'idiosynchronic' to refer not only to a particular language, but also to dialects and sub-dialectal forms. For the term 'idiosynchronic' was intended to be a theoretical – or mythical – response to the point that it was not simply national languages which could be thought of as synchronic systems, but *any* system of language which achieved the required stability. Once it was perceived that it was not simply national languages that retained the stability and determinancy required for the status of *langue* to be thrust upon them, then it became clear that dialects and sub-dialectal forms would also have to be recognized as idiosynchronic systems in order to reassert some order of stability at the sub-national level of heteroglossic difference.

That linguistic differences had produced practical difficulties for linguists is undoubted. For example one Victorian linguist, struggling with the problem of dialectal differences asserted: 'If the question is asked, what is a dialect? No scientific or adequate definition can be given. For all practical purposes this will suffice. A language is a big dialect, and a dialect is a little language' (Meiklejohn 1891: 7). Although this definition is in fact quite close to that given by Saussure it does not have any of the scientific air of his foundation of the 'idiosynchronic system'. None the less linguistic heterogeneity caused difficulties since as Whitney commented, 'in a true and defensible sense, every individual speaks a language different from every other'. All speakers have their own particular forms of pronunciation, vocabulary and grammar, since: 'The forms of each one's conceptions, represented by his use of words is different from any other person's; all his individuality of character, of knowledge, education, feeling, enters into this difference.' (Whitney 1800 : 154). British linguists of the early twentieth century, still working in a non-Saussurean tradition, were also to note such differences:

> 'No two persons pronounce exactly alike. The difference may arise from a variety of causes, such as locality, early influences, social surroundings, individual peculiarities and the like'
>
> (Jones 1909: 1).

Another attributed linguistic differences to 'differences of interest and occupation', 'differences of class', 'difference of place and abode', 'difference of age', and 'differences of fashion . . . and even sex' (Wyld 1907: 42). Thus in the face of this mass of heterogeneity the only possibility that linguists saw as being available to them was to systematize: to homogenize differences by assigning particular clusters of them to the 'idiosynchronic systems' theorized by Saussure and thus to introduce a natural order into an aggregation 'which lends itself to no other classification' (Saussure 1983: 10). And, of course, the implications of such a methodology were not restricted to the study of language alone and were to be extended to the users of language. The striving for order, stability and homogeneity whch had produced such marked effects on the differences of language also led to the positing of determinate groups of speakers, bound to a particular 'idiosynchronic system', and recognizable as distinct sociological groups. A good example of the effects of such methodology is evinced in Wyld's important work in British linguistics, formulated without reference to Saussure's text, on the process of the 'differentiation of dialect' and the role of 'speech communities' in it. He argued that,

> If we define *Speech Community* as a group of human beings between whom social intercourse is so intimate that their speech is practically homogeneous, then whenever we find appreciable speech differences we must assume as many communities, and it will follow that there will be as many Dialects as communities.
>
> (Wyld 1927: 47)

Not only does this set out the rationale for much of the modern study of sociolinguistics, it also sets the stage for the appearance of that modern linguistic hero, the Ideal Speaker-Hearer:

> Linguistic theory is conceived primarily with an ideal speaker-listener in a completely homogeneous speech community, who knows its language perfectly and is unaffected by such grammat-

ically irrelevant conditions as memory limitations, distractions, shifts of attention and interest, and errors (random or characteristic) in applying his knowledge of the language in performance.

(Chomsky 1965: 14)

It is possible to perceive in this Chomskyan premise the familiar pattern of exclusion and reduction which also occurred in Saussure. But is it not the case that Jones and Wyld, along with later formal sociolinguistic theorists, were aware of the problems of linguistic differences and attempted to incorporate them within their studies? It might at first sight appear that this is the case but a closer examination will reveal the familiar processes of reductive systematization. For rather than noting such linguistic differentiation and the difficulties it poses for any attempts to systematize language, both Jones and Wyld, and their later descendants, simply incorporate them by expanding the set of 'idiosynchronic systems'. Along with national language and dialect the linguists formulated other systems: the sociolect, the idiolect, register and contextual style. In this way nothing was to fall outside the all-encompassing systematic web of linguistics. Nothing could be so heterogeneous as not to have a place in some homogeneous system or other. And nothing could be allowed to disrupt the myth of staticity in language which was the prerequisite for the scientificity of its study.

The main concern of the first part of this essay, however, is not with the familiar Saussurean distinctions between *langue* and *parole*, nor synchrony and diachrony. The main concern will be with the less familiar, but certainly as crucial, distinction and privileged ordering of 'internal' and 'external' linguistics. It is this privileged Saussurean hierarchy which it is the aim of this essay to disturb by a process of inversion and reordering. The effect will be to return history to its central position in the study of language and to cast further doubt on the possibilities of a 'science of language'.

The hierarchical privileging of 'internal' over 'external' linguistics is clearly necessary to the task of delimiting the object of linguistics. Saussure argues that,

linguistic questions interest all who work with texts – historians, philologists, etc. Still more obvious is the importance of linguistics to general culture: in the lives of individuals and societies, speech is more important than anything else. That linguistics should continue to be the prerogative of a few specialists would

35

be unthinkable – everyone is concerned with it in one way or another.

(Saussure 1983: 7)

Given the importance of language, then, along with the Baconian warning that 'no other subject has fostered more absurd notions, more prejudices, more illusions, or more fantasies' (ibid.) it follows that it is necessary to rule out all extraneous factors in its study. Hence arises the distinction between 'internal' linguistics (the proper, scientific study of language) and 'external' linguistics (dealing with factors that have an influence upon, but are not essential to, language). It is, as Saussure argues, a question of precise delimitation and exclusion: 'My definition of language presupposes the exclusion of everything that is outside its organisation or system – in a word of everything known as external linguistics' (ibid.: 20). It is, however, as he also points out, a delimitation which appears to be counter-intuitive since 'external linguistics is none the less concerned with important matters, and these demand attention when one approaches the study of language'. Yet the process of exclusion and deliberate refusal of such 'important matters' is required before the object of the new science can be allowed to appear in its full glory.

It is important to specify exactly what is excluded in the relegation of 'external linguistics', and what 'important matters' are held to have no place in the study of language. First 'there are all the respects in which linguistics links up with ethnology. These are all the relations which may exist between the history of a language and the history of a race or civilisation.' Second in the process of the ordering of the topics to be silenced are 'the relations between languages and political history'. Examples are 'major historical events such as the Roman Conquest', 'colonization', the internal politics of a country' and the claim that 'advanced states of civilisation favour the developments of certain special languages (legal language, scientific terminology, etc.)'. The third important matter ruled out is the fact that 'a language has connections with institutions of every sort: church, school, etc'. And finally the true scientist of language has to ignore 'everything which relates to the geographical extension of languages and to their fragmentation into dialects' (ibid.: 21–2).

That such a process of exclusion was necessary to the Saussurean project should be evident, as is the fact that he did not reject the whole area of 'external linguistics' as useless or uninteresting. What will be contested here, however, is the validity of this particular process of exclusion. This will take the form of challenging Saussure by taking him at his word and attempting to demonstrate that the significance of language 'in the lives of individuals and societies' may well be 'a factor of greater importance than anything else'. It will be a claim that the 'important matters' of 'external linguistics', which 'demand attention when one approaches the study of language', such as language and its relation to the history of a race or civilization, to political history, to institutions and to human geography, are the very questions with which we should remain in the study of language. The point will not be that we should concentrate on 'external' aspects rather than those 'internal' factors outlined by Saussure, but that we should see those 'external' factors – so brutally excluded – as constituting the object of the study of language. Rather than being additional or supplementary factors, they are precisely what give us something to study in the first place. Not optional extras, then, to be taken up by linguists in search of a break from formal scientificity, but the very features which enable us to see and hear the bare outlines of what might tentatively be called 'the object of linguistics'. For once we have removed, as Saussure's scientific project demands that we do, the 'external' factors from the study of language, we are left with very little to talk about. If the difficulties of approaching the full historical becoming of language are methodologically ruled out in advance, then we are left with nothing but 'scientific', reductive, formalism.

3 DUMB HISTORY, ARTICULATE LANGUAGE AND OTHER MYTHS OF DESIRE

It has been argued so far that Saussure's 'science of language' was facilitated only by a series of demarcations and prohibitions which brought about the manageable myths required by linguists. Yet it is also the case that the historical study of language – at least in so far as it was practised in Britain in the nineteenth and early twentieth centuries – was mythological. Therefore the aim of this section will be to demonstrate the mythological concerns of the other 'science of language' in this period. And again the limit of permissible discourse in the new science will be of central importance: its silence and articulation, its denials and involuntary expressions.

The 'Science of Language', Max Müller argued in 1861, 'is a science of very modern date'. He was referring of course to comparative philology and its late entrance to British intellectual life:

Its very name is still unsettled, and the various titles that have been given to it in England, France and Germany are so vague and varying that they have led to the most confused ideas among the public at large as to the real object of the new science. We hear it spoken of as Comparative Philology, Scientific Etymology, Phonology and Glossology. In France it has received the convenient but somewhat barbarous name of *linguistique*. If we must have a name for our science, we might derive it either from *mythos*, word, or from *logos*, speech. But the title of Mythology is already occupied.

(Müller 1862: 27)

Despite Müller's reluctance to name the new 'science', 'mythology' was regarded as a possibility and only the fact that it had been appropriated to another discourse prevented it from becoming accepted ('mythology', referring to a field of knowledge dealing with myths, was a coinage of the 1830s). In fact 'mythology' would have been an interesting name for the new 'science of language' and not simply for etymological reasons. The study of language was indeed to be a study of *mythos* in the Greek sense of 'anything delivered by word of mouth'; but it was also a study of *myths* in the sense of powerful discourses which achieve particular effects in the social realm. Thus 'mythology' in the sense that I am using it here is not the later Greek sense of the poetic or legendary tale which is opposed to the historical account, an opposition veering towards that between falsity and truth, but related to Barthes' use of it in the sense of 'a type of speech chosen by history'. Müller was to be proved correct: 'mythology' would have been a better term than the convenient 'linguistique' on the grounds that the latter suggests a study solely concerned with language whereas the former suggest a study of language in relation to other discourses whose effects are felt within social life.

One of the most important mythical legacies of the Romantic period was that which posited language as a site of history. This, combined with the formal historical stress of the comparativists, gave language major significance in nineteenth-century British cultural debates. On the one hand was the notion that a proper historical account could give language its own order, coherence and continuity; and on the other the sense that language itself could resolve the problems of history. Davies, writing in the *Transactions of The Philological Society* in 1855, declared that 'a good philology is one of our best media for determining obscure questions of history' (1855: 283). His words were echoed in J. W. Donaldson's argument that,

It may seem strange that anything so vague and arbitrary as language should survive all other testimonies, and speak with more definiteness, even in its changed and modern state, than all other monuments however grand and durable.

(Donaldson 1839: 12)

The importance of this legacy was that it meant that language seemed to offer a direct link to the past since it was through language that history spoke most effectively. For the nation of course such a conversation with the past was crucial since it lent a sense of continuity and coherence to the national history. Donaldson illustrates the point when he argues in the same text that:

Though we had lost all other history of our country we should be able to tell from our language, composed as it is of a sub-stratum of Low German with deposits of Norman French and Latin . . . that the bulk of our population was Saxon and that they were overcome and permanently subjected to a body of Norman invaders.

(ibid.)

Now although this is a powerful claim it is in fact deceptive since linguistic evidence on its own could not reveal historical knowledge quite as directly as is desired here. Even such terms as 'sub-stratum' and 'deposits' indicate that there is already a chronology at work which would have to be gained from other sources. To put the problem more bluntly, a historian approaching such evidence with no corroborating facts would have an impossible task in deciding which is the substratum and which the deposits: came first – the Low German or the Norman French and Latin? The linguistic evidence alone would not show and would need to be interpreted from within an already extant ordering of discourse and history. Yet this problem was ignored in the theoretical contention that even if all other historical sources were to be destroyed, our own synchronic *etat de langue* would still offer us history lessons.

The reason for the strength of this belief was that history was held to reside *in* language and thus, 'often where history is utterly dumb concerning the past, language speaks' (Mathews 1880: 226). The study of language offers the best hope for the historian since it moves beyond the narratives of history to a closer and more reliable examination of their materials. Thus the hermeneut could trust the history *in* words rather than the historical narratives constructed *with* words since although it is possible to create false historical narratives, language itself cannot lie about history since its very being is historical. As Latham put it succinctly, language is 'a material history' (Latham 1862: 750).

This powerful myth then was a legacy from an earlier period and was one that was to be deployed in various significant ways in the nineteenth century. The tempting idea that language is the ground in which the signs of history are simply and directly displayed had not yet struck the problem of discovering that what one digs out of 'material history' depends at least in part on what one is looking to find. The objection that language does not simply reveal history as one digs into it, but offers materials which can be ordered and arranged according to various patterns and structures in order to gain particular purposes and effects had not yet been made. It was that freedom which presented the study of language with its enormous mythological power.

One area in which the study of language was made to exercise this power was the set of discourses around the British nation-state. It was in this field that one of the most powerful of myths was to be consolidated: language as the political unconscious of the nation. The conception that a language reflected the national character was a firmly held belief which had been inherited from 'romantics' such as Diderot and Von Humboldt. Formulating it in the mid-nineteenth century, however, the British linguist Graham defined a language as:

> The outward expression of the tendencies, turn of mind, and habits of thought of some one nation, and the best criterion of their intellect and feelings. If this explanation be admitted, it will naturally follow that the connexion between a people and their language is so close, that the one may be judged of by the other; and that the language is a lasting monument of the nature and character of the people.
>
> (Graham 1869:ix)

The belief that language and national character are inextricably intertwined is another example of the processes of homogenization and identification in the study of language. So much so that the homogenized unity of the language of any particular national community was taken to be the criterion of its cultural safety and purity:

> It is evident therefore that unity of speech is essential to the unity of a people. Community of language is a stronger bond

than identity of religion or government, and contemporaneous
nations of one speech, however formally separated by differences
of creed or of political organisation, are essentially one in
culture, one in tendency, one in influence.

(Marsh 1860:221)

Given these beliefs it is predictable that much of the nineteenth-
century historical work on language in Britain should have been
directed towards tracing a 'unity of speech' in the English language.
This project of 'the history of the language' (a project whose very title
gives away its aim in advance by the double use of the definite article),
and that of its historical progeny the *New/Oxford English Dictionary* and
the field of English literary studies, was precisely to trace a continuity
in 'the English language' which could then be matched with that of
'the English nation'. Its central concepts – 'standard English' and
'good literature' – were concepts, much like Saussure's own necessary
starting points, based on delimitation and rejection. However, the
point of the centralizing tendency of such work can be postponed for
the moment since it will be necessary first to present an account of the
powerful myth of language and nationality.

If it is true that in this period and field of linguistic research it was
history that was viewed as having fallen silent, to be rescued from
oblivion by the expressive nature of language, it is important to see
precisely what language was saying on history's behalf and thus to
specify the secrets of history which the language articulated. The
answer is that the language was telling the secrets of the English
nation: its unity, coherence, greatness and permanence. For when the
English language revealed its secrets it did so only in order to cement
the national identity:

It is of course our English tongue, out of which mainly we
should seek to draw some of the hid treasure which it contains . . .
we cannot employ ourselves better. There is nothing that will
more help to form an English heart in ourselves and others.

(Trench 1851:24)

It told the history of a 'modern nation which is fit to lead the world,
especially in the very matter of language' (Skeat 1895–8:415). And it
articulated this history by drawing parallels between the strengths of
the language and those of its speakers, since as one linguist put it,
there is 'a certain conformity between the genius of our institutions
and that of our language' (Trench 1855:43). Or as another confirmed,

the language 'carries with it the cherished and sanctified institutions of its native soil' (Harrison 1848:378). The main strength of the language, mirrored in the national self-image, was its liberalism: 'The English language, like the English people, is always ready to offer hospitality to all peaceful foreigners – words or human beings – that will land and settle within her coasts' (Meiklejohn 1886:279). The imperial language and nation then will not only welcome peaceful foreigners but will also not omit to shoulder its share of the white man's linguistic burden. Thus: 'To make amends for all this borrowing, England supplies foreigners (too long enslaved) with her own staple – namely the dictions of free political life' (Kington-Oliphant 1873:339). The language, like the nation, was not to be ashamed of its 'borrowings' but to put them on display as the markers of superiority:

> We do not wish to discard the rich furniture of words which we have inherited from our French and classic eras; but we wish to wear them as trophies, as the historic blazon of a great career, for the demarcation and amplification of an imperial language whose thews and sinews and vital energies are essentially English.
>
> (Earle 1901:63)

It was a language which embodied in its spread the fortunes of the nation and its future:

> That language too is rapidly becoming the great medium of civilization, the language of law and literature to the Hindoo, of commerce to the African, of religion to the scattered islanders of the Pacific. The range of its influence, even at the present day, is greater than ever was that of the Greek, the Latin, or the Arabic; and the circle widens daily.
>
> (Guest 1882:703)

'The language', that constructed ideal with its magical properties, is precisely mythological in the sense of belonging to a discourse, or number of discourses, which exercise powerful effects in the social realm. 'The language' here becomes the site of dissemination for desired, and in this sense therefore mythical, solutions to particular historical problems. In the face of conflict 'the language' offered unity, in times which threatened a break with the past it preached continuity, in times of political struggle it extolled the virtues of liberalism, and in times of doubt it offered boundless optimism. It was in fact the perfect myth, in two of the senses of the word: it was a type of speech chosen by history and its form was that of a poetic, legendary tale. For as one of the foremost linguistic mythologers of nineteenth-century Britain recognized, words 'are not merely arbitrary signs, but living powers' (Trench 1851:3).

4 THE IMPOSSIBLE SCIENCE

This essay has presented an account of two differing fields of knowledge both of which claimed the title of the 'science of language'. It has been argued that in both cases the basis of their interest in language has been mythical: on the one hand requiring mythical entitites in order to guarantee 'scientificity', and on the other dealing with the articulate forms by which history is represented to itself and to others. In this concluding section there will again be a stress on these two sciences in order to stress their common links and perceptions and to indicate the problems of attaining to a science of language. In this the texts of Bakhtin will be of central importance.

One of Bakhtin's central tenets is that 'verbal discourse is a social phenomenon social throughout its entire range and in each and every of its factors, from the sound image to the furthest reaches of abstract meaning' (Bakhtin 1981:259). At first sight such a belief might appear to be in line with Saussure's own distinction between the language itself (*langue*) and speech (*parole*) since in making this distinction, Saussure argues, 'we distinguish at the same time: (1) what is social from what is individual and (2) what is essential from what is ancillary and more or less accidental' (Saussure 1983:14). However, there is a major difference between Bakhtin's central tenet and that of Saussure since although they may both express apparently similar beliefs about the social nature of what it is which is to be addressed in their investigations (praxis for Bakhtin, an 'object' for Saussure), they are at odds when it comes to the problem of how to interpret the term 'social'. For Saussure the question of social being reduces to one of common factors, of sameness and collective and identical self-reproduction. When he posits language as a social phenomenon Saussure means precisely this:

A language, as a collective phenomenon, takes the form of a totality of imprints in everyone's brain, rather like a dictionary of which each individual has an identical copy. Thus it is something which is in each individual, but is none the less common to all . . . . This mode of existence of a language may be represented by the following formula:

$$1 + 1 + 1 + 1 \ldots = I \text{ (collective model).}$$

(ibid.:19)

Thus in any given 'speech community', all its individuals 'will establish amongst themselves a kind of mean; all of them will reproduce – doubtless not exactly, but approximately – the same signs linked to the same concepts'. For Saussure it is the case that both language and society are aggregations of sameness; to use Marx's metaphor, society for Saussure is like a sack of potatoes in which all the potatoes are of the same size and shape. Moreover in this view of society a form of crude egalitarianism is held to exist since given that the language is a 'social fact', to use Durkheim's terminology, it must mean that it operates equally as a constraint (the essence of Durkheim's theory in regard to this concept) for all members of society. Thus a language is an imposition on all the members of a community which they are powerless to resist since, in Saussure's words, 'no society has ever known its language to be anything other than something inherited from previous generations which it has no choice but to accept'; 'the continuous efforts required in order to learn one's native language point to the impossibility of radical change'; 'linguistic facts are rarely the object of criticism, every society being usually content with the language it has intended'; and a language 'is part and parcel of the life of the whole community, and the community's natural inertia exercises a conservative influence upon it'. For these reasons any language is radically egalitarian since: 'at any moment of time, a language belongs to all its users. It is a facility unrestrictedly available throughout a whole community' (ibid.: 72–4).

For Saussure then the social nature of a language amounts to this: it is inextricably tied to a particular social group (ideally a nation) whose own unified and homogeneous form mirrors that of the language. In Bakhtin's account, however, Saussure's view of a language starts off on the wrong step by banishing precisely its social features. The exclusion of any concern with language and race, language and political history, language and institutions, language and human geography – along with all the other areas banished to the realm of 'external linguistics', means that the field of enquiry is already heading in the wrong direction. For Bakhtin, language is constantly under the influence of many social forces pulling in different directions and this means that rather than seeking to identify the unit of a language and its speakers, the linguist must pay attention to the heteroglossic differences of language and languages. Such differences arise out of the interests of distinct social groups and stem from Bakhtin's view of any social formation as constructed by a conflictual struggle between such interest groups. Rather than viewing society as a unified mass of individuals, Bakhtin sees it as the site, and object, of conflict. An example of the opposed methodology of these two theorists is given when Saussure comments on the 'literary development of a language':

> This is a phenomenon of general importance, since it is insepar-able from political history. A literary language is by no means confined to the limits apparently imposed on it by literature. One has only to think of the influence of the salons, of the court, and of academics.

(ibid.:22)

In a sense this is a typically Bakhtinian perspective in its stress on the social extension of literary language and its propagation in particular institutions. However, the flaw in Saussure's work, that which allows him to perceive only the unities of language, is that he excludes precisely such viewpoints from his investigations. For Bakhtin on the other hand it is precisely such perceptions which allow him to see the diversity amongst apparent unity, the 'internal stratification present in every language at any given moment of its historical existence'. It presents him with his material for study:

> The internal stratification of any single national language into social dialects, characteristic group behaviour, professional jargons, generic languages, languages of generations, tendentious languages, languages of the authorities, of various circles and of passing fashions, languages that serve the specific sociopolitical purposes of the day, even of the hour.

(Bakhtin 1981:263)

If Bakhtin and Saussure disagree on the question of the social nature of language what of the position of the first scientists of language, in particular the British historical linguists? Again, at first sight there appear to be promising links between such historical work on language and that of Bakhtin, for Trench's comment that words are 'not merely arbitrary signs, but living powers' seems related to the Bakhtinian belief in the power-laden nature of verbal discourse. Yet the promise turns out again to be a disappointment and for familiar

45

reasons. The principal reason is that the British linguists also saw language and society as unified. As was pointed out earlier in the essay they argued for an essential unity between the greatness, liberality and coherence of the language and nation. They saw the present, in the linguistic and the social realms, as forming a seamless continuity with the past, and it was for this reason that they insisted that

> eyes should be opened to the Unity of English, that in English literature there is an unbroken succession of authors, from the reign of Alfred to that of Victoria, and that the English which we speak *now* is absolutely *one* in its essence, with the language that was spoken in the days when the English first invaded the island and defeated and overwhelmed its British inhabitants.
>
> (Skeat 1873:xii)

The epic past, 'the absolute past of national beginnings and peak times' in Bakhtin's phrase, is conjoined with an epic present in this view of history. It is an easy continuity of achieved greatness and permanence.

However this is not to argue that these linguists were not interested in the differing forms of language since their work did in fact often mark the exciting beginnings of an investigation of heteroglossia. Max Müller, for example, warned that

> as political history ought to be more than a chronicle of royal dynasties, so the historian of language ought never to lose sight of those lower and popular strata of speech from which those original dynasties spring and by which alone they are supported.
>
> (Müller 1862:51–2)

And much of the work carried out by such linguists did indeed concentrate upon the dialects of English, as evinced in the texts published by the English Dialect society and principally its *English Dialect Dictionary*. However, despite such attention to heteroglossia, it is none the less the case that their work, like Saussure's was based on the quest for unity in a language. For the work on dialects was posited upon the fundamental premise that they were deviations from the central form of the language. Skeat, one of the foremost dialectologists, defined 'dialect' in this way: 'In relation to a language such as English, it is used in a special sense to signify "a local variety of speech differing from the standard or literary language"' (Skeat 1912:1). The phrase 'standard language' was in fact a coinage of these linguists in the 1850s and was a necessary methodological concept for their work. It was invented – in precisely the same way that *langue* served for Saussure – in order to introduce stability and unity into an apparently heterogeneous mass.

Their view of the language and its unity with the society to which it belonged was to become an illustration of Bakhtin's theoretical stance. For Bakhtin the idea that a language could be a unity was a construction which served particular interests. And in their work on the 'standard language' the British historical linguists exemplified this view. For the 'standard language' which was their object of study soon shifted from its status as the literary language to a particular form of the language restricted to a specific class. Again this process of exclusion and restriction was carried out under the banner of scientificity, as Ellis's comments on the concept of a received form of pronunciation demonstrate:

> there will be a kind of mean, the general utterance of the more thoughtful or more respected persons of mature age, around which the other words seemed to hover, and which, like the averages of the mathematician, not agreeing precisely with any, may for the purposes of science be assured to represent all.
>
> (Ellis 1869–89:Pt 1, 13)

Like Saussure's 'linguistic state' Ellis's object can only be brought about by the denial of difference and the writing of a mythical, 'representative', mean. The development of the concept of the 'standard Language', as illustrated in *The Oxford English Dictionary* definition, reveals the continuation of this process:

> a variety of the speech of a country which by reason of its cultural status and currency, is held to represent the best form of that speech . . . .
> *Standard English*: that form of the English language which is spoken (with modifications, individual or local) by the generality of the cultured people of Great Britain.

Thus the language, as presented in its standard form, became united not with the whole of society but with the dominant class. It is once more a unity which is based on exclusion: the language, as opposed to its dialects, is that spoken by the cultured generality and not any other speakers. As Bakhtin's work would suggest, this hierarchical exclusion has specific group interests at heart and they are often expressed by the linguists in moralistic terms:

47

By 'good English' we mean those words and those meanings of them and those ways of putting them together, which are used by the best speakers, the people of best education; everything which such people do not use, or use in another way, is bad English.

(Whitney 1877:3)

For Bakhtin such historical work would indeed have been alive to words as 'living powers' in the social realm. But from his perspective the flaws which had characterized such historical work as yet were two: first, to think that the language could be identified solely with one group, and, second, to posit an impossible unity between language and nation. Both Saussure and the historical linguists made the same mistake from a Bakhtinian perspective since rather than registering a unitary language, which is how they saw their different sciences of language, they were helping to form one. Thus the positing of both *langue* and the 'standard language' as static unities, possible only by an act of deliberative blindness to difference, is an engagement in the politics of language rather than its scientific study.

In his essay 'Discourse in the novel' Bakhtin presents a historical critique of the type of linguistic research discussed in this article. Its salient point, he argues, is that

> linguistics, stylistics and the philosophy of language – as forces in the service of the great centralizing tendencies of European verbal-ideological life – have sought first and foremost for *unity* in diversity. This exclusive 'orientation toward unity' in the present and past life of languages has concentrated the attention of philosophical and linguistic thought on the firmest, most stable, least changeable and most mono-semic aspects of discourse.
>
> (Bakhtin 1981:274)

In Bakhtin's view, however, this 'orientation toward unity' has diverted this form of thought away from the nature of language. It has led it to posit a form of *monoglossia* as the usual state of a language, a staticity of being rather than historical becoming. And it thus becomes the theoretical expression of certain political tendencies which have particular interests in view – for, as Bakhtin argues:

> Unitary language constitutes the theoretical expression of the historical processes of linguistic unification and centralization, an expression of the centripetal forces of language. A unitary language is not something given [*dan*] but is always in essence

posited [*zadan*] – and at every moment of its linguistic life it is opposed to the realities of heteroglossia.

(ibid.:270)

The conflicts present within any particular language are banished by *monoglossia*. Or at least appear to be, for the struggle between centripetal forces which seek unity and centrifugal forces which reflect differing social interests, can never be absolutely resolved. At differing times, in different political contexts, the forces acting in language will have differing effects: sometimes *monoglossia* will triumph, sometimes *heteroglossia* will appear with all its contradictory elements. If, however, it is the case that *monoglossia* can triumph on occasions – as I have attempted to show in this essay – then it is also the case that this must be a temporary victory. For the nature of language remains in the last instance heteroglossic and dialogical – despite all the best efforts of monoglossic, centralizing tendencies. Any instance of language, any utterance in Bakhtin's view, 'cannot fail to brush up against thousands of living dialogic threads' and thus register the heteroglot struggle between differing viewpoints and contradictory forces. As Bakhtin puts it,

> at any given moment of its historical existence language is heteroglot from top to bottom: it represents the co-existence of socio-ideological contradictions between the present and the past, between differing epochs of the past, between different socio-ideological groups in the present, between tendencies, schools, circles and so forth, all given a bodily form.
>
> (ibid.:291)

The social life and historical becoming of language make it impossible that *monoglossia* could triumph over *heteroglossia* in any absolute sense. Though of course even a non-absolute victory can give the winner certain rights and possibilities. And thus in a real sense language never can be unitary though it can be constituted as such by the sorts of discursive practices that Saussure and the historical linguists undertook. But then such a unitary language as that engendered by both science and myth is unitary, according to Bakhtin, 'only as an abstract grammatical system of normative forms, taken in isolation from the concrete, ideological conceptualisations that fill it, and in isolation from the uninterrupted process of historical becoming that is characteristic of all living language' (ibid.: 288). The repression of history, its absence in any other than a distorted and distorting form,

49

has led to a crucial inability in the 'science of language'. It has produced a science which has not yet become aware of its proper field since the dialogic aspect of discourse and the forces linked with it have not yet been brought within its scope. It is a science, ironically enough, still without an object.

The science of language then is an impossible and self-contradictory science. For although Bakhtin argues that 'only a single and unitary language, one that does not acknowledge other languages alongside itself, can be subject to reifications', which appears to open up the possibility of finding such a language to be the object of scientific knowledge, it has been the purpose of this paper to argue that such a unitary language is already a construction, a product of the practices of linguistics (amongst other practices). The object of linguistics which Saussure discovered was in fact twice removed from the reality of language: it had been united by the repression of *heteroglossia*, and it had then been reified as a stable 'thing' of the world. As regards the historical science of language, it is likewise an impossibility since it too banishes *heteroglossia*, produces a unitary language, and gives that unitary language a single ideological task. It is a clear example of the firm linkage of ideological meaning to language which is the defining factor of 'mythological and magical thought' according to Bakhtin.

With the failure of these two sciences, then, there arises the necessity of a new task – that of allowing history and language to speak: to tell of their differences, their forces, the institutions which support them, the groups which struggle for them. And much more besides. As one of the historical linguists put it: 'Each language has a history of its own, and it may be made to tell us its own *life*, so to speak, if we set the right way to work about it' (Craik 1861: 1).

The task remains to be performed.

3

Ideologizing Saussure: Bloomfield's and Chomsky's readings of the *Cours de linguistique générale*

John E. Joseph

1 INTRODUCTION: MISREADING AND IDEOLOGY

The history of linguistics is largely a history of misreadings, of failed communication between authors and readers, exacerbated by the illusion that communication has successfully occurred. From readings of Plato's *Cratylus* as a defence of linguistic naturalism by scholars in the Renaissance and after, to Chomsky's (1966) interpretations of some of those same Renaissance and Enlightenment thinkers as prefiguring his own versions of rationalism and nativism, to the peculiar understanding of Chomsky's competence-performance dichotomy by applied linguists in the 1960s and 1970s (see Newmeyer 1989), innumerable lines of failed communication have circumscribed the study of our primary medium of communication.

Whether semi-intentional or genuinely accidental, these misreadings are rarely neutral. Texts are not processed by empty brains, but by minds already stocked with set ideas, *a priori* categories, prototypes – and, perhaps most importantly, agenda. In other words, misreadings are usually ideologically determined.

This is not a negative criticism against the field of linguistics or its history. Misreading as defined above is an inevitable occurrence, particularly where author and reader are separated by generation and culture. Most literary critics have accepted the premise that texts do not have an inherent meaning, but that meaning is created upon each individual act of reading, by a reader who brings his or her unique mind and life experience to bear on the text. Certainly there is no reason why this should be less true in a non-fictional genre like linguistics than in fiction; indeed, given the power of agenda and the polemicism of the field, it may be more true.

In this sense, misreading is not to be construed as error. It is quite possibly integral to change and progress. And by no means is it restricted to linguistics. Misreading is a function of disciplines proportionately as they are theoretical rather than applied, abstract rather than practical, and founded upon a tradition of discourse rather than a tradition of action. Hence theology is excessively prone to it, while stonemasonry remains relatively unaffected. Physics, psychology and linguistics fall somewhere in-between.

Misreading does not render a field less scientific. Stonemasonry is not generally held to be more or less 'scientific' than theology; scientificness is not an appropriate criterion by which to contrast the two disciplines. Rather, it is on the abstract-practical scale that they differ. Thus, to suggest that significant misreadings have shaped the history of linguistics, and that these misreadings may have ideological motivation, is in no way to argue about the field's scientificness. As we stressed in the Introduction, ideology in one form or another is omnipresent in linguistics as in most other types of thought. The crucial distinction to be drawn is between linguists who acknowledge their ideological stances and those who do not. Just as the failure to recognize misreading produces the illusion of successful communication, the failure to acknowledge ideology creates the illusion of an objective, 'pure' sphere of enquiry. In both cases it is neither ideology, nor misreading, but *illusion* that compromises the integrity of the science, and that it is healthy to dispel.[1]

The ubiquity and inevitability of misreading do not guarantee that it will occur always and everywhere in equal measure. Some readers are more prone to it than others, notably those who, like Chomsky (1966), have an urgent agenda. And some authors evoke misreading more than others, above all those who do not write the books with which they are most closely identified and, worse, die before others write them. Such was the case with Socrates, Jesus Christ, and Mongin-Ferdinand de Saussure (1857–1913). Jesus and Saussure, their thought recorded by several hands, pose especially great problems of exegesis: the lack of a single authoritative text makes for uncommon breadth of interpretation.

In Saussure's case, this openness may run deeper still, being a characteristic part of his thought. This was the opinion of Jakobson (1971 [1969]: 744): 'But perhaps the genuine greatness of this eternal wanderer and pathfinder lies precisely in his dynamic repugnance towards the "vanity" of any "definitive thought" .' Jakobson intended for 'this eternal wanderer' to describe Saussure in his lifetime, and while it seems to have been an accurate portrayal (see further Joseph

1989a), it applies even better to Saussure in the decades following his death and the publication of the *Cours de linguistique générale* (henceforth *CLG*). Certainly no linguist in the twentieth century has undergone as many ideologically-driven readings as Saussure – a combined result of the revolutionary nature of his thought, the way in which it was preserved, and the fact that he was not on the scene as an academic-political force to protest the most egregiously ideological misreadings.

In this study I shall focus on how Saussure has been read by the two most influential American linguists of this century, Leonard Bloomfield (1887–1949) and Noam Chomsky (b. 1928). In both cases, but especially in Chomsky's, we shall see how their readings of Saussure evolved in tandem with their theoretical stance – that is, I think it is fair to say, with their ideology of language. The point is not to reveal the 'error' of a particular reading. It is to show in a constructive way the uses to which Saussure has been put in the development of modern linguistic science, and to consider the ideologies motivating those uses.

2 BLOOMFIELD AND SAUSSURE

Two quite contradictory statements on Bloomfield's relation to Saussure appeared in print in 1987, Bloomfield's centenary year. One, by Roy Harris, notes that while in his 1923 review of the *CLG* Bloomfield 'acknowledges Saussure as the founder of modern general linguistics' (Harris 1987b: xii–xiii), in his 1933 book *Language* 'Saussure is given a single passing mention in an introductory chapter on the history of linguistics' (Harris 1987b: xii).

> The reason for the disparity between Bloomfield's eulogy of Saussure in 1923 and his virtual dismissal of Saussure ten years later is not difficult to explain. The Bloomfield of the 1923 review is Bloomfield in his pre-behaviourist period; and in his pre-behaviourist period Bloomfield was a follower of the psychologist Wundt. So the 1923 review gives us a reading of the *Cours* as viewed by an American Wundtian who was also a Germanic philologist of the traditional stamp (and a student of Amerindian languages as well). But ten years later Bloomfield had rejected Wundt in favour of Watson. His reading of Saussure had altered accordingly. Saussure was now read not as the adventurous founder of modern linguistics, but as a perpetuator of the endemic psychologism of late-nineteenth-century approaches to language.

That later Bloomfieldian reading was to dictate the relationship between American and European versions of structuralism for the next quarter of a century.[2]

(Harris 1987b: xiii)

The other statement is by Bloomfield himself, in a letter to J. Milton Cowan dated 15 January 1945 which Cowan published as a sample of a serious letter from Bloomfield in an article devoted mainly to his humorous correspondence (Cowan 1987). After suggesting some corrections in the wartime Russian grammar Cowan was writing under his supervision, Bloomfield lamented:

Denunciations are coming thick & fast; I expect to be completely discredited by the end. There is a statement going round that de Saussure is not mentioned in my *Language* text book (which reflects his *Cours* on every page). Also that it does not deal with *meaning* – it seems there is no chapter on this topic. I do not intended [*sic* in Cowan] to give any recognition to falsehood of this kind or to discourses which contain them or are based on them.

(Cowan 1987: 29)

Although one is naturally inclined to take Bloomfield's own word as definitive, it should be noted that only Harris's statement is in accord with the standard histories of twentieth-century linguistics;[3] that a cursory reading of Bloomfield (1914) and (1933) seems to substantiate Harris's, and not Bloomfield's, view; and that authors' reactions to negative reviews can often be less than rational. Even allowing that Bloomfield has engaged in some counter-hyperbole (thus Koerner 1989: 441), today's reader is at a loss to detect pervasive Saussurean influence in Bloomfield (1933). Yet Bloomfield's one extant statement about his debt to Saussure can hardly be dismissed out of hand.

This seeming paradox stems in part from an illusion: we imagine that what Bloomfield thought of as Saussure's 'reflection' corresponds to our own late-twentieth-century conception of Saussure. We may even fall into the trap of imagining that Bloomfield's or our own conception of Saussure corresponds to the historical Saussure, or that such a construct as the 'late twentieth-century conception of Saussure' is anything more than a vague abstraction. This is familiar territory: we are contrasting Saussure as *langue* with Saussure as *parole*. And just as we cannot determine the nature of *langue* except through evidence from *parole*, our best evidence for understanding conceptions of Saussure will come from actual individual readings. I shall proceed, therefore, to conduct a close examination of Bloomfield's most detailed writings on the *CLG*, Bloomfield (1923), (1926) and (1927).

3 BLOOMFIELD (1923): SELF-DEFENCE

In his 1923 review of the *CLG* (on which see further Koerner 1989), Bloomfield makes a number of revelatory statements. The opening paragraphs grant recognition to Saussure's importance, though in a form hardly stronger than the ordinary academic niceties for a deceased senior colleague.

> It is gratifying to see a second edition of de Saussure's posthumous work on language; the popularity of the book betokens not only an interest in language, but also a willingness of the scientific public to face linguistic theory . . . .
> . . . in lecturing on 'general linguistics' he stood very nearly alone, for, strange as it may seem, the nineteenth century, which studied intensively the history of one family of languages, took little or no interest in the general aspects of human speech.
>
> (Hockett 1970: 106)

From here to the last sentence of the review, when he declares that Saussure 'has given us the theoretical basis for a science of human speech' (ibid.: 108), virtually every statement allows for an ambiguous reading. Where, for instance, does Bloomfield locate Saussure's importance? Plainly not in any novelty – let alone revolution – of approach; rather:

> The value of the *Cours* lies in its clear and rigorous demonstration of fundamental principles. Most of what the author says has long been 'in the air' and has been here and there fragmentarily expressed; the systematization is his own.
>
> (ibid.: 106)

He then describes some of these already known ideas that the *CLG* merely systematized: 'It is known that the historical change in language goes on in a surprisingly mechanical way, independent of any needs, desires, or fears of the speakers' (ibid.).

Saussure would have agreed with the sentiment, but would have broadened it further to include independence of potential effects on language structure. He would have baulked at the term 'historical change' and perhaps 'mechanical', which differs from 'automatic' by an implied metaphor. We know that the value of the term 'mechanical' in Bloomfield's work is determined by the opposition mechanistic–mentalistic, and we cannot assume that Bloomfield's position on this score corresponds to Saussure's. The next idea 'in the air' is that:

> Outside of the field of historical grammar, linguistics has worked only in the way of a desperate attempt to give a psychologic interpretation to the facts of language, and in the way of phonetics, an endless and aimless listing of the various sound-articulations of speech.

(ibid.: 106–7)

Even though Bloomfield would often repeat these criticisms over the years, in point of fact they apply quite well to Bloomfield (1914). Herein may lie a clue to the ambiguous nature of this review: Bloomfield cannot hail the theoretical advances of the *CLG* without implicitly acknowledging the shortcomings of his own major work. The next sentence, containing Bloomfield's most biting remark, seems to bear out this possibility: 'Now, de Saussure seems to have had no psychology beyond the crudest popular notions, and his phonetics are an abstraction from French and Swiss-German which will not stand even the test of an application to English' (ibid.: 107). Saussure would not, in other words, have been in a position to criticize Bloomfield (1914) were Bloomfield not ready to concede its weaknesses. With characteristic adeptness, Bloomfield then turns a stinging criticism into an apparent compliment: 'Thus he exemplifies, in his own person and perhaps unintentionally, what he proves intentionally and in all due form: that psychology and phonetics do not matter at all and are, in principle, irrelevant to the study of language' (ibid.).

So Bloomfield rescues his own work from the two Saussurean principles which would seem to discount it, by a two-front deflection: he trivializes the *CLG*'s rejection of psychology and phonetics by declaring them to have been fundamental principles already in the air – thus apparently known by Bloomfield himself – then makes it clear that Saussure could have passed no worthwhile judgement in these areas anyway. The implication is that Saussure's rejection of psychology and phonetics may result from his utter incompetency in these areas. Bloomfield emerges as superior to Saussure on every conceivable score.[4]

While the next two paragraphs, which give some details of the

CLG, are less manipulative, one is struck by how many individual words along the way are not Saussurean, but eminently Bloomfieldian:

the language of a community is to be viewed as a system of signals. Each signal is made up of one or more units; these units are the 'sounds' of the language. Not only has each signal a definite meaning . . . but the combination of these signals proceeds by definite rules and itself adds definite elements of meaning . . . . All this is a complex and arbitrary system of social habit imposed upon the individual, and not directly subject to psychologic interpretation. . .

(ibid.: 107)

'Signals' is evidently a translation of *signes*; but the English term suggests the notion of a stimulus, with its behaviouristic implications. As for constituent 'units', the *CLG* speaks only in a vague way of *linearité*. If 'these units are the "sounds" of the language', then Bloomfield must have in mind only the *signifiant*, and not the *signifié*. His statement that 'each signal has a definite meaning' undoes, by its wording, the dynamics of the Saussurean *signe*, for which it is equally and crucially true that each meaning has a definite signal. That Bloomfield does not make this reverse claim is significant, given his bias against semantics; for although this bias may not have been absolute (see Matthews 1986), Bloomfield would certainly have been hesitant to acknowledge an autonomous existence for meanings. In the last sentence of the citation, the word 'habit' clearly belongs to Bloomfield rather than Saussure.[5]

This second half of the review would seem to support the hypothesis that Bloomfield's Saussureanism might differ in key ways from what most of us conceive as a Saussurean position today. Whether or not it is objectively there, Bloomfield found in the *CLG* a linguistic system operating on 'signals', and a fundamental rejection of psychologism. The first part of the review helps us to see in a more general way how strong the *CLG*'s impact must have been for Bloomfield: Saussure's principal tenets, if correct, could not fail to cut the legs out from under Bloomfield's major study (1914). Bloomfield's agenda is, quite naturally, the defence of his own work. Like most good reviewers, he cloaks his criticism of Saussure in a sophisticated veil of deference and patronage. Yet even the closing remark ('de Saussure has here first mapped out the world in which historical Indo-European grammar (the great achievement of the past century) is merely a single province; he has given us the theoretical basis for a science of human speech' (ibid.: 108)) pales as a compliment when we remember how little importance Bloomfield actually accords to a 'theoretical basis' divorced from practical applications (see following section).

4 BLOOMFIELD (1926) AND (1927): SAUSSURE THE BEHAVIOURIST

The first important paper by Bloomfield to incorporate the behaviourist theories of A. P. Weiss is the 1926 proposal for a 'postulational method' which 'saves discussion, because it limits our statements to a defined terminology; in particular, it cuts us off from psychological dispute' (Hockett 1970: 128–9). Saussure and Sapir are here acknowledged for having taken 'steps toward a delimitation of linguistics' (ibid.: 129n.). 'Thus', Bloomfield notes, 'the physiologic and acoustic description of acts of speech belongs to other sciences than ours' (ibid.: 129). All these sentiments echo their first utterance in the review of the *CLG*; they are followed by the first presentation of a behaviourist scenario in the 1933 mould: 'to certain stimuli (A) a person reacts by speaking; his speech (B) in turn stimulates his hearers to certain reactions (C). By a social habit which every person acquires in infancy from his elders, A-B-C are closely correlated' (ibid.). The term 'social habit' comes directly from the 1923 review. Already in 1926, then, ideas which Bloomfield earlier associated with Saussure occur with only fleeting and indirect acknowledgement.

Pace Harris, no 'dismissal' of Saussure should be inferred from this, for another paper of the same period (Bloomfield 1927, destined to meet as much neglect as the 1926 paper was to exert influence) deals with Saussurean doctrine in detail and still in positive terms. Bloomfield (1927) clarifies some key questions regarding his understanding of the *CLG* and its impact for American structuralism. It begins with a declaration of Wundt (1900) as the greatest work in linguistics of the first quarter-century (Hockett 1970: 173); the footnoted list of seventeen 'lesser' works includes Bloomfield (1914) and Saussure (1922). Weiss (1925) does not figure in the list, presumably because it is not exclusively linguistic, but it nevertheless dominates the article's first section ('The underlying method').

Bloomfield notes some positive aspects of the work of the linguists in his list, among which that 'they do not in their actual work use the troublesome introspective terminology; they are not disturbed by the impossibility, today, of reducing human conduct to physiologic (neuro-logic) terms; yet they employ no extra-material forces' (ibid.: 174).

Note especially the restriction to 'actual work', as opposed to theorizing, where the 'introspective', 'extra-material' psychological terminology did still predominate. That such theorizing is the target of Bloomfield's critique should be borne in mind when reading his 'eulogy' of the *CLG* as providing 'the theoretical basis for a science of human speech' (see above). Although linguistics occupies 'a strategic position from which to attack the study of man' (ibid.), the linguists he has listed – including Wundt, Saussure and himself as of 1914 – 'do not make this attack. They accept the finalism and supernaturalism of individual psychology, with many variations, only to discard it, of course, as soon as they approach the actual subject matter of linguistics' (ibid.).

That is, the psychology expounded in their introductory chapters does not spill over into the later chapters on linguistic analysis. The doubling of 'supernaturalism' with the logical positivistic term 'finalism' will recur throughout the article.

The linguist cannot accept 'individual psychology, with many variations' because 'it tries to explain on an individual basis phenomena which he knows to be historically conditioned by the social group' (ibid.). The statement sounds perfectly Saussurean, yet Bloomfield means it to apply not only to Saussure but to Wundt's *Völkerpsychologie* (apparently counted here as a mere variation of individual psychology), to Bloomfield (1914), and in fact, we soon learn, to every approach not founded upon behaviourist precepts. Neither individual nor social psychology pertains to the 'plane of abstraction' on which 'social patterns, linguistic and other' exist and operate:

> We do not trace all the vocal utterances of an individual from birth . . . . We do not trace the usage of a linguistic form in a community, act by act. Once the individual has acquired the habit of using a certain linguistic form, we assume that under certain constellations of [physical stimulus, purely personal condition of the individual at the time, and extra-linguistic group-habits] he will utter it.
>
> (ibid.: 175)

Again, the first part of this statement is perfectly Saussurean, and would not have come from Bloomfield during his earlier, Wundtian phase. It is enlightening to see Saussurean ideas used as the logical justification for introducing the postulates of behaviourism. Bloomfield believes that linguists should depend upon no psychological theory in any case, but should make psychologists come to them, as it were. Again, this statement is comprehensible only if we separate behaviourism from psychology, since Bloomfield (1933) is built directly upon behaviourist theory.

At the end of section I, Bloomfield makes two statements, one foreshadowing his 1933 book ('For Weiss, the social group is an organism of a higher order than the many-celled individual') and another recapitulating his review of the *CLG* ('a psychology is not necessary in linguistics') (ibid.: 176). He then offers the strong claim that the Weissian view is 'a sketch of what I take to be the implications of the actual practice . . . of all linguists, whatever be their views on psychology' (ibid.). Again, the divorce of actual practice from theorizing is essential.[6]

Part II, 'The Problem of Meaning', deals most directly with the *CLG*, in which meaning is not reckoned as much of a problem at all, as Bloomfield at first appears to recognize:

> In what way does the word *apple* 'mean' or 'refer to' an apple, when none is present? Why is the dictionary definition nevertheless sufficient? This problem is psychologic rather than linguistic and is for our science best dealt with by some convenient postulate. It is, of course, solved with magic ease if we are satisfied with the answer that, when the physical apple is not present, a 'mental image' or 'concept' of an apple takes its place.
>
> (ibid.: 177)

That 'mental image' or 'concept', introduced into linguistic thought by Aristotle, restored to prominence by the *CLG*, and ridiculed by Bloomfield, is – astonishingly – ascribed by Bloomfield not to Saussure, but to Ogden and Richards (1923). The fact that their famous triangular diagram of meaning contains as one of its apices 'Thought or Reference' (to which Bloomfield adds the parenthetical gloss '[image, concept, or thought of an apple]') is why Bloomfield says they 'take us not one step ahead' (ibid.). The other two apices are 'Referent' (Bloomfield: '[. . . the actual physical apple]'), and 'Symbol' (Bloomfield: '[the word *apple*]'). Yet historically the 'Referent' is Ogden and Richard's addition to – or re-pre-Aristotelianization of – the Saussurean system (see Harris 1987b: 62–3), which consists only of terms equivalent to 'Thought or Reference' (*signifié*) and 'Symbol' (*signifiant*). Having undone the centrality of Saussure's *signifié* and restored the physical object to the system, Ogden and Richards ought to have got credit, not blame, in Bloomfield's eyes!

But Bloomfield saw things very differently: for him, Saussure's system consisted not of two units, but of four. 'De Saussure's system is more complex: (1) actual object, (2) concept, (3) acoustic image, (4) speech utterance . . .' (Bloomfield 1927:177). He clearly favours Saussure over Ogden and Richards, but the undesirable 'concept' is still there. Bloomfield then clarifies that (4) is *parole*, while 'the segment formed by the two purely mental terms (2) and (3) is *langue*, the socially uniform language pattern' (ibid.). 'Mental' is another loaded term for Bloomfield, an indication that he could not possibly accept the system as thus far presented.[7]

In Bloomfield's next move we see him rescue Saussure from the charge of mentalism; it is, I believe, the single most important passage in understanding Bloomfield's unique reading of Saussure. Again, the problem is that two terms of Saussure's system, 'concept' (*signifié*) and 'acoustic image' (*signifiant*), are 'purely mental': 'De Saussure's careful statement lays clear the point at issue: What he calls 'mental' is exactly what he and all other linguists call "social" ' (ibid.). That is, *signifiant* and *signifié* both belong to *langue*; *langue* is a social construct; therefore *signifiant* and *signifié* are social constructs. So far Bloomfield is swimming within a Saussurean lacuna: the failure to resolve the ambiguity between *langue* as a pre-eminently social fact and as an individual mental attribute. But he goes further: 'there is no need for the popular finalistic terms. We shall do better to drop (2) and (3) and speak instead of a socially determined correspondence between certain features of (1) and (4)' (ibid.).

Since 'actual objects' and 'speech utterances' obviously have their 'social' side as well – actual objects, either by their presence or their absence, provoke utterances, which constitute social intercourse – we can simply dispense with their 'mental' quality. This done, there remains no reason to distinguish actual object from concept, and speech utterance from acoustic image. We have not only got rid of the undesirable finalistic terms 'concept' (*signifié*) and 'acoustic image' (*signifiant*) but have shown that they never really belonged in Saussure's system at all, that Saussure, at bottom, was not a mentalist.

Bloomfield continues to argue the case that Saussure did not really mean for *signifiant* and *signifié* to be taken as a fundamental part of his system – again promoting 'actual practice' to primacy over mere theorizing:

> In his actual practice, de Saussure strictly rules out the meta-physical terms. . . . Or again, Osthoff's explanation of verbal first members of compounds arising in several Indo-European

61

languages, an explanation typical of the linguist's avoidance of mentalism, is for de Saussure paradigmatic.[8]

(ibid.: 177–8)

The upshot of this section is that Saussure's linguistic system, as viewed by Bloomfield, is precisely the system we are accustomed to identifying as that of Bloomfield (1933). Bloomfield is not offering an improvement upon Saussure's system; he is saying that Saussure's system is actually thus, and that the unfortunate addition of two redundant and unnecessary metaphysical terms should not brand Saussure as a mentalist, for fundamentally he is not one. The Saussurean system reduces to 'a socially determined correspondence between certain features of (1) [actual object] and (4) [speech utterance]' (ibid.: 177). Saussure does not escape blame entirely; for his unnecessary use of the mentalistic terms he is still taken to task (together with the Bloomfield of 1914) for having accepted 'the finalism and supernaturalism of individual psychology, with many variations' in theoretical excurses, even though abandoning it in actual analysis.

Bloomfield's repeated condemnation of linguists who do not practise what they preach gives us further cause for believing that not only is his theoretical system of 1933 grounded in his idiosyncratic understanding of the *CLG*, but, further, that he will have attempted to integrate this system directly into his analytic practice. If this was in fact the case, then the history of European-American linguistic relations in the twentieth century is in for considerable rewriting.

To return, by way of conclusion, to the statement by Harris which opened section 2: the 'eulogy of 1923' is more ambiguous and less generous than eulogies are wont to be; the 'dismissal of Saussure ten years later' is nonexistent, as Cowan (1987) correctly attests. It is true that 'the 1923 review gives us a reading of the *Cours* as viewed by an American Wundtian', but it also supplies a partial motive for Bloomfield's dismissal of Wundt. It appears to be from the *CLG* that Bloomfield acquires his dictum that linguistics does not need psychology. Bloomfield read Saussure as introducing a radical new social aspect, and then found the formalization of that aspect in behaviourism. It is not the case that his reading of Saussure altered between 1923 and 1933 because of his reorientation from Wundt to Weiss; rather, his reorientation from Wundt to Weiss seems to have been propelled by his reading of Saussure, which, in so far as the written record allows us to determine, underwent no substantial change. Certainly Bloomfield (1927) makes clear that Saussure is not a perpetuator of psychologism, but a behaviourist *avant la lettre*.

On his final point Harris is surely right: the 'Bloomfieldian reading was to dictate the relationship between American and European versions of structuralism for the next quarter of a century'. The sense is, however, turned on its head. The 'Bloomfieldian reading' in question was not a dismissal, but an idiosyncratic interpretation that at its crux – the resolution of *signifiant* and *signifié* into 'speech utterance' and 'actual object' – veers far from the path of orthodox Saussureanism.

5 CHOMSKY AND SAUSSURE

Chomsky's *Knowledge of Language* (1986), a synthesis of many facets of his linguistic work, includes his first attempt in several years to situate this work relative to the earlier structuralist tradition. This occurs primarily in Chapter 2, 'Concepts of language', devoted largely to establishing the distinction between 'I[nternalized]-language' (the grammar in the mind of an individual speaker) and 'E[xternalized]-language' (the 'commonsense' (ibid.: 15) notion of a language like 'English', which Chomsky terms an 'artificial construct' (ibid.: 26, 27, 29, 31) and a 'mere artifact' (ibid.: 26), having 'no corresponding real-world object' and thus existing 'at a higher order of abstraction' than I-language (ibid.: 27)). Whereas for Chomsky I-language is the proper focus of linguistic enquiry, 'modern [non-Chomskyan] linguistics' failed to make the distinction between the two (ibid.: 16).

> Modern linguistics commonly avoided these questions by considering an idealized 'speech community' that is internally consistent in its linguistic practice. . . . No attempt is made to capture or formulate any concept with the sociopolitical or normative-teleological aspects of informal usage of the term 'language'. The same is true of approaches that understand language to be a social product in accordance with the Saussurean concept of 'langue'.

> (ibid.)

The last sentence is ambiguous: it is not immediately apparent whether 'The same is true . . . ' refers just to the preceding sentence ('No attempt is made to capture or formulate any concept . . . ') or to the whole paragraph, including the positing of an idealized speech community. The second interpretation must be correct, however, if the passage is to be deemed consistent with a later reference to 'the familiar Saussurean-Bloomfieldian idealization to a homogeneous speech community' (ibid.: 147).[9]

Because of its failure to distinguish the two modes, structural linguistics ended up studying the mere epiphenomena of E-language.

> Structural and descriptive linguistics, behavioral psychology, and other contemporary approaches tended to view a language as a collection of actions, of utterances, or linguistic forms (words, sentences) paired with meanings, or as a system of linguistic forms or events. In Saussurean structuralism, a language (*langue*) was taken to be a system of sounds and an associated system of concepts; the notion of sentence was left in a kind of limbo, perhaps to be accommodated within the study of language use.
>
> (ibid.: 19)

Again, the final sentence, with the reference to Saussure, is ambiguous. Is Chomsky equating a 'system' of sounds and concepts with the 'collection' of actions, utterances, or forms referred to previously, or making a distinction between specifically Saussurean structuralism and its later offshoots? Is Saussure receiving two criticisms (for dealing with mere collections of forms, and for not incorporating the sentence into *langue*), or one criticism (the latter) and one plaudit (for dealing with systems rather than mere collections)?

The second interpretation is evidently the correct one, again assuming consistency with Chomsky's next reference to Saussure:

> It should be noted that familiar characterizations of 'language' as a code or a game point correctly toward I-language, not the artificial construct E-language. A code is not a set of representations but rather a specific system of rules that assigns coded representations to message-representations. Two codes may be different, although extensionally identical in the message-code pairings that they provide. Similarly, a game is not a set of moves but rather the rule system that underlies them. The Saussurean concept of *langue*, although far too narrow in conception, might be interpreted as appropriate in this respect.
>
> (ibid.: 31)

Here, it is specifically the concern of *langue* not with a 'set' of elements but with 'the rule system that underlies them' that Chomsky appreciates, while lamenting the failure to include syntax within this system.

If Saussure functions as a minor precursor for the I-language concept, the major precursor is 'Otto Jespersen, who held that there is some "notion of structure" in the mind of the speaker "which is definite enough to guide him in framing sentences of his own", in

64

particular, "free expressions" that may be new to the speaker and to others' (ibid.: 21–2, citing Jespersen 1924). Saussurean *langue* is 'far too narrow' because it does not explicitly provide for the possibility of such creativity, nor indeed for the sentence (ibid.:19, see the citation on p. 18). 'Saussurean structuralism had placed Jespersen's observation about "free expressions" outside of the scope of the study of language structure, of Saussure's *langue*' (ibid.: 32).

In sum, Chomsky appears to accept one feature of Saussurean linguistics –

(1) the characterization of *langue* as an underlying system rather than as a set of elements

– but to reject at least two others:

(2) that it takes *langue* to be a social product, necessitating a fictitious idealized speech community and preventing it from capturing 'the sociopolitical and normative-teleological aspects' of E-language;

(3) that it does not include sentences or 'free expressions' within the domain of *langue*.

In none of these cases is it self-evident that the statement represents correct or incorrect linguistic theory, or that it accurately characterizes the *CLG*. In contrast to feature (1), consider the following opinions:

> It seems that Saussure regarded *langue* as essentially a storehouse of signs (e.g., words, fixed phrases) and their grammatical properties, including, perhaps, certain 'phrase types'.

> Modern linguistics is much under the influence of Saussure's conception of *langue* as an inventory of elements (Saussure, 1916, 154, and elsewhere, frequently) and his preoccupation with systems of elements rather than the systems of rules which were the focus of attention in traditional grammar and in the general linguistics of Humboldt.

> The distinction I am noting here is related to the *langue-parole* distinction of Saussure; but it is necessary to reject his concept of *langue* as merely a systematic inventory of items and to return rather to the Humboldtian conception of underlying competence as a system of generative processes.

The preceding citations are, of course, from none other than Noam Chomsky (1963: 328; 1964c: 23; 1965: 4).[10] They accuse *langue* of precisely the characteristic which Chomsky (1986: 31) credits it with not having.

Similarly, feature (2) above, wherein *langue* is rejected on account of its being a 'social product' necessitating an idealized speech community, represents a turnaround for Chomsky. In the period just discussed, when Chomsky rejected *langue* as being just an inventory of signs, he nevertheless accepted it for correlating with his own notion of individual linguistic competence:

> In a work that inaugurated the modern era of language study Ferdinand de Saussure (1916) drew a fundamental distinction between what he called *langue* and *parole*. The first is the grammatical and semantic system represented in the brain of the speaker; the second is the actual acoustic output from his vocal organs and input to his ears.
>
> (Chomsky 1963: 327)

> The perceptual model A is a device that assigns a full structural description D to a presented utterance U, utilizing in the process its internalized generative grammar G, where G generates a phonetic representation R of U with the structural description D. In Saussurian terms, U is a specimen of *parole* interpreted by the device A as a 'performance' of the item R which has the structural description D and which belongs to the *langue* generated by G.[11]
>
> (Chomsky 1964c: 26)

The *CLG*'s characterization of *langue* as a 'social fact' was never mentioned by Chomsky in this period.

Feature (3) has remained a relatively steady critique in Chomsky's comments on Saussure over the years. Yet at one time he deemed it a minor problem which could be compensated for, so as to produce a perfect conjunction between Saussure's concept of language and his own:

> Second, our conception of *langue* differs from Saussure's in one fundamental respect; namely, *langue* must be represented as a generative process based on recursive rules. . . . Once we reformulate the notion of *langue* in these terms, we can hope to incorporate into its description a full account of syntactic structure.
>
> (Chomsky 1963: 328)

I have cited these sets of conflicting opinions not to suggest that Chomsky's views on Saussure deconstruct, but rather to show how they have evolved over a period of more than twenty years. I assume that Chomsky's views of 1986 represent a more highly developed phase of his thinking, a closer approximation to the truth of things, just as his linguistics of 1986 represent a closer approximation to the structure of universal grammar than did his very different linguistics of 1965.[12] Obviously, to accept Chomsky's 1986 positions is to admit that his 1965 positions were at least incomplete, and where the two are contradictory, that the 1965 positions were less adequate. And indeed, the 1986 statements turn out to be better supported by actual statements in the *CLG*, at least in the case of (1) and (2).

Thus we can infer on the basis of Chomsky's own recent work that certain of his statements about Saussure from the 1960s are inadequate, that they represent misreadings relative to his more recent views. We can then proceed to enquire into their history, including their possible ideological motivations. The development of Chomsky's views on Saussure between 1963 and 1968 has been briefly sketched, and certain of their inaccuracies noted, by De Mauro (1972: 400–4). However, De Mauro does not indicate how the misreadings and the evolution of Chomsky's Saussureanism might be connected. He is content with an inventory of Chomsky's surface statements, if you will, without seeking their deep underlying explanation.

6 CHOMSKY (1963) THE SAUSSUREAN

Chomsky's interest in the early history of linguistics began around 1960, at which time he read the *CLG* and Godel (1957), along with much else (Chomsky, personal communication). As a student he knew Saussure only by name, since with a few exceptions the pre-post-Bloomfieldian tradition (including Bloomfield's own work) was ignored in the ahistorical atmosphere of the time. Chomsky recalls hearing occasional references to Saussure in lectures by and conversations with Jakobson, whom he met in the early 1950s, but indicates that such references were less frequent than one might suppose. Thus Chomsky's personal discovery of Saussure postdates by several years the formation of his linguistic worldview, which by his own account maintains the essence of what it was in the early to mid-1950s (see Chomsky 1979: 113; 1986: 5).

The earliest references to the *CLG* in Chomsky's work occur in his long 1963 article 'Formal properties of grammars'. As noted by De Mauro (1972: 400), section 1.1 of that article, which contains the three (1963) passages cited above, constitutes 'une véritable profession de foi saussurienne', wherein Chomsky explicitly equates Saussure's

67

system with his own. 'Our discussion departs from a strict Saussurian conception in two ways' (1963: 328) — *just* two ways, with neither being an obstacle incapable of resolution. Chomsky goes on to equate *langue* directly with 'a grammar that generates sentences with structural descriptions; that is to say, . . . the speaker's linguistic intuition, his knowledge of the language' (ibid.: 329).

This article represents Chomsky's first extensive attempt to align himself with a pre-Bloomfieldian precursor. In the early 1960s, Chomsky's main opposition was the linguistic establishment dominated by the former students of Bloomfield, many of whom tried to portray Chomsky as a Young Turk with no respect for the great tradition they were upholding. Chomsky defused this weapon by finding a tradition older than theirs with which to align his own views. What he found was the *CLG*. It allowed him to portray the neo-Bloomfieldians as the true upstarts, and himself as the defender of traditional linguistic enquiry.

Thus, the agenda behind Chomsky (1963) is to highlight every possible correlation between the *CLG* and Chomsky's own work. The principal misreading motivated by this agenda is the claimed identity of Chomskyan linguistic competence with Saussurean *langue*. Chomsky (1963) completely ignores two of the most salient features of *langue*: first, that it has both an individual and a social aspect, neither of which can be conceived of without the other (cf. Chomsky 1986: 16); second, that it has both a synchronic and a diachronic aspect (*CLG* 24).[13] The *CLG*'s description of *langue* as 'la partie sociale du langage, extérieure à l'individu' (*CLG* 31) points up a major flaw in Chomsky's equation of *langue–parole* with competence-performance. Whereas in the *CLG langue* represents the social aspect of language and *parole* the individual aspect, in Chomsky's work competence represents the individual aspect, with all social facts regarding language being relegated to the (always marginalized) domain of performance. By 1986, when 'competence' and 'performance' have disappeared from Chomsky's lexicon, it is finally licit to recognize the social side of *langue*.

But even in 1963 Chomsky does bring up one lacuna in the *CLG*: the failure to assign syntax and recursive rules to *langue*. Syntax being precisely the area of his greatest impact upon the study of language, Chomsky, by noting this particular difference between his work and the *CLG*, shows that not only is he the heir to the pre-Bloomfieldian tradition, but that he has already improved upon this tradition where it was weakest.

With hindsight, the *CLG* was a less than ideal choice as an anchor point for Chomsky, since it was widely considered to be a cardinal text of structuralism, including the Bloomfieldian variety. Bloomfield himself was not averse to the idea, judging from his attempt to reconcile Saussure's thought with his own (see section 4 above). Chomsky risked having his linguistics understood as 'true' structuralism, versus the 'false' structuralism of the neo-Bloomfieldians, when in fact it was from structuralism of any sort that he wished to escape.

7 CHOMSKY (1962–4):
REACHING FURTHER BACK

In 1962, after writing the 1963 paper, Chomsky delivered a plenary address to the Ninth International Congress of Linguists that is generally credited with having propelled him to worldwide prominence within the field. The paper exists as a preprint distributed to those attending the Congress (Chomsky 1962), and in three published versions, all of which differ from the preprint and from each other. Of these, Chomsky (1964a) is closest to the (1962) version; (1964b) contains all of the (1964a) revisions plus a considerable amount of new material on the history of linguistics; and (1964c) reproduces (1964b) with some very minor adjustments.

Chomsky (1962) makes comments on the *CLG* that are superficially very similar to those of the earlier (1963) paper. He continues to claim that his view of language 'differs from that of de Saussure in two respects' (1962: 512), and after discussing them he presents his models of language perception and acquisition as 'Still remaining within the classical Saussurian framework, as modified above' (ibid.: 513). Nevertheless, rather than formulate his own system in terms of *langue* and *parole* as in the (1963) article, Chomsky presents them first in his own words, then translates them into 'Saussurian terms' (ibid.).

The slight distance he thereby puts between himself and Saussure coincides with his first passing references to other nineteenth-century linguists, namely Wilhelm von Humboldt and Hermann Paul. He first quotes Paul to the effect that rote memory plays a trivial role in language production (ibid.: 509; cf. 1964c: 8); but his next citation of Paul, this time juxtaposed with Humboldt, is a criticism of the two scholars for failing to take account of 'creativity' in language production (1962: 512; cf. 1964c: 22).

However, between the preprint and the Congress proceedings, Chomsky's attitudes toward Saussure and Humboldt seem to have reversed. To his discussion of creativity he adds several pages summarizing Humboldt's conception of language (1964a: 918–21), and states that 'one can distinguish two conflicting views regarding the essential nature of language in Nineteenth Century linguistic theory', Humboldt's view of an underlying *Form* in language (ibid.: 918–20), and William Dwight Whitney's view of language as an inventory of elements (ibid.: 921). To Whitney's view Chomsky annexes Saussure and structural linguistics (ibid.: 921–2); to Humboldt's view he joins his own thought: 'It is just this point of view concerning the essential nature of language that underlies and motivates recent work in generative grammar' (ibid.: 920).[14]

At the same time, Chomsky finally drops the statement that his approach differs from Saussure's in two ways. The result is that, while he still maintains a general identification of generative grammar with *langue* and remarks on Saussure's 'lucidity' in distinguishing competence from performance (ibid.: 915), the critique of *langue* as 'basically a store of signs with their grammatical properties' grows in significance. What had been a minor obstacle to a reconciliation of the Saussurean and Chomskyan positions becomes an insurmountable barrier.

The change in attitude is often subtly expressed: Chomsky no longer says that his model of perception and acquisition remains within 'the classical Saussurian framework', but merely 'the classical framework' (1964a: 922). Indeed, Chomsky takes pains to modify his earlier characterization of the *CLG* as placing syntax clearly in the domain of *parole* (see section 8 below). Yet the net outcome is that Chomsky (1964a) no longer conveys the impression that its author desires to align himself with what he sees as a Saussurean position.

This development continued in Chomsky (1964b and c), which carried the search for a historical anchor back from the nineteenth to the seventeenth century. It is here that Chomsky first introduced Descartes, Cordemoy and the Port-Royal Grammar, suggesting a 'Cartesian' linguistic tradition that would culminate with Humboldt before being undone by Whitney, the Neogrammarians *et al.* Although the references to Saussure are left unchanged in Chomsky (1964b and c), the addition of considerable chunks of new material on the 'Cartesians' (and on later chapters of Humboldt) combine to dwarf Saussure's significance – a far cry from Chomsky (1963). And when Chomsky expanded this material into a book, *Cartesian Linguistics* (1966), Saussure received only a couple of passing mentions (1966: 12, 55).

Evidently Chomsky's interest in Humboldt was connected to the work of John Viertel, one of his colleagues on the MIT Machine Translation Project in the late 1950s (and twenty years later the translator of Chomsky 1979), who had undertaken a large-scale study of Humboldt's linguistic thought (see Chomsky 1979: 135; and the reference to Viertel's work in Chomsky 1964a: 920, 1964b: 59, 1964c: 21). It is also possible that John Verhaar's (1962) paper on Saussure and Humboldt to the Ninth International Congress of Linguists helped Chomsky to clarify the differences between their theoretical positions, though the concerns of Verhaar's paper are quite different from those of Chomsky's additions to his original text.

But to locate sources of Chomsky's interest in Humboldt is not to find motives for his abandonment of Saussure. One motive is mentioned at the end of section 6: the fact that the *CLG* was widely considered to be the cornerstone of structuralism, from which Chomsky wished to distance his own position as much as possible. This problem may well have come to a head at the International Congress, its large European contingent dominated by self-avowed Saussureans. Despite Chomsky's (1963) claim of kinship with Saussure, it is hard to imagine that the European linguists' knowledge of the *CLG* would have prepared them to be less startled than their American structuralist counterparts by Chomsky's ideas.

In any case, what Chomsky needed was not Saussurean allies, but a historical anchor point, a solidly respected linguistic tradition to which to marry his own theoretical stance. The Humboldtian tradition still had practitioners, but unlike the Saussureans they were largely confined to Germany and isolated from the mainstream of the field. In noting this tactical advantage I do not mean to imply that Chomsky's interest in Humboldt was insincere; to the contrary, it has never wavered in the more than a quarter-century since the 1962 Congress. But the political convenience presented by following Humboldt rather than Saussure was no less real.

8 CHOMSKY (1965–79) THE ANTI-SAUSSUREAN

In terms of the preceding argument, the 'Cartesians', with no living tradition, represented an even more advantageous historical anchor for Chomsky. The critics of *Cartesian Linguistics* were strident, but tardy: for by the late 1960s, Chomsky had in effect vanquished the former students of Bloomfield for dominance in the field. Henceforth most of his serious rivals were to be the former students of Chomsky.

The period of Chomsky's most intense interest in the 'Cartesians' coincides with his most strident remarks about Saussure. By this time Chomsky's agenda had become just the opposite of what it had been in his 1963 article: to lump Saussure and the neo-Bloomfieldians together in one great 'modern linguistics' demonology, framed by the Descartes-to-Humboldt tradition and its generative revival. Recalling that feature (1) above suggests that Chomsky's earlier statements about Saussure viewing *langue* as a mere inventory of elements constitute a misreading, we have here an apparent motivation for that misreading. To a paragraph detailing certain seventeenth- and eighteenth-century opinions about how word order directly recapitulates the 'natural order of thoughts', and therefore can be excluded from grammar, Chomsky adds the comment: 'It is worth noting that this naive view of language structure persists to modern times in various forms, for example, in Saussure's image of a sequence of expressions corresponding to an amorphous sequence of concepts' (Chomsky 1965: 7–8).

This is an extremely strong form of feature 3. Even in Chomsky (1964a, b, c), remarks about the *CLG* not placing syntax explicitly in the domain of *langue* are considerably qualified: '[Saussure] appears to regard sentence formation as a matter of *parole* rather than *langue*, of free and voluntary creation rather than systematic rule (or perhaps, in some obscure way, as on the border between *langue* and *parole*)' (Chomsky 1964a: 921; 1964b: 59–60; 1964c: 23).

I think that most Saussureans would accept this as a fair comment. The *CLG* is very unclear on this point, reflecting an ongoing evolution in Saussure's thought over the period of the lectures on which the book is based.[15] Godel (1957: 168–79), whom Chomsky cites more than once, suggests that the endpoint of this evolution would be a view according to which all syntagms, including sentences, belong to *langue* at least potentially (see also De Mauro 1972: 468–9, n. 251). Naturally, ambiguity in a text leaves it particularly vulnerable to ideologically driven readings. *Language and Mind* (1968, expanded edition 1972), which caps Chomsky's period of intense interest in the 'Cartesians', presents syntax as part of *parole*, with no qualifiers other than the words 'occasionally' (first sentence) and 'not strictly' (second sentence):

> He [Saussure] occasionally expressed the view that processes of sentence formation do not belong to the system of language at all – that the system of language is restricted to such linguistic units as sounds and words and perhaps a few fixed phrases and a small number of very general patterns; the mechanisms of sentence

formation are otherwise free from any constraint imposed by linguistic structure as such. Thus, in his terms, sentence formation is not strictly a matter of *langue*, but is rather assigned to what he called *parole*, and thus placed outside the scope of linguistics proper; it is a process of free creation, unconstrained by linguistic rule except insofar as such rules govern the forms of words and the patterns of sounds.

(Chomsky 1968/1972: 19–20)

The last comment is not supported by *CLG* (172–3), which states in no uncertain terms that at least some prepositional phrases, verb phrases, and even sentences within *langue* are constrained by linguistic rule. Chomsky goes on to imply that Saussure has taken a resolute position on the placement of syntax within *parole* – 'In taking this position, Saussure echoed an important critique of Humboldtian linguistic theory by the distinguished American linguist William Dwight Whitney, who evidently greatly influenced Saussure' (Chomsky 1968/1972: 19–20)[16] – when in fact it is the lack of a clear position on Saussure's part that causes the *CLG* to waver. Finally, perhaps Chomsky's strongest published statement about Saussure comes in a 1976 interview, when discussing Jespersen's idea of 'free expression': 'Here he went a good deal further than the structuralists, including Saussure, who had only quite primitive things to say on this subject' (Chomsky 1979: 156).

9 CHOMSKY (1986) THE NEO-SAUSSUREAN?

In this instance, Chomsky's (1986: 19) moderate comment that 'In Saussurean structuralism . . . the notion of sentence was left in a kind of limbo, perhaps to be accommodated within the study of language use' can be taken to indicate that the 1965–72 statements were a misreading, and that his 1963–4 hedgings were closer to the truth.[17]

We have seen misreadings used to justify exaggerated claims both of Chomsky's kinship with Saussure (1963), and of the differences between them (1964–76). The remaining question is what has 'unmotivated' the misreadings of the latter period, making possible the more balanced and accurate views of Chomsky (1986)?

We are still too close to the changes in question to be certain that we are judging them accurately and impartially. But the following facts are clear. Chomsky's rejection of Saussure beginning with the 1964 articles rested fundamentally upon the notion of a well-defined deep

73

and surface structure related by a set of transformational rules, a notion which Chomsky felt was compatible with the linguistic views of the 'Cartesians', but not with those of the structuralists. One of the principal developments in generative grammar since the 1960s has been the placing of severe restrictions on transformations (reduced in government-and-binding theory to only one – move-α – with a whole module, bounding theory, devoted to limitations on its application) and consequently a de-emphasis on the contrast between deep and surface structure, which has in fact been reformulated as a three-way distinction of D-structure, S-structure, and surface structure since Chomsky (1980). The history of these changes and what motivated them is reviewed in Newmeyer (1986: 145–69) and Chomsky (1979: 169–79). The point is that, although followers of GB disdain to admit it, the result has been, not a return to, but at least a turn back in the direction of, the sort of 'flat' structure which once had made Saussure the possessor of an 'impoverished and thoroughly inadequate conception of language' (Chomsky 1968: 20).[18]

The differences between Chomsky's earliest and most recent comments regarding Port-Royal are instructive in this regard. In 1964, Chomsky claims to find an important component of his theory actually present in the Port-Royal grammar: 'In particular, we find the observation that the semantic content of a sentence is represented only in an unexpressed deep structure, based on elementary underlying strings, in the *Grammaire générale et raisonnée* of Port-Royal (1660)' (Chomsky 1964c: 15).

In 1986, when 'semantic content' (redubbed Logical Form) has been reassigned to S-structure, the level at which transformational rules (i.e. instances of move-α) have already applied, the description of the Port-Royal grammar changes accordingly: 'The seventeenth-century Port-Royal grammar and logic, for example, incorporated devices similar to phrase structure and transformational rules in this sense and used them to explain the semantic properties of sentences and to develop a theory of inference' (Chomsky 1986: 65). One detects a change in tone as well: the 'devices' in question are merely similar, rather than (implicitly) identical. The preceding citation occurs, significantly, in an account of the long-since abandoned Extended Standard Theory, and is followed by a review of the restrictions that were to be placed on transformations.

In sum, there is abundant evidence that Chomsky – like Bloomfield, Saussure and probably every other linguist – has read according to his agenda. So much of his intellectual development is on the public record that his work provides an exceptional body of evidence for how an individual's readings change in parallel with shifts in his or her ideology. Chomsky adopted Saussure as a historical precursor at a propitious moment in the course of his work, citing aspects of Saussurean thought that corresponded to that work and ignoring most of those that did not. Shortly thereafter, having found preferable precursors, he reversed the emphasis on those aspects and progressively distanced himself from Saussure. Now, further changes in generative theory have freed Chomsky to reread certain virtues into the Saussurean viewpoint – a viewpoint maintained in its 'pre-Chomskyan' form in so few quarters that even its proponents, at least the realistic ones, have long since ceased to imagine that it might one day re-emerge as a threat to the generative position.

10 CONCLUSION

Given the extent of Saussure's influence, there are virtually as many important readings of him as there have been important linguists in this century. While the processes seen at work in Bloomfield's and Chomsky's readings (as well as in those of dozens of other readers who might have been chosen; for examples see Joseph 1989a, b, c) are unusually extensive for reasons alluded to in section 1 above, they are nevertheless extensions of the basic problem of 'misreading' throughout disciplines, particularly those which are oriented toward the abstract rather than the practical.

This being the case, the present article should self-deconstruct: my readings of Bloomfield and Chomsky are not offered as 'true' in any kind of objective sense. They have been shaped by my agenda of locating ideologically determined readings. Yet I believe, perhaps too optimistically, that awareness of one's own ideological bent at least removes one major obstacle to clarity of thought. At the same time I realize, perhaps too pessimistically, that publishing this chapter guarantees its misreading: some linguists will insist on seeing it as a negative criticism of the field and its history no matter how fervently I protest to the contrary. But let me try one last time: a discipline is scientific to the extent it is able to dispel its illusions. No discipline has ever or will ever dispel all illusions. Unless on this ground one is ready to declare that no discipline is a science, then linguistics is most assuredly a scientific enterprise.

NOTES

I am grateful to Robert Austerlitz, Charles Hockett, Konrad Koerner and Rulon Wells for useful comments on sections 2, 3 and 4 when I first presented them in a different form at the 1987 LSA meeting (see Joseph 1989d); to Noam Chomsky for supplying valuable information regarding his early interest in Saussure (section 6); to Fr Frank Dinneen for some first-hand reminiscences of the Ninth International Congress of Linguists (section 7); and to Talbot Taylor for helpful criticisms and general encouragement. Any errors of fact or interpretation are entirely my responsibility.

1 A number of my own ideologies are on display in the foregoing paragraphs: for example, that misreadings are inevitable, productive, ideologically driven; that revealing them strengthens, rather than weakens, work in the field.

2 It was not J. B. Watson but Albert Paul Weiss (1879–1931) whose behaviourist psychology became Bloomfield's model. Harris acknowledges further on that 'it would be a mistake to infer from the way in which Bloomfield's *Language* deliberately ignores Saussure that Saussurean ideas left no trace in American academic linguistics of the interwar period. Bloomfield himself admitted to Jakobson that reading the *CLG* was one of the events which had most influenced him (De Mauro 1972: 371)' (xiii–xiv).

3 For example, De Mauro (1972: 371–2): 'Mais la mention isolée du nom de Saussure dans *Language* [Bloomfield 1933] autorise à maintenir que commence là l'éclipse de Saussure, caractéristique de la linguistique post-bloomfieldienne . . . . Il y a en effet chez les bloomfieldiens la crainte de retomber dans le mentalisme en quittant le terrain behavioriste et en parlant de langue.'

4 Bloomfield concludes this paragraph with a seeming metacommentary; my notes appear in brackets: 'Needless to say, a person who goes out to write down an unknown language [as Bloomfield had done, but Saussure had not] or one who undertakes to teach people a foreign language [likewise a more central concern for Bloomfield than Saussure] must have a knowledge of phonetics [as Saussure did not], just as he must possess tact [as Bloomfield's tactics admirably demonstrate!], patience, and many other virtues; in principle [but not in practice!], however, these things are all on a par, and do not form part of linguistic theory.' In the light of Bloomfield's practice over the next twenty-five years, it is hard to see that he could have intended a sincere endorsement here.

5 Bloomfield goes on to give a fairly accurate account of *Langage–langue–parole*; then makes a couple of small errors: he equates *linguistique diachronique* with 'historical linguistics' when the clear intent of the *CLG* was to put the two in opposition (see Harris 1987: 89); then describes it in terms of 'change in the system of *la langue*', when the *CLG* took such pains to correct the notion of change to that of concurrence and replacement within *la parole*.

6 Two further justifications are given for this stance: (1) 'In discussing certain fundamental problems, such as that of meaning, which could be

dealt with by [behaviourist] postulates, linguists are accustomed to appeal directly to psychology'; (2) 'every now and then, before some knotty problem, a linguist will lay down the long-tried tools of his trade, not to sharpen or improve them, but to resort instead, for the nonce, to incantations about whose value no two even of the psychologic shamans will agree'. This appears to be an attack on the 'introductory chapters' of the books he is discussing, where general principles are outlined before their application – or rather non-application, abandonment – to the analysis of data. The 'incantations' correspond to what he will label and dismiss as 'mentalism' in 1933.

7 Meanwhile, let us note that the additional complexity he sees in Saussure's system over Ogden and Richards's resides in the 'acoustic image', which could not fall clearly into either their 'Thought or Referent', with which it shares the feature of being purely mental, or their 'Symbol', with which it shares linguisticness.

8 To be precise, the second argument is not pertinent, for it applies to a diachronic shift, something which the *CLG* maintains does not occur within *langue*, but in *parole*.

9 In the book's only other reference to Saussure besides those discussed in this section, Chomsky dismisses as 'unintentionally comical' the charge by Harris (1983) that 'the standard idealization (which he ascribes to Saussure-Bloomfield-Chomsky) reflects "a fascist concept of language if ever there was one", because it takes the "ideal" speech community to be "totally homogeneous" ' (Chomsky 1986: 47n.). But cf. Crowley and Cameron, this volume.

10 The two earlier versions of Chomsky (1964c) show minor stylistic variations in the passage cited (Chomsky 1964a: 922, 1964b: 60).

11 The corresponding passage in Chomsky (1964a: 923) and (1964b: 61–2) omits the word 'full' in the first sentence.

12 Chomsky (1986: 5) characterizes such progress as 'a healthy phenomenon indicating that the discipline is alive, although it is sometimes, oddly, regarded as a serious deficiency, a sign that something is wrong with the basic approach' (see also Chomsky 1979: 175–6). Exactly the same may be said of his opinions regarding Saussure.

13 These also happen to be two features of language to whose study Chomsky has never made any direct contribution, although indirectly his ideas have had a tremendous impact on diachronic enquiry and a considerable impact on sociolinguistics.

14 Koerner (1988) questions the accuracy of Chomsky's identification of Humboldt's view with his own.

15 To cite just one statement by Saussure from the *CLG* source materials: 'Ce n'est que dans la syntaxe en somme que se présentera un certain flottement ici entre ce qui est donné dans la langue et ce qui est laissé à l'individuel. La délimitation est difficile à faire' (Engler 1968–74: 2022C).

16 Regarding Whitney's influence on Saussure, see Joseph (1988).

17 As Chomsky (1986: 5) has commented regarding the development of generative theory, 'there have been many changes and differences of opinions, often reversion to ideas that had been abandoned and were later reconstructed in a different light' (see also Chomsky 1979: 176).

18 Throughout the period of restricting the power of the transformational component, and ever since, Chomsky has insisted that elimination of the component is not a desideratum. Certainly it continues to play a key role in virtually every module of GB theory. The important point for my argument is simply the indisputable fact that this component has been greatly reduced in power and in work performed, and in this sense is relatively less significant within the overall model than it was in the mid-1960s. Beyond this, the considerable success of the transformation-free model of Generalized Phrase Structure Grammar can be taken as additional evidence of the component's diminishing appeal to the linguistic community at large. See further the contrastive studies in Droste and Joseph (1990).

4

Demythologizing sociolinguistics: why language does not reflect society

Deborah Cameron

1 INTRODUCTION

As Roy Harris, from whom I borrow the notion of 'demythologizing', has observed:

> A concept of a language involves, and is most often clearly manifest in, acceptance or rejection of what requires explanation about the ways in which languages work. This means that a concept of a language cannot stand isolated in an intellectual no-man's land. It is inevitably part of some more intricate complex of views about how certain verbal activities stand in relation to other human activities, and hence, ultimately, about man's place in society and in nature.
>
> (Harris 1980: 54)

Harris's own work represents an attempt to explore the 'intricate complex of views' that underpin the western tradition of language study. He identifies what he calls a 'language myth' (Harris 1981): a collection of taken-for-granted propositions about the nature and workings of language from which particular questions 'naturally' follow, and lead in turn to particular kinds of solutions. For example, if one accepts the Lockean idea of communication through language as 'telementation', the transference of messages from one mind to another, the obvious question is 'how can this be accomplished?' and the natural solution is to model language as a 'fixed code' located in the mind of every speaker.

Harris's project of 'demythologizing' linguistics consists essentially in making explicit the hidden assumptions which underlie linguists' models, showing that they are historical constructs (rather than immutable truths given by the nature of language itself) and subjecting them to critical scrutiny. By adopting a different concept of a language, Harris points out, we would inevitably commit ourselves to asking quite different questions and proposing quite other solutions. In Harris's view this is exactly what linguistics ought to do; but I should perhaps add that we do not have to agree with Harris's outright rejection of current linguistic orthodoxy to accept his critical method as a valid and useful tool for reflecting on our practice.

In this chapter, I want to reflect on the practice of sociolinguistics (by which I mean, more or less, the 'variationist' or 'quantitative' paradigm associated with the work of Labov; whether this is an unreasonably narrow definition of the term 'sociolinguistics' is a question to which I shall return). In a demythologizing spirit I shall ask what assumptions about language and society underpin work in the quantitative paradigm, why sociolinguists have invested in these assumptions and whether they are useful, or even tenable. I shall argue that if sociolinguistics is to move forward, or indeed to realize fully its current objectives, it will need to shift its views 'about how certain verbal activities stand in relation to other human activities' – a move whose consequences for sociolinguistic methodology and theory may well prove quite radical.

Let me say immediately that I do not wish to deny the value of work in the quantitative paradigm. Indeed, there is an irony in my attempting to demythologize sociolinguistics, since sociolinguistics itself was conceived as a demythologizing exercise. The name Labov once gave it – 'secular linguistics' – implies a conscious desire to challenge sacred linguistic dogmas.

The doctrine Labov was most concerned to challenge was that of 'the ideal speaker-hearer in a homogeneous speech community' (I use the familiar Chomskyan formulation, but the central point that linguistics must idealize its object in order to describe it goes back through the structuralist paradigm and to Saussure). Labov debunked this as myth by showing that language is not homogeneous, either at the level of the speech community or the individual grammar. Rather, it possesses 'structured variability'. 'Structured' is important here: it means the variation found in language is not a matter of 'free' or random alterations (which mainstream linguists had recognized but excluded from consideration on the grounds that they were superficial, hence uninteresting, and difficult to model elegantly) but is, on the contrary, systematic and socially conditioned. Labov's work demonstrated that variation could be modelled, and that the analysis of variation provided insight into the mechanism of language change. In other words, he argued convincingly that to accept the myth of the ideal speaker-hearer in the homogeneous speech community was not merely to screen out a few surface irregularities, but rather to miss a fundamental general property of language.

By insisting on the importance of heterogeneity, and developing methods for analysing it, sociolinguistics clarified questions of real theoretical importance which were not addressed in any principled way by existing paradigms. Like all myths, the myth of idealized homogeneity had foregrounded some things, making them easier to 'see', while rendering other things (like variation and change) impenetrably obscure. Labov's work may with justice be called 'demythologizing' because it pointed this out, and began the task of bringing what was obscure into the light. But the approach he founded is not without myths and blindspots of its own. Quantitative sociolinguistics has certainly clarified some aspects of language in society. But other aspects remain mysterious, the crucial questions unanswered, or even unasked.

What are these crucial questions? Very briefly, they concern the reasons *why* people behave linguistically as they have been found to do in study after study. Sociolinguistics does not provide us with anything like a satisfactory explanation. The account which is usually given – or, worse, presupposed – in the quantitative paradigm is some version of the proposition that 'language reflects society'. Thus there exist social categories, structures, divisions, attitudes and identities which are marked or encoded or expressed in language use. By correlating patterns of linguistic variation with these social or demographic features, we have given a sufficient account of them. (The account may also be supplemented with crudely functionalist ideas – that speakers 'use' language to express their social identity, for instance – or with a slightly less crude model in terms of group 'norms' at both macro- and micro-levels.)[1]

Two things about this kind of account are particularly problematic. The first problem is its dependence on a naive and simplistic *social* theory. Concepts like 'norm', 'identity' and so on, and sociological models of structures/divisions like class, ethnicity and gender, are used as a 'bottom line' though they stand in need of explication themselves. Secondly, there is the problem of how to *relate* the social to the linguistic (however we conceive the social). The 'language reflects society' account implies that social structures somehow exist before language, which simply 'reflects' or 'expresses' the more fundamental categories of the social. Arguably however we need a far more complex model that treats language as *part of* the social, interacting with other modes of behaviour and just as important as any of them.

Before I return to these problems in more detail, it is necessary to ask why sociolinguistics has become caught up in them – why has the quantitative paradigm invested in the whole notion of 'language reflecting society'? This takes us back to the question of what socio-linguistics is, and how the field has been defined.

2 'SOCIOLINGUISTICS AND SOCIOLINGUISTICS': THE RISE AND RISE OF THE QUANTITATIVE PARADIGM

As I pointed out above, to make sociolinguistics synonymous with the Labovian quantitative paradigm is to beg the question. There are other approaches to the study of language in society (such as ethno-graphy of speaking, discourse analysis, sociology of language) which surely have some claim to the title 'sociolinguistics' so that my definition could be construed as unnecessarily narrow and restricted, not to say biased.

To the criticism of narrowness and bias, however, I would respond by asserting that my definition of sociolinguistics reflects a historical (and academic-political) reality: over the last fifteen years the quantitative paradigm has so successfully pressed its claims to the central and dominant position in language and society studies, that for most people in the field (and especially most *linguists* in the field) 'sociolinguistics' does indeed mean primarily if not exclusively 'Labovian quantitative sociolinguistics'. The effect of this shift, for as we shall see it *is* a shift, is to privilege and even to mythologize one kind of approach to linguistic variation.

It is instructive to look at what has happened to the discipline known as 'sociology of language'. Today it is sometimes assumed that this never existed as a separate enterprise – that it was merely a terminological variant of sociolinguistics, since discarded by common consent. But a look at the literature gives the lie to that idea. Joshua Fishman, for example, one of the leading practitioners of sociology of language in the 1960s and early 1970s, draws a distinction between the two approaches (Fishman 1968: 6). He conceives of sociolinguistics as a type of linguistics, a way of studying language; sociology of language by contrast need not be done by people trained in linguistics and will always take problems of society and social theory as a starting point.

In so far as any distinction has been maintained, it seems to have become one of content rather than theoretical orientation. Sociology of language concerns itself with macro-social language questions (language choice and planning, for instance) while sociolinguistics deals with the microanalysis of variation (for an explicit statement to this effect see Hudson 1980: 5; for a recent (and rare) example of a sociology of language text see Fasold 1984, which is however titled *The Sociolinguistics of Society* – perhaps the term 'sociology of language' no longer sells books to linguists?). Fishman regards this development with considerable disfavour. In a review of Fasold 1984 (Fishman 1986) he attacks the content-based distinction as inherently ill-founded and criticizes Fasold for paying insufficient attention to social theory *per se*. But what all this illustrates is that, apart from a few dissenting voices like Fishman's, there has been a shift in the consensus about what properly constitutes the study of language in society, and it is a shift away from the sociological towards the more purely linguistic.

If further evidence is needed, one can point to any number of textbooks by influential authors in which the primacy of linguistic over social issues is vigorously asserted (Hudson 1980; Trudgill 1978 and 1983). In a rather bizarrely titled introductory essay called 'Sociolinguistics and sociolinguistics', Trudgill puts his notion of what he calls 'sociolinguistics proper' in the following terms: 'All work in this category . . . is aimed ultimately at improving linguistic theory and at developing our understanding of the nature of language . . . very definitely *not* "linguistics as a social science"' (1978: 3).

Now there is of course nothing wrong with trying to improve linguistic theory and our understanding of the nature of language; it is also quite true that sociolinguistics of the sort Trudgill advocates has enabled progress to be made (see pp. 80–1 above). But one might ask: why this assiduous policing of the disciplinary borders? What is at stake in the emphatic denial of 'linguistics as a social science'? Is Trudgill's stand well-motivated in terms of the overall aims of sociolinguistics, or is it determined by somewhat different considerations?

In my view, what Trudgill says (and he is typical enough) can be interpreted as part of an understandable concern about the academic prestige of sociolinguistics. Many sociolinguists would like to lay claim to the sort of prestige mainstream linguistics has achieved over the last twenty-five years; conversely, they would like to distance themselves from the more dubious reputation of contemporary sociology. Academic prestige is dependent on various factors, but one of them is *scientific status*:

a prestigious discipline will tend to possess qualities associated with science (however erroneously) such as theoretical and methodological rigour, 'objectivity', abstraction and so on. One achievement of the so-called Chomskyan revolution has been to appropriate this sort of status for linguistics more successfully than previous or alternative paradigms. Little wonder, then, that sociolinguistics should concentrate on the 'linguistics' to the virtual exclusion of the 'socio'.

It is also relevant, however, that mainstream linguists are sceptical of the sociolinguists' claim to share their glory. Sociolinguistics is in some respects a 'poor relation'; in the accepted university curriculum it is peripheral or optional where mainstream grammar is 'core' knowledge, while in terms of prestige it is frequently dismissed as mere 'butterfly collecting'.[2] Sociolinguists therefore find themselves in a position where they have to 'prove' the validity of what they do to their own academic colleagues in the mainstream; this again encourages them to be as 'rigorous' and 'objective' as possible (for instance, to make heavy use of statistical techniques) and, most importantly, to let linguistics set the agenda for research.

The trouble with concentrating on the purely linguistic and es-chewing approaches tainted with the 'social science' tag is that sociolinguistics, however you try to define it, remains the study of language *in society*. Linguistic variation cannot be described sensibly without reference to its social conditioning; and if sociolinguistics is to progress from description to explanation (as it must unless it wants to be vulnerable to renewed charges of 'butterfly collecting') it is obviously in need of a theory linking the 'linguistic' to the 'socio'. Without a satisfactory social theory, therefore, and beyond that a satisfactory account of the relationship between social and linguistic spheres, sociolinguistics is bound to end up stranded in an explanatory void.

Faced with the problem of explaining variation, and in the absence of a well-thought-out theory of the relation of language and society, sociolinguists tend to fall back on a number of unsatisfactory positions: they may deny that anything other than statistical correlation is necessary to explain variation, they may introduce *ad hoc* social theories of one kind or another, or they may do both. Let us look more closely at the way these positions are taken up in practice and at their adequacy or otherwise as explanatory strategies.

3 EXPLANATION AND THE LIMITS OF QUANTIFICATION: THE CORRELATIONAL FALLACY

In the quantitative paradigm, statistical correlations are used to relate frequency scores on linguistic variables to nonlinguistic features both demographic (class, ethnicity, gender, age, locality, group structure) and contextual (topic, setting, level of formality). For instance, it is well known that rising frequencies of 'prestige' variants like postvocalic [r] in New York City correlate positively with rising social status and rising levels of formality. This kind of regularity is called a 'sociolinguistic pattern'.

Sociolinguistic patterns are essentially descriptive statements about the distribution of certain variables in the speech community. The question remains how to explain that distribution. As Brown and Levinson (1987) have noted, it is commonplace to take correlation as the terminal point of the account. Thus it could be claimed that my score for the variant [r] is explained by the fact that I belong to a particular social category – say, working-class women of Italian descent aged 50+ and living in New York City – and am speaking in a particular context, say a formal interview with a linguistic researcher. The variable (r) acts as what Scherer and Giles (1979) call a 'social marker'. This whole 'explanation' clearly rests on the perception that 'language reflects society': I shall refer to it as the 'correlational fallacy'.

Why is it a fallacy? Because the purported explanation does not in fact explain anything. Someone who subscribes to the sort of account given above has misunderstood what it means to explain something. One does not explain a descriptive generalization (such as 'older working-class female Italian New Yorkers in formal interviews have average (r) scores of n%') by simply stating it all over again. Rather, one is obliged to ask in virtue of what the correlation might hold. Any account which does not go on to take this further step has fallen into the correlational fallacy.

It is precisely at the point where the further step becomes necessary that *ad hoc* social theories are likely to be invoked. A sociolinguist might assert, for instance, that by using n% of (r), older working-class female Italian New Yorkers are expressing their identity as older working-class female Italian New Yorkers; or they are adhering to the norms of their peer group, or possibly (as in the case of a formal interview) the norms of the larger society which dictate a more standardized speech on certain occasions.

There are various difficulties with these suggestions, not all of which can be gone into here in the detail they deserve, but certain problems can at least be sketched in. Take, for example, the notion of speakers expressing a social identity. It is common currency among sociolinguists, but a social theorist might pose some awkward questions about it: do people really 'have' such fixed and monolithic social identities which their behaviour consistently expresses? Furthermore, is it correct to see language use as expressing an identity which is separate from and prior to language? To put the point a little less obscurely, is it not the case that the way I use language is partly *constitutive* of my social identity? To paraphrase Harold Garfinkel, social actors are not sociolinguistic 'dopes'. The way in which they construct and negotiate identities needs to be examined in some depth before we can say much about the relation of language to identity.

The suggestion that people's use of language reflects group norms is a more useful one; it recognizes that human behaviour needs to be explained not in terms of invariant causes and effects but in terms of the existence of social meanings, in the light of which people act to reproduce or subvert the order of things. Unfortunately the account of normativity to be found in sociolinguistics is a curious and extremely deterministic one (a claim which will be illustrated below). There is also the question of where linguistic norms 'come from' and how they 'get into' individual speakers – a problem which becomes all the more acute when, as is often the case, the alleged norms are statistical regularities of such abstraction and complexity that no individual speaker could possibly articulate them either for herself or any other member of the speech community. So once again, the whole issue of norms requires a less *ad hoc* and more sophisticated treatment than it has on the whole received from sociolinguists.

Many of the problems to which I have referred here are also addressed by Suzanne Romaine in an article titled 'The status of sociological models and categories in explaining linguistic variation', which stands as an indictment of the correlational fallacy in socio-linguistics (Romaine 1984). In her article, Romaine adduces four typical studies in the quantitative paradigm (Labov 1963; Gal 1979; Milroy 1980; Russell 1982) and points out a link between them: they all explain linguistic variation and change in terms of group structure and membership. Tight-knit groups (technically, dense multiplex networks) promote language maintenance whereas looser ties permit linguistic change.

An illustration may make this clearer. Lesley Milroy (1980) devised what she called a 'network strength scale' to measure the integration of her Belfast informants into their peer group. Points were scored for such things as having strong ties of kinship in the neighbourhood; working at the same place as your neighbours; spending leisure time with workmates; and so on. Individuals scored between 0 and 5 for network strength, and high scores were found to correlate positively with the use of certain vernacular variants. People who were less well integrated – for instance because they had been rehoused, were employed outside the neighbourhood where they lived or had no work at all – used fewer of these vernacular features. This led Milroy to conclude that people in her survey behaved linguistically as they did because of the normative influence of their peer group. Their scores on linguistic variants were determined by how strong or weak the peer group influence was. Tight-knit groups where people spend a lot of time with each other (and less with anyone else) are efficient norm-enforcing mechanisms – hence the finding that they promote the mainte- nance of traditional vernacular rather than permitting innovation to creep in.

All this may seem obvious enough, but as Romaine enquires, what kind of an *explanation* is it? The social network is a theoretical construct which cannot therefore 'make' any individual speaker do anything. Yet if we take away the idea of the network's ability to enforce linguistic norms, all we are left with is statistical correlations. Of these Romaine comments: 'the observed correlations between language and group membership tell us nothing unless fitted into some more general theory' (1984: 37).

What is this 'general theory' to be? Clearly, it needs to engage with the whole issue of how individuals relate to groups and their norms – in Romaine's words, it must make reference to 'rationality, intentionality and the function of social agents and human actors' (ibid.: 26). Is it then a theory of individual psychology, which seeks to explain how actors make rational decisions in the domain of linguistic behaviour? This kind of 'rational choice' line is the one often favoured by sociolinguists who do go beyond correlation (cf. Brown and Levinson's explanation (1987) of politeness phenomena in terms of strategies for satisfying universal psychological needs to maintain 'face'). But while an account of individual psychology may be necessary, I think Romaine recognizes it is not sufficient. There is another, neglected area which properly belongs to the study of language in society but which cannot be addressed within the current assumptions of the quantitative paradigm.

Romaine hints at this when she makes the following observation:

> It is legitimate to recognise that an agent's social position and his relations with others may constrain his behavior on a particular occasion in specific ways. . . . People are constrained by the expressive resources available in the language(s) to which they have access and by the conventions which apply to their use. (1984: 37).

This can be interpreted as an argument for social or sociological levels of explanation as well as individual or psychological ones. For what Romaine alludes to here is the fact that speakers 'inherit' a certain system and can only choose from the options it makes available. Social agents are not *free* agents, but this does not mean we have to go back to the notion that they are sociolinguistic automata. Rather, we should ask ourselves such questions as 'what determines "the expressive resources available" in particular languages or to particular groups of speakers? Who or what *produces* "the conventions which apply to their use"? How – that is to say, through what actual, concrete practices – is this done?'

To address such issues seriously requires us to acknowledge that languages are regulated social institutions, and as such may have their own dynamic and become objects of social concern in their own right. With its emphasis on microanalysis and its suspicion of social theory, sociolinguistics tends to push this kind of perspective into the background. But if we seek to understand people's linguistic behaviour and attitudes – and, after all, changes in the linguistic system must at some level be brought about by the behaviour and attitudes of actual speakers – an approach to language in society which foregrounds questions like Romaine's is desperately needed. A demythologized sociolinguistics would incorporate such an approach as a necessary complement to quantification and microanalysis. It would deal with such matters as the production and reproduction of linguistic norms by institutions and socializing practices; how these norms are appre-hended, accepted, resisted and subverted by individual actors and what their relation is to the construction of identity.

At this point it is helpful to consider in concrete terms how an approach like this would work and what its advantages might be. I shall therefore turn to a case in point: the changes in linguistic behaviour and in certain language systems brought about by the reformist efforts of contemporary feminists. These developments exemplify a kind of linguistic change with which quantitative sociolinguists do not feel at ease, and in relation to which conventional accounts within the 'language reflects society' framework appear particularly lame.

4 A CASE IN POINT: SEXISM IN LANGUAGE

Over the last fifteen years the question of 'sexism in language' has been a hotly contested topic both inside and outside professional linguistic circles. What is at issue is the ways in which certain linguistic subsystems (conventional titles and forms of address, parts of the lexicon and even of grammar, for instance) represent gender. Feminists have pointed out that the tendency of these representations is to reinforce sexual divisions and inequalities. Salient facts about English include, for example, the morphological marking of many female-referring agent nouns (*actress, usherette*); the availability of more sexually pejorative terms for women than men (Lees 1980); the non-reciprocal use of endearment terms from men to women (Wolfson and Manes 1980); and, most notoriously, the generic use of masculine pronouns (Bodine 1975).

It should not surprise us that phenomena like these are widely understood as an instance of 'language reflecting society'. 'Society' holds certain beliefs about men and women and their relative status; language has 'evolved' to reflect those beliefs. Feminists have tried to argue that more is going on than passive reflection: sexist linguistic practice is an instance of sexism in its own right and actively reproduces specific beliefs. But nonfeminist sociolinguists have notably failed to take their point.

This becomes particularly evident in discussions of recent changes in English usage – changes which have occurred under pressure from feminist campaigns against sexism in language. For some time, the view of many linguists was that reforming sexist language was an unnecessary, trivial and timewasting objective, since language merely reflected social conditions. If feminists concentrated on removing more fundamental sex inequalities, the language would change of its own accord, automatically reflecting the new nonsexist reality.[3] (This, incidentally, suggests a view of language which might have been supposed to be obsolete in twentieth-century thought, and which we might label 'the organic fallacy': that language is like an organism, with a life of its own, and evolves to meet the needs of its speakers. Exactly how language does this remains a mystery.)

More recently however it has become obvious that linguistic reform as proposed by feminists has enjoyed a measure of success. For instance, it is clear that generic masculine pronouns are no longer uniformly used by educated speakers and writers; even such authoritative sources as Quirk *et. al.* (1985) acknowledge the existence of alternatives such as singular *they* and *he or she*. What do sociolinguists make of this change in English pronominal usage? Astonishingly, they tell us it has happened 'naturally', as a reflection of the fact that women's social position has radically altered in the last two decades (cf. Cheshire 1984: 33–4 for a statement to this effect).

It is worth pointing out in detail what is wrong with this sort of claim. One immediate flaw in the argument is that it is patently untrue: without campaigns and debates specifically on the issue of sexism *in language*, linguistic usage would not have altered even though other feminist gains (such as equal pay and anti-discrimination legislation) were made. Historically speaking there is certainly a connection between feminist campaigns for equal opportunities and for nonsexist language, but the one has never entailed the other, nor did either just reflect the other. To repeat the crucial point once more: language-using is a social practice in its own right.

It should also be pointed out that a change in linguistic practice is not just a reflection of some more fundamental social change: it is, itself, a social change. Anti-feminists are fond of observing that eliminating generic masculine pronouns does not secure equal pay. Indeed it does not – whoever said it would? Eliminating generic masculine pronouns precisely eliminates generic masculine pronouns. And in so doing it changes the repertoire of social meanings and choices available to social actors. In the words of Trevor Pateman (1980: 15) it 'constitutes a restructuring of at least one aspect of one social relationship'.

Another problem with the 'language reflects society' argument in relation to changes in English usage is that it makes language change a mysterious, abstract process, apparently effected by the agency of no one at all (or perhaps by the language itself – the organic fallacy rides again). This overlooks the protracted struggle which individuals and groups have waged both for and against nonsexist language (and the struggle continues). It ignores, for instance, the activitity of every woman who ever fought to put 'Ms' on her cheque book, every publisher, university committee or trades union working party that produced new institutional guidelines on the wording of documents, not to mention every vituperative writer to the newspapers who resisted, denounced or complained about nonsexist language.

The general point here is that there are instances – this is one – where we can locate the specific and concrete steps leading to an observable change in some people's linguistic behaviour and in the system itself. We can discover who took those steps and who opposed them. We can refer to a printed debate on the subject, examine the arguments put forward on both sides (and it is interesting that those arguments tended to be about language rather than gender: not 'should women be treated equally' but 'what do words mean and is it right to change them?'). The 'language reflects society' model obscures the mechanisms by which sexist language has become less acceptable, evacuating any notion of agency in language change. Crucially, too, the model glosses over the existence of social conflict and its implications for language use. Here as elsewhere in sociolinguistics the underlying assumption is of a consensual social formation where speakers acquiesce in the norms of their peer group or their culture, and agree about the social 'needs' which language exists to serve.

It would of course be wrong to claim that all linguistic change is of this kind – organized and politically motivated efforts to alter existing norms and conventions. But some linguistic changes *are* of this kind, and sociolinguistics should not espouse a concept of language which makes them impossible to account for.

5 TOWARDS A DEMYTHOLOGIZED SOCIOLINGUISTICS

The campaign against sexism in language is one instance of a type of metalinguistic practice which we might call 'verbal hygiene' (other examples might include Plain English movements or Artificial Language movements; systems regulating the use of obscenity and insults (cf. Garrioch 1987); and, of course, prescriptivism, standardization and associated activities). Such practices are referred to in sociolinguistic work in passing if at all: doubtless it is thought that they are unlikely to advance linguistic theory, and should therefore be left for sociologists to research.

Yet if the arguments put forward above have any force, it may not be so easy to prise apart the concerns of linguistic theory and those of the sociologist. We have seen that sociolinguists make casual but significant use of notions like 'norm' and 'social identity' in order to explain the variation and the attitudes they observe. And I have argued that one of the problems with this is that we are left with no account of where norms 'come from' and how they 'get into' individual speakers – it is not good enough simply to situate them in some vague and ill-defined 'society', as though society were homogeneous, monolithic and transparent in its workings, and as if individual language users were pre-programmed automata. A detailed investigation of language-users' metalinguistic activities – for instance, forms of 'verbal hygiene' – might well tell us a good deal about the production of norms and their apprehension by individuals.

It is striking, for example, that sociolinguists very often refer to the (overt) 'prestige' of standard English and assume this is impressed on speakers by normative instruction carried out mainly in schools; yet I know of no study of how (or even whether) the norms of standard English are inculcated by teachers. Dannequin (1988) has researched this question in France, and the resulting paper is extremely informative – a model of demythologizing.

Metalinguistic activities and beliefs have received, at least in urban western societies, less attention than they merit. For it is surely a very significant fact about language in these societies that people hold passionate beliefs about it; that it generates social and political conflicts; that practices and movements grow up around it both for and against the *status quo*. We may consider the well-attested fact that many people, including those with minimal education, read a dictionary for pleasure; that there is a vast market for grammars, usage guides and general interest publications, radio and TV programmes about the English language; that many large-circulation newspapers and periodicals (such as the *Readers Digest*) have a regular column on linguistic matters.

Most researchers in the quantitative paradigm are of course well aware of these facts, and more generally of people's keen interest in linguistic minutiae. With some honourable exceptions, though, they tend to treat laypersons' views on usage as manifestations of ignorance to be dispelled, or of crankishness and prejudice to be despised. The axiom that linguistics is 'descriptive not prescriptive', together with the methodological principle that a researcher should influence informants as little as possible, prevent sociolinguists taking folk linguistics seriously. Arguably, though, practices like dictionary reading and writing to the papers on points of usage are striking enough to demand analysis: first, not unnaturally, they demand investigation.

And this is the task I would set for a demythologized sociolinguistics:

to examine the linguistic practices in which members of a culture regularly participate or to whose effects they are exposed. As well as being of interest in itself, this undertaking would help us to make sense of the process noted by Romaine: the constraining of linguistic behaviour by the social relations in which speakers are involved and the linguistic resources to which they have access. We might also discover how language change may come about through the efforts of individuals and groups to produce new resources and new social relations. For language is not an organism or a passive reflection, but a social institution, deeply implicated in culture, in society, in political relations at every level. What sociolinguistics needs is a concept of language in which this point is placed at the centre rather than on the margins.

NOTES

1 'Macro' norms would include the prestige of standard and the stigma of nonstandard variants, constructed at the level of the whole society (education, media and so on); 'micro' norms would be of the sort alluded to by Labov (1972) and Milroy (1980) whereby close-knit peer groups sanction deviations from local rules of language use.

2 In the UK sociolinguistics is also under-resourced in terms of grant support; Newmeyer 1986 claims this is not so in the US, but that (if true) reflects not the prestige accorded to the field by linguists but the potential state agencies see in it for social control. Cf. Turner 1988.

3 Although this view among linguists is difficult to document from published sources, the point has been made to me in conversation by innumerable professional colleagues, many of whom have also expressed misgivings about linguistic reform on the grounds that it is prescriptive and linguists should therefore eschew it.

Part II

THE LINGUISTICS OF SELF-IMAGE

5

Celso Cittadini and the origin of the vernacular: the convergence of science and subjectivity

Michael T. Ward

1 INTRODUCTION

The work of the late-cinquecento philologist Celso Cittadini offers a striking example of the motivation of linguistic theory by pre-existing belief. In an attempt to assert the worth of the Italian vernacular, Cittadini rejected common conceptions of its origin, finding in inscriptional evidence confirmation of an alternate view. While his pronouncements may seem to constitute just another episode in the protracted controversy known as the Italian 'Question of the Language', Cittadini stands apart for his greater attention to significant data and its utilization than to subtleties of argumentation. Although his philological investigation was guided by a hypothesis regarding his language's development, the sophistication of its results distances Cittadini from theorists of his own and preceding eras.[1]

Cittadini is well known as a participant in the linguistic debates of the sixteenth century, and his work has been viewed as anticipating the discoveries of later historical linguistics. Despite such recognition, there have been few studies devoted to his theories, and what examinations do exist contain certain inaccuracies.[2] The present discussion will focus on key aspects of Cittadini's *Trattato della vera origine, e del processo, e nome della nostra lingua (Treatise on the True Origin, and Process, and Name of our Language)* and *Trattato degli articoli, e di alcune altre particelle della vulgar lingua (Treatise on the Articles and Some Other Particles of the Vernacular Tongue)* (both published in 1601), dissertations which furnish an undisputedly authentic view of his perspective.[3] I hope that my analysis of his complex and sometimes imprecise exposition will permit a fuller appreciation of his significance for the field of language science.

In the following pages Cittadini's perspective on four broad topics will be addressed: his conception of a bi-level structure in Latin, corresponding chiefly to social stratification (section 2); his portrayal of the largely independent evolution of each linguistic stratum (section 3); his treatment of specific orthographic and phonetic modifications across the centuries (section 4); and his involvement in the 'Question of the Language' (section 5).

2 THE BI-LEVEL STRUCTURE OF LATIN

Fundamental to an understanding of Cittadini's stance is his postulation of a two-tier construction within the Latin language. Very early in the *Vera origine* there appears a clear statement of this view:

> At all times, both earlier and later, there were in Rome two types of language. One, rough and half barbarous, was found among the populace, that is, unlearned Romans and foreigners, or those of the lower classes, and uneducated country folk. The expressions and words of this variety were rejected by writers and noble speakers, and have remained, for the most part – except for word-endings – in the mouths of the Italian people, without distinction of commonness or nobility. . . . The other language variety was cultivated by art and was pure Latin, found among writers and noble speakers, and the learned.
>
> 1601: 2r–v)[4]

Cittadini claims that although it is chiefly the language of the Roman populace which has been maintained (with modification) through the centuries, the only written examples of this variety in its ancient stage are found in inscriptions and epitaphs; Roman authors, however, attest to its existence (ibid.: 2v). Forestalling the objection that this lack of concrete evidence means the absence of a separate vernacular Latin,[5] Cittadini observes that even great diligence has saved no more than one out of a thousand books in the more valued cultured variety. Thus it is not surprising that documentation of the other medium should be scant (ibid.: 43r–44r).

For the most part, we are told, the constituent elements of cultivated Latin disappeared, in the process leading to the development of the modern vernacular. The quality of the cultured species depended on the effort exerted by the learner, for acquisition was possible only through study of the rules of grammar and of the works of good authors (ibid.: 2v, 35r). Those who did not engage in such pursuits could only communicate 'barbarously, that is vulgarly, as is often found in ancient inscriptions' (ibid.: 35r).[6]

Although Cittadini's exposition is at times a bit vague, I believe that Figure 1 accurately reflects his conception of Latin and its development. Because his description is essentially that of a situation of diglossia, I will use the designations 'High' and 'Low', respectively, to refer to the classical and colloquial media.[7]

There are certain slight inconsistencies in the treatises examined, principally regarding terminology, which complicate interpretation.[8] To disregard Cittadini's statements concerning the eternal presence of two Latin languages would make it possible to claim that he envisioned a split between them occurring only during the late 'Romana' period (instead of much earlier; see Figure 1). However, Cittadini is most insistent in his affirmations.[9] Furthermore, his discussion presents an apparent contradiction, which will be addressed shortly. While claiming the perpetual existence of two strata, he nevertheless focuses on only one of the levels in portraying the successive stages of the language.

In his postulation of a separate vernacular Latin tongue, Cittadini adduces much evidence of what he refers to as 'non-Augustan Latin', contrasting this variety with the elevated classical language. Non-Augustan Latin comprises two groups of items: archaic forms predating what is in his system the third stage of the 'Romana' period; and non-standard features dating from during and after this third stage. As will be seen, the divisions numbered 1–4 in Figure 1 refer mainly to the cultivated variety. That is, Cittadini's depiction of these stages is based on the testimony of texts employing the High language. None the less, it is possible for him to rely on citations from the pre-Augustan period in support of the assumed vernacular continuum,

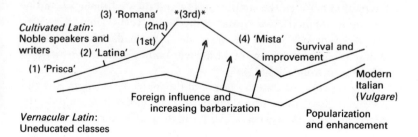

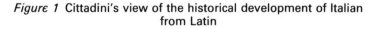

Figure 1 Cittadini's view of the historical development of Italian from Latin

because he evidently regarded the High and Low systems as much closer in structure during early periods than subsequently.

The first body of testimony to non-classical Latin is quite small, we are told. Extant fragmentary evidence of the oldest stages fails to show the original forms because of subsequent modification. Thus the earliest reliable data on previous structures come from first- and second-stage 'Romana', and include elements of certain ancient verse compositions, and the few complete, unchanged words found on Duilius' *columna rostrata* (ibid.: 4r–8r).[10]

The second principal manifestation of an ancient vernacular consists of grammarians' comments on aberrant usage, non-classical constructions present in Latin documents, and irregular features found in inscriptions. Many of the authors Cittadini cites lived long before the arrival of the Goths, he hastens to point out (ibid.: 41v), and thus attest to traits present even during a remote period of the language. Included among figures referred to in this context are Cicero, Apuleius and Isidore of Seville. Cittadini also notes that the vernacular was mentioned in the declaration of the Council of Tours, in a plea for communication in the language of the people (ibid.: 35r–37r, 41v–42v, 44r–46v).

Cittadini's study of inscriptions and epitaphs furnished additional evidence for the existence of an early Low language. Many of these, he states, date from before the rule of Constantine (ibid.: 47v), or originated between this time and that of Honorius (ibid.: 50v). Composed chiefly in the official medium, the inscriptions nevertheless clearly show 'barbarous, that is, vernacular, Latin words, and others half-vulgar, as well as barbarized Latin terms' (ibid.: 47v).[11] The vernacular forms cited by Cittadini evince non-classical features involving vowels, consonants, morphosyntax and lexicon, although he does not differentiate among such classes. He does make specific reference to fluctuation between the simple vowel *e* and the diphthong *ae*, and to the absence of final *-d*, *-m*, *-s*, and *-t* (this last, in verbs) (ibid.: 47r–52v, 71r–72r). The lack of final *-s* is mentioned in particular as a noteworthy characteristic of 'the usage of the ancient Latin vernacular, which has come down to us' (ibid.: 49v).[12]

In specifying the dates of origin of the inscriptions cited, and the time periods of the authors mentioned, Cittadini is attempting to prove the existence of a colloquial Latin not connected to the invasion of Italy by barbarian groups. Modern scholarship, too, relies on such epigraphical and textual evidence in postulation of non-classical structures, but Cittadini's outlook is particularly innovative given the environment in which he worked. While today few dispute that Romance derives chiefly from unembellished Latin, Cittadini was forced to struggle against an opposing cinquecento concept. According to this predominant outlook, Italian resulted from the corruption of classical Latin by external, chiefly Germanic, forces. It is, of course, Cittadini's perspicacity in recognizing the nature of Italian that is responsible for his renown.[13]

3 THE INDEPENDENT EVOLUTION OF THE TWO STRATA

Cittadini traces the developments both of the cultivated medium and of the language used by the common people, trajectories which he portrays as largely independent. In the first chapter of the *Vera origine* we read that Latin had four principal stages: 'Prisca', 'Latina', 'Romana' and 'Mista' (ibid.: 1v). Here Cittadini is relying on the suppositions of respected authorities (in particular, he claims, on those of Isidore (*Etymologiae* IX, i, 6)). The first two stages were employed by the oldest inhabitants of Italy, and during the reigns of the kings of Latium and of Rome, respectively. Cittadini further subdivided the third epoch, 'Romana', into three periods: (1) through the time of Ennius and Plautus; (2) through that of Caecilius and Terence; and (3) through the era of Virgil and Livy. The last of these subdivisions, termed 'Augustan Latin', represents for Cittadini the culmination of Roman expressive elegance. 'Mista', we are told, designates the language which entered Rome with the men and culture of the provinces, following the expansion of the empire and extension of citizenship to all inhabitants. The introduction of non-Roman influence marked an immediate decrease in the purity of speech, an impoverishment subsequently exacerbated by further barbarization (ibid.: 1v–4r, 33v).

In this portrayal of the four-stage trajectory of Latin, Cittadini clearly has in mind principally that variety employed by the upper classes. Although such focus is nowhere stated explicitly, it is apparent from his insistent references to literary production, well-known authors, and quality of expression, in this context. If we take seriously Cittadini's affirmations that there always existed two levels within Latin, it must be assumed that his vision holds for an increasing separation between High and Low languages beginning slightly before, or during, the 'Romana' period, as the cultivated medium was enriched through increasing literary use. This would have created a radical split between the two strata during 'Romana' 's third stage, when Augustan Latin achieved its greatest elegance (as shown in Figure 1). As will be discussed below, the passage from 'Romana' to 'Mista' signified for our author a sudden downturn in the cultured language due to a corrupting influence working through the lower social and linguistic level.

Cittadini's concentration on the literary language in his depiction of four successive stages is reflected in the statement that after the time of Honorius, the use of 'pure Latin' (here, that of the upper classes) declined even more radically than before, due to deficiencies on the part of teachers and lack of talent in students. The cultured medium was retained, we are told, only among a few monks and clerics, and these individuals too were guilty of using neologisms and words destroyed by barbarians. After the demise of the majority of those who still possessed Latin elegance, hardly anyone's language surpassed that of the common people, whose speech was 'full of barbarisms and solecisms' (ibid.: 68v).[14] The beauty of the cultivated ancient tongue was not, however, permanently lost, Cittadini maintains. He observes that it had always been used to some extent, in both speech and writing, and in his own day was the object of a good deal of attention worldwide (ibid.: 53r, 61v, 63v, 66v–67r, 68v).

As has been mentioned, Cittadini was convinced that despite certain changes the modern vernacular constituted an extension of the ancient Low variety.[15] Except for the articles, the endings of certain words, and other 'temporary and foreign' elements, the two vernaculars are almost the same language, he maintains, 'in substance, that is, regarding the body of the words, not in accidence, that is, in the endings of the terms' (ibid.: 39v–40r).[16] Cittadini contradicts the view of the majority of his contemporaries (who saw Italian as the result of Latin's contamination) by emphasizing that the development of their language did not take place suddenly. Instead, he states, there was at work here a continuous process involving generations of speakers (ibid.: 60r, 68r–v).[17] It should be noted that Cittadini's allowance for linguistic change also distinguishes him from earlier theorists who alleged that the ancient vernacular was identical to the Italian of their day.[18]

In accord with his belief in the continuity of a colloquial stratum within Latin, Cittadini claims greater similarity between the modern and pre-Augustan tongues than between the ancient languages and that variety employed by Cicero (ibid.: 38r). As proof of this, Cittadini offers archaic items from the inscription on Duilius' column, contrasting them with the classical equivalents, and provides the Old Latin, modern vernacular, and late 'Romana' versions of a random series of terms. His argumentation supports the idea that he conceived of a close relationship between High and Low languages existing at an early stage, followed by marked elevation of the cultivated medium (ibid.: 37v–38r, 39r).

Cittadini's hypotheses incorporate the assumption that change in language is natural and inevitable.[19] As a prime factor in linguistic development he cites the instability and variability of the human will (ibid.: 37v), and affirms that languages, like all things, must have 'a beginning, growth, period of equilibrium, increase, and descent' (ibid.: 37r).[20] In addition to recognizing the role of such natural evolution, he sees as highly important for Italian the influence exerted by those who entered Rome from other lands, territories both within and beyond the peninsula. Although the effects were felt first in the Low variety, the corruptive impact was strong enough that the High language suffered damage as well. Cittadini's conception of the significant function of corroding forces actually bears some resemblance to that of theorists who focused on Germanic invasion, despite his overt disagreement with them. The dissension primarily concerns the time period in which corruption occurred and the agents held to be responsible.

The *Trattato della vera origine* begins with this declaration:

> The majority of those who have expressed themselves, or do so now, regarding the vernacular tongue claim that it had its origin when the Barbarians – that is, the Goths at first, or the Langobards later – tyrannically occupied Italian lands, and not before. They say that our language is a corruption of Latin. This is not true. Rather we hope to show fully and clearly that our tongue had another beginning, one much older.
>
> (ibid.: 1r–v)[21]

Cittadini's opposing thesis, of course, is that of the essential identity of modern and ancient vernaculars. Peculiarly Italian features not present in the ancestor, such as the articles and characteristic word-endings, come not from a recent foreign presence, but

> from ancient times . . . from the presence of Barbarians who lived as friends and citizens; and also from that of slaves and similar people, whose language the Roman inhabitants of the city wished to speak, perhaps for reasons of novelty, as does

happen. With this they came to ruin the purity of their native language.

(ibid.: 40r–v)[22]

An additional influence was exerted by the speech habits of Roman soldiers, those returning to their native land after long absence as well as those from the provinces brought to Rome for purposes of defence (ibid.: 41v, 69v). Contributing to the development of Italian were the normal instability of worldly institutions, and a general lack of care regarding language, most evident during the decline of the empire (ibid.: 68r). Cittadini's description of the later development of the modern tongue includes an assertion that the languages of various invading groups (such as the Langobards, Franks, Greeks, Normans, Germans, Bretons, French and Spanish) occasioned a series of unspecified modifications (ibid.: 53r–v).

Corruption of the Low language was principally responsible for decline of the High variety, as the latter experienced foreign influence through the filter of the vernacular. Despite Cittadini's lack of explicitness, it must be assumed that he regarded speakers of the colloquial tongue as conduits for the innovations imported by new-comers, themselves members of the lower classes. Furthermore, although hypothesized dates of language change remain imprecise, our author evidently saw an impact on the High variety beginning during the 'Romana' period, with the negative effects felt most strongly after the institution of universal citizenship (which occasioned descent to the 'Mista' stage). We are told that the language of Livy must have been quite different from that of Polybius some 200 years before, during which time 'the Romans associated continuously with many and diverse generations of Barbarians, which they had not done previously' (ibid.: 7r–v).[23] Cittadini cites a series of Latin authors' complaints concerning foreign cultural and linguistic influence (ibid.: 33v–34r, 42v–43r), claiming that barbarization (clearly, of both varieties of Latin) had already begun to take place by the age of Cicero and Caesar (ibid.: 34r–v). This pause in the ascent of the High variety may be envisioned as a plateau encompassing the third period of the 'Romana' stage (as shown in Figure 1). The eventual outcome of barbarian impact, we read, was that the classical tongue, too, underwent change, 'in such a way that not much of its ancient Latinity remained' (ibid.: 42v).[24]

4 ORTHOGRAPHIC AND PHONETIC CHANGE

In addition to tracing general trends of development, the *Vera origine* and *Trattato degli articoli* provide evidence concerning specific spelling and sound changes through the centuries. Although a wealth of data is supplied, only salient features of Cittadini's treatment can be outlined here. The orthographical modifications mentioned relate to the cultivated language of literature and of official inscriptions. Here Cittadini cites observations of Latin grammarians and relies heavily on epigraphs he adduced in the portrayal of Latin's successive stages. Noteworthy in this discussion is that while Cittadini correctly identifies as spelling changes such developments as the introduction of Latin medial consonant doubling (ibid.: 12v, 18v), he also characterizes an evolution in third singular verb endings (*-et* > *-it*) as merely a change in orthographical convention (ibid.: 18v). Cittadini's treatment of diphthongs fails to distinguish geminate vowels (used at an early period to represent Latin long vowels) and true diphthongs; regarding the latter group, the base form which Cittadini claims to be represented by the digraph is generally that long vowel found in classical inscriptions. Thus rather than seeing here evidence of sound change, he appears to regard pronunciation as stable across the centuries, with evolution occurring only in its representation (ibid.: 14v–16r, 19r–20r). Much of the data on orthographical change is provided in support of Cittadini's repeated claims that early texts were modified by those of later periods for the purpose of modernization (ibid.: 7v–7av, 10r–15r; '7a' refers to the second of two pages, each numbered '7').

Cittadini's discussion of specific sound changes naturally centres on changes he perceives in the ancient vernacular, leading to creation of Italian. Nevertheless, the starting point for most of the developments delineated is a form identical to that of classical Latin. This practice, not unknown to modern Romance linguists, may be related in Cittadini's case to the concept of a previous closeness of High and Low varieties, prior to their divergence; perhaps he presumes that the elements cited were not dissimilar in the two cognate languages before these media separated. This would accord with his use of such adjectives as 'discarded' and 'removed' in the description of certain final consonants absent from ancient vernacular forms (ibid.: 50r, 51r).[25] He takes pains to note that all of the intermediate terms he hypothesizes are attested in ancient inscriptions, of which he has made copies, and that his conjectures are deduced from such epigraphical data (ibid.: 58v, 70v–71r).

Throughout his discussion of inscriptions, but more fully in a chapter of the *Vera origine* intended to demonstrate the origin of Italian in vernacular Latin, Cittadini describes a series of evolutions in verbs, noun groups and unclassified forms.[26] Although he does not utilize the terminology of modern language science, he points out such phenomena as syncope (e.g., *quomodo* > *como*: 73r), reduction of consonant groups (e.g., *domna* > *donna*: 51r), loss of final consonants (e.g., *habeas/habeat* > *abea*: 51r), intervocalic lenition (e.g., *scribet* > *scrive*: 58r) and reinforcement (e.g., *hodie* > . . . *hoggi*: 58r), as well as various vocalic changes (e.g., *quiescit* > *quiescet*: 52r; *cum* > *con*: 73r; *quaero* > *chero*: 73r). Nevertheless, Cittadini is also capable of postulations such as that of a leap from *precessero* to *precedettero* (50r–v), the capricious addition of final -*e* in the formation of *imperadore* (58v) and of final -*o* in that of *facciono* (58r–v), and the convoluted modification necessary in the trajectory *posuer* > *posuerà* > *ponerà* (51r). We see no evidence that he attributes importance to the role of analogical factors in the evolutions he depicts.

Also in chapter 23 of the *Vera origine*, and more extensively in the first sections of the *Trattato degli articoli*, Cittadini traces the development of definite articles and forms of similar origin. Noteworthy in its similarity to modern treatments is his insistence on the central role of *hic, iste,* and *ille* in the creation of Italian articles and pronouns, following weakening of their demonstrative force and reinforcement through combination (ibid.: 57v–58r, 70r–73v).[27] Notable too are his unhesitating recognition of certain particular developments (e.g., *illorum* > . . . *loro*: 73r; *ista nocte* > *stanotte*: 58r), and an evidently keen interest in regional variation.[28] None the less, his view that the Latin demonstratives had been used exactly as are the articles they produced (but only in the academic environment), and were introduced by mistake into common speech (ibid.: 68v–69r), is not consonant with later ideas. Some postulations appearing here indicate that Cittadini saw sound change as less restricted than do more modern linguists: for example, the devoicing and repositioning of final -*d* in *hoc istud*, leading to *cotesto* (in a possibly conscious effort to avoid the unpleasant combination *oe*) (ibid.: 58r). In his comments on geographical variants, Cittadini's postulation of a developmental sequence Latin > Neapolitan/Sicilian > Roman > Sienese/Tuscan (ibid.: 72r–v) is interesting, even if completely discordant with the modern view.

5 THE QUESTION OF THE LANGUAGE

The final chapter of the *Vera origine* defines Cittadini's position with respect to the 'Question of the Language'. In this conclusion he affirms that, based on the evidence he has presented, 'it can quite rightly be concluded that the modern vernacular . . . is to be termed "vulgar" ' (ibid.: 60r).[29] Shaping his approach to the matter of terminology is his view that the various tongues of Tuscany and Italy differ not in substance but merely in accidental features. Thus it is natural that Cittadini should see the term 'Florentine' as too restrictive. The language of Florence, used without replacement of unacceptable elements by others from cognate systems, is not a praiseworthy instrument, we are told. In addition, many individuals from areas outside this city have produced works worthy of imitation. 'Tuscan' is a similarly insufficient term, for all vernacular speakers participate in the language, and great writers have included the best elements from many tongues. Cittadini quotes Dante's list of defects in various Tuscan dialects (*De vulgari eloquentia* I, xiii), stating that in the absence of such imperfections it would indeed be possible to speak of a Tuscan tongue. The term 'courtly' is inapplicable because there is no universality or permanence in the courts: use of this denomination would require additional specification of place and time, and thus there would be different languages, not just one (as the vernacular undoubtedly is). 'Italian' is an unacceptable name because it applies equally well to Latin, it lacks specificity, and – just as the parent language was spoken throughout Italy but still called 'Latin' – the widespread modern tongue should not lose its proper appellation (ibid.: 60r–64r).

If the name of a language is to relate to that of the territory in which it is spoken, Cittadini states, the region considered should be the most worthy. The modern vernacular should be called 'vulgar Latin', since 'Latin' is derived from 'Latium' and it is in this important area that the modern language too is spoken naturally. The designation can be shortened to 'vulgar' because the colloquial variety is, at present, more common than 'grammatical Latin'. Cittadini maintains that the entire *Vera origine* supports his conclusion (ibid.: 64r–66v).[30] This view, he claims, is the only one possible for those who can escape the bonds of subjectivity and approach linguistic study 'with sound judgment, and free of partiality' (ibid.: 60r).[31]

While, as seen in preceding sections, Cittadini's treatises reflect much of what may be termed a scientific perspective, it is obvious that he was not free of an essentially unscientific preoccupation. Various features of his presentation show the influence of the decades of debate composing the 'Question of the Language', discussions often marked more by personal bias than by sound reasoning. These traits include an insistence on factors such as beauty and elegance in linguistic matters, a concern with the corruption of language and the possibility of recovering lost glory, and a conviction of the superiority of certain dialects, particularly those of Rome and his native Siena. The impact of the language question is seen also in Cittadini's decision to make his considerations on nomenclature constitute the 'conclusion' of his longer treatise, as well as to mention the topic at the very outset (ibid.: 2v). The formal separation of his remarks on terminology from his observations on linguistic history does not obscure the pervasive influence of Cittadini's milieu.

In the description of a Latin tongue comprising two levels, the tracing of independent evolutions for each stratum, the delineation of various orthographic and sound changes, and the assignment of an appropriate appellation for the modern vernacular, Cittadini's *Trattato della vera origine* and *Trattato degli articoli* evince a notable merger of subjectivity and science. Undertaking his investigation of Latin and Italian with strong preconceptions regarding the merits of the latter, Cittadini elaborated a hypothesis which contrasted sharply with dominant views of the day. His exposition demonstrates a noteworthy reliance on meaningful evidence and aptitude in its employment, features which differentiate his approach from the approaches of previous scholars. The latter, no less ideologically driven yet substantially less scientific, cannot however be dismissed out of hand. They formed an essential foundation and stimulus for the better theories that would supersede them.

NOTES

1 Scaglione (1988), while noting the extent to which Cittadini's theories constitute a reaction against existing notions, has observed that he succeeded in freeing Romance philology from the prison of the 'Question of the Language'.
2 Main points of Cittadini's outlook are discussed briefly in the standard surveys of Italian grammatical theory and the *Questione della lingua*: Vivaldi 1894–98: vol. 1, 116–22 and 1925: vol. 1, 147–52; Trabalza 1908: 283–90; Kukenheim 1932: 173, 181, 187, 190–1, 197; Hall 1942: 20–1, 47; and Vitale 1978: 106–7. Cittadini's contribution is also outlined by Vitale 1955: 44–7 and Di Franco Lilli 1970: 1–10. The most complete descript-

ions to date of his perspective have been supplied by Schlemmer's notes accompanying a 1983 facsimile of the *Vera origine* (Cittadini 1601), and Faithfull's (1962) instructive article on seicento linguistic theory, neither of which, however, is entirely satisfactory.

3 Cittadini's later *Origini della toscana favella* (1604; revised edition 1628) has been the object of controversy due to its resemblance to certain unpublished grammatical treatises by his predecessor Claudio Tolomei. For details, see Sensi 1892; D'Ovidio 1893; Trabalza 1908; Vannini 1920; Vivaldi 1925; Sbaragli 1939; Weiss 1946; Faithfull 1962; and Cappagli and Pieraccini 1985.

4 'Per ogni tempo, e prima e poi, furono in Roma due sorte di lingua. L'vna rozza e mezzo barbara, laquale era propria del vulgo, cioè de' Romani e de' Forestieri Idioti, o vogliamo dir della gente bassa, e de' contadini senza lettere; i cui modi di dir, e le cui voci erano rifiutate, da gli Scrittori, e da' dicitori nobili, e fuor che le passioni di esse principalmente, e per la maggior parte sono rimaste nelle bocche de gli Italiani huomini senza distintione di vilta, o di nobiltà . . . e l'altra coltiuata dall'arte e pura latina, la quale era propia de gli Scrittori e de' dicitori nobili, e letterati.' A statement at 37r repeats this hypothesis.

5 This was a popular argument against the existence of a colloquial Roman tongue, appearing (in very similar form) in Pietro Bembo's 1525 *Prose della volgar lingua* (2nd edn: 84) – a work which Cittadini himself annotated. In fact, it is probable that our author specifically intended to refute the opinions which the Cardinal had expressed (see Vivaldi 1894–8: vol. 1, 117; and Faithfull 1962: 244).

6 'barbaramente, cioè volgarmente, come si truoua vsato non poche volte nelle antiche iscrittioni'.

7 Ferguson's (1959) well-known study describes bilingual (or bidialectal) situations involving Arabic, Swiss German, Haitian Creole and Greek. He distinguishes High and Low varieties on the basis of function, prestige, use in literary endeavours, mode of acquisition, degree of standardization, stability, grammatical structure, lexicon and phonology.

8 For example, certain declarations appearing on 37v, 39r and 63v.

9 Other modern scholars have interpreted Cittadini's pronouncements differently. Vitale (1955: 45, 47), for example, sees Cittadini's theory as involving principally vernacular Latin, from which would spring the relatively insignificant cultured variety. Similarly, Schlemmer (Cittadini 1601: 22) claims that Cittadini's view accords with Coseriu's schematization (1978: 268 [not '168']), depicting 'literary Latin' as an offshoot of the continuum 'archaic Latin' → 'vulgar' or 'popular Latin'.

10 This column was erected in honour of Gaius Duilius, consul in 260 BC and victor at Mylae (First Punic War). It exists only in the form of a copy found in the Roman Forum in 1565, a reproduction generally dated to early imperial times; its inscription duplicates the archaic original only imperfectly (see Gordon 1983: 124–7).

11 'parole barbare, cioè volgari, latine, ed altre mezzouolgari, non che latine imbarbarite'.

12 'l'vsanza del propio fauellare antico de' Latini, il quale è peruenuto fino a noi'.

13 Cittadini's innovation is emphasized by Trabalza 1908: 288; Vivaldi 1925: vol. 1, 151; Kukenheim 1932: 197; Vitale 1955: 42, 47; Faithfull 1962: 244; Di Franco Lilli 1970: 8; and Schlemmer (Cittadini 1601: 31–3).

14 'piena di barbarismi e di solecismi'.

15 Despite assertions to the contrary (e.g., Vivaldi 1925: vol. 1, 148), Cittadini never claims the exact equivalence of ancient and modern vernaculars.

16 'auueniticcie, e forestice'; 'in sostanza, cioè ne' corpi de' vocaboli, e non ne gli accidenti, cioè nelle passioni delle voci'. Similar statements appear throughout the text.

17 Cittadini's conception of linguistic development as an ongoing, gradual evolution represents an advance over the previous dominant outlook. Even Tolomei, whose influence our author acknowledges, saw language change as involving what can be called *generatio*, in contrast with Cittadini's belief that such modification entailed *alteratio* (Faithfull 1962: 248–53). On the significance of Lodovico Castelvetro's views for those of our author, see Vivaldi 1894–8: vol. 1, 115–16; Vitale 1955: 43–4; and Faithfull 1962: 248–53.

18 This theory, discussed throughout the quattrocento and refuted in Bembo's *Prose* (1525: 80–5), is usually said to have been espoused by the influential Humanist Leonardo Bruni, who allegedly maintained that the language of oratory and the theatre must have been incomprehensible to the populace. (See Tavoni 1982, however, for an alternative view of Bruni's claims.)

19 Dante had made the same observation nearly three centuries earlier (*De vulgari eloquentia* I, ix). As is evident throughout Cittadini's exposition, he was quite familiar with Dante's works, even having translated the Florentine's principal linguistic treatise (see Trabalza 1908: 288, n. 1; Vivaldi 1925: vol. 1, 149; Weiss 1946: 47; and Di Franco Lilli 1970: 3, n. 4, and 8). Cittadini's striking innovation in this facet of his discussion is a greater emphasis on the natural evolution of linguistic systems, including the cultivated medium – change made apparent through his familiarity with centuries of Latin inscriptions.

20 'principio, augumento, stato, accrescimento, e mancanza'.

21 'La maggior parte adunque di coloro, i quali della nostra lingua hanno ragionato, o ragionano perche vogliano che la lingua vulgare . . . hauesse cominciamento, quando i Barbari, cioè, i Goti prima, o i Longobardi apresso tiranneuolmente il dominio d'Italia occuparono, e non prima; e che ella sia vn corrompimento della Latina fauella: il che non esser molto vero; anzi essa nostra lingua hauer'altro cominciamento, e più antico assai hauuto, speriamo di fare apparir viè più che chiaro, e pianamente.'

22 'ab antico . . . da quella [conuersation] de' Barbari, che ci stauan come amici, e come Cittadini; ed anco da quella de' serui, e d'altre genti simili, la cui lingua per vaghezza di nouità volendo forse, come auuiene, parlare i Romani habitatori fermi della Città, ne veniuano a guastar la purità della natia loro latina'.

23 'i Romani conuersarono continuamente con più e diuerse generationi di Barbari; il che da prima fatto non haueuano'.

24 'di maniera, che non le rimase molto di quel suo primo antico latinismo'.

25 'gettata via'; 'leuata'.

26 Here, however, we are warned not to expect a full treatment of the topic, but only examples of the changes which took place. Bembo, Castelvetro, and Leonardo Salviati are cited as having written authoritatively about the formation of the vernacular, although Cittadini expresses his disagreement with their basic premise (origin of the language in the combination of Latin with other tongues) (57r–v).

27 Most preceding theorists saw the vernacular articles as derivations from non-Latin systems, especially Greek or Germanic (see, for example, Vivaldi 1925: vol. 1, 149 and note 2).

28 Cittadini's views on geographical differentiation within Tuscany are expressed (albeit briefly and, as the author admits, incompletely) in *Degli idiomi toscani*, not published prior to Gigli's 1721 collection of Cittadini's works.

29 'si può con molta ragione concludere, che ella . . . debba esser chiamata . . . vulgare'. The selection of 'vulgare' actually represents a reprise of the term preferred by Bembo, in whose *Prose* the chief concern is defence of the vernacular (and consideration of terminology is minimal). Ironically, it was the Cardinal who popularized the theory of corruption against which Cittadini so vigorously reacts.

30 Cittadini's discussion of terminology responds to more than eighty years of disputation; principal exponents of the designations which our author rejects, and their main works, are as follows: 'Florentine', Nicolò Machiavelli (*Discorso o dialogo intorno alla nostra lingua*, 1515); 'Tuscan', Claudio Tolomei (Il Cesano, published 1555); 'Courtly', Baldassarre Castiglione (*Il Cortegiano*, 1524); 'Italian', Giangiorgio Trissino (*Il Castellano*, 1529) (Vitale 1978 provides an overview of these scholars' theories). Cittadini, along with critics such as Scipione Bargagli (to whom the *Vera origine* is dedicated), Diomede Borghesi, Orazio Lombardelli, and Adriano Politi, belonged to the Sienese School of philologists. These individuals followed Tolomei's lead in rejecting Florentine exclusivity, often advocating instead a more widely Tuscan approach to the matters disputed (see Vitale 1978: 105–10; Weiss 1946; and Faithfull 1962).

31 'con sani occhi di mente, e senz'affetto di parte'. Despite the impartiality of which Cittadini boasts, the *Vera origine's* dedication proudly proclaims that the work has been composed in the vernacular of Siena. Our author specifies that this is not the language commonly employed in his day (even by men of letters), but the Sienese of the time separating Dante and Boccaccio, with allowance made for rejection of antiquated items and of those not generally accepted. Cittadini maintains that older Sienese texts (of which he furnishes a short catalogue) are equal to those produced in any other Tuscan city (preliminary pages 2r–3v).

6

Ideology and the 'clarity' of French

Pierre Swiggers

1 INTRODUCTION

In 1785 the Piedmontese scholar Carlo Denina, who was very active in promoting the use of French in the Italian Savoy,[1] wrote the following in his pamphlet *On the Character of Languages, in Particular of the Modern Ones* (*Sur le caractère des langues et particulièrement des modernes*): 'Everybody agrees on the precision of the French language. . . . Since people commonly attribute to the French language, more than to any other language, the properties of clarity, neatness and precision, one is eager to know the reason for this' (Marazzini 1985: 16–18). The first reason, in Denina's view, is a historical and 'internal' one: the language that developed out of Latin in northern Gaul had lost all its final vowels, and this made it necessary to mark syntactic functions by using particles and auxiliaries, and by functionalizing the syntactic position of words within the sentence.

> It became necessary to distinguish nouns by the use of articles, and persons of the verb by the use of pronouns, and to arrange words in such a way that one could understand the sentence and its meaning. For this reason it became customary to put the subject or nominative before the verb, and if I am not mistaken, this is the real cause of the analytic order in construction of which the French language is so proud.[2]

But Denina is aware of the danger of regarding the S-V (O) order as the 'natural' one. There is first the fact that this order is the one *imposed* or *recommended* by rhetoricians and teachers of eloquence. He also points out that this order is not universal in French, reputed for its clarity: reading through Voltaire's work, one finds 'an order of construction which is really inversed', as shown for instance by the opening sentence of the second volume of the *Essai sur l'histoire universelle* quoted by Denina: '*Régnoit alors en Allemagne Frédéric I, qu'on nomme communément Barberousse*'. To this Denina adds the following comment:

> Now it is true that [*vivoit* and] *régnoit* are not active verbs preceded by their accusatives. But it is not infrequent that the active verb is preceded by its accusative, with a pronoun added in a slightly pleonastic way: *cet homme je l'ai vu*. In these cases the pleonasm lends greater clarity and precision to the sentence. But this does not prove that the French language, by its own genius, is more precise than the Italian; it just shows that French writers have polished their style somewhat more. La Mothe was right in his address to the French Academy: 'Les langues n'ont point de génie[3] par elles-mêmes. Ce sont les écrivains célèbres qui par l'usage qu'ils en font, établissent ces préventions confuses, auxquelles dans la suite on laisse usurper le nom de principes.'

(Marazzini 1985: 19–20)[4]

Denina's text is interesting in various respects. First, it is an external, but overtly 'francophile' testimony to the qualities of the French language, written at a time when French was the cultural interlingua in western Europe and also in the heyday of the controversy on 'direct and natural word order' (see Ricken 1978). Moreover, Denina's text is theoretically very interesting in that it uses the concept of 'genius of a language', and appeals to a word-order-based typology of languages. Finally, the passages translated here reflect a more 'sociological' and less hypostasizing view of the 'clarity of French': the *clarté* is not a language-internal property, but an *a posteriori* aspect of the French language, which has its ground in a style and a usage elaborated by generations of writers.

Carlo Denina was a perspicacious observer of the European linguistic scene, and a gifted analyst. He consciously avoided the qualification 'natural'[5] in speaking of (French) word order, and instead of promoting some languages and discriminating against others, he stressed the universality of linguistic expression[6], thus bridging the gap between Aristotle's 'hermeneutic' philosophy of language and Humboldt's 'energetic' language metaphysics. He was also sensitive to the more colloquial speech styles and the special effect their redundancies produce (the sentence *cet homme je l'ai vu* is, from the socio-communicative point of view, very different from *j'ai vu cet homme*). But one wishes Denina had dug further into the problem, so as to lay bare the fragile foundations of the 'clarity and precision' of French. It is somewhat ironical that in 1784, one year before the publication of Denina's *Sur le caractère des langues et particulièrement des modernes*, Rivarol could write in his *Discours sur l'universalité de la langue française* (1784): 'what is not clear, is not French' (*ce qui n'est pas clair n'est pas français*). Rivarol's dithyramb on the clarity of French was the outgrowth of a linguistic and philosophical concern with structural properties of a language; but an outgrowth which had left behind it the technicalities of previous analyses, and which had turned a cautious and well-contained appraisal of French into a void myth. The purpose of this chapter is to trace the development of this myth, and to point to some landmarks testifying to the under- or overdetermination of facts by ideology.

2 SUNRISE

The Renaissance saw the beginning of language comparison – in the natural and more superficial sense – and of attempts to characterize languages in terms of phonetic, morphological and syntactic properties. In most cases the context in which this type of analysis was pursued was either a pedagogical one, as was the case of language manuals stressing some differences between, say, English and French, or a practical-scientific one, as in treatises on the orthographical system to be used for a particular language (compared with other, most often cognate languages). In other cases, the context was a purely descriptive one – thus directly contributing to the autonomization of vernacular grammar – a case in point being Louis Meigret's comparison of French and Latin word order in his 'Treatise of French Grammar' (1550)[7]:

> If we consider in detail the style of the Latin language and that of our tongue, we will find them to be opposite in that we normally end our sentence or utterance with what comes first in Latin. And if we consider the order of nature, we will find that the French style comes much closer to it than the Latin. As a matter of fact, in Latin, one normally puts the object before the verb, after which follows the subject; in this way, the patient, which by the order of nature should be last in the sentence, comes first in speech; and the agent, which logically should be first, comes last; as a matter of fact, the agent logically comes before the action or passion (= undergoing of action), since it is the starting point of its motion.[8] The speaker of Latin in

speaking elegantly will say *Gallos vicit Caesar* ('Caesar slew the Gauls'); keeping the same order this would give us in French *les Gaulois a vaincu César*,[9] meaning *César a vaincu les Gaulois*. Moreover, speakers of Latin put causes before consequences, whereas we most often state facts before we come to the causes. It is true that causes come before effects, but the latter are the first to affect man's senses. For this reason it has been necessary for man to gain knowledge about the facts and events of nature, before seeking the causes thereof; it would be unreasonable to argue about the causes of someone's death before being certain of the bare fact. But I do not want to criticize the Latin style, nor should one be inelegant and styleless in speaking or writing Latin. But on the other hand it is also unreasonable to become addicted to it, and not to adopt a much more easy and convenient way of 'construing'[10] our language, according to the order which nature respects and which speech usage has established.[11]

Meigret's statement was, ideologically speaking, a rather neutral one, although one can say that it fits well within his attempt to loosen the description of the French language from its ties with the Latin model. Besides, we find a similar observation in Jean Garnier's grammar of French (*Institutio gallicae linguae*, 1558), written in Latin, and adopting almost slavishly the Latin model.[12] The situation is, however, different in the case of Henri Estienne's work (see Clément 1898). Henri Estienne, son of the famous printer and Humanist scholar Robert Estienne, was a meticulous observer of language properties, and an excellent translator with first-hand knowledge of several classical and modern languages. He noted some interesting typological 'parallels' between French and classical Greek (such as the existence of a definite article, and a rather strict word order), but his specific contribution to the myth of French clarity is coloured by his ideological position with respect to the court. At the time Estienne was active the French court was strongly Italianized – much to the dismay of the Protestant-minded Humanists, including Estienne – and this situation brought with it a loss of purity of the French language. This then was the era of a second 'defence' of French, this time not against the classical languages, but against a 'collateral' idiom, viz. Italian. In comparing French and Italian Estienne stressed the advantages of the former, the 'precellence' of which was grounded in the transparency (or univocity) of the written image. Italian, on the other hand, is characterized by ambiguity: 'I mean the ambiguity for the eye: e.g., *atto* can mean "apt" and "act". . . . And *addotto* can stand for [Latin] *adductus* ("adduced" = Italian *addotto*), and for [Latin] *adoptavit* ("he adopted" = Italian *adottò*)"' (Estienne 1579: 51–2, translated with additional glosses).

Estienne's focus was a very specific and limited one: it was restricted to the (occasional) ambiguity of written language, abstraction being made of the possible use of diacritic signs.[13] His view was not grounded in a theory of language (as linked with thought), nor was it supported by an analysis of other linguistic levels. But in using univocity vs. ambiguity he paved the way for more ambitious attempts to justify the clarity of French.

3 SUNSHOWER: BATHING IN LIGHT (DESPITE SOME CLOUDS)

The most important seventeenth-century theorization of linguistic problems was the achievement of the Port-Royal *solitaires*.[14] The *Grammar* (1660) and the *Logic* (1662) constitute a coherent tool for the use and the analysis of (chains of) symbols expressing and conveying thoughts. The basic principle of the Port-Royal theory is that of the arbitrariness of the linguistic signs:

> The third division of signs is that into natural signs, which do not depend on man's fantasy, such as an image appearing in the mirror, which is a natural sign of the person it represents, and into other signs, which exist only by institution and established convention, be it that they have some distant relationship with the thing signified, or that they do not have any at all. In this way words are the signs of thought by institution, and so are the written characters the signs of words.
>
> (Port-Royal 1662: I,IV)

This is a statement about the *transparency* of language, as a system open to every speaker: the transparency of language is grounded in the conscious use of the total set of linguistic signs, which are arbitrary at the level of their constitution. In the passage from *constitution* to *use*, structural arbitrariness is overridden by pragmatic intentionality. Overridden or, better, 'completed': as a matter of fact, the transparency of the linguistic system is the essential condition for the truthful (and univocal) 'loading' of the semiotic structure. This makes clear why the Port-Royal authors do not raise the fundamental methodological question with respect to their theory, viz. that of the well-founded nature of a theory of general grammar. There simply was no reason for them to raise it: given that the system of linguistic signs has been constituted in order to express ideas and thoughts and since it is used intentionally with that function, one cannot have doubts about the conformity of the respective segmentations. The task of the grammarian-philosopher is then to rephrase, in a systematic way, the control exerted by the speaker over the system of signs he uses. Signs, the essence of which consists in exciting the idea of the thing presented by the idea of the 'representing thing' (the *representans*), have an intimate link with men's knowledge:

> The sign, since it is always either certain or probable, should find its area of being within knowledge. In the sixteenth century, signs were thought to have been placed upon things so that men might be able to uncover their secrets, their nature or their virtues; but this discovery was merely the ultimate purpose of signs, the justification of their presence; it was a possible way of using them, and no doubt the best; but they did not need to be known in order to exist: even if they remained silent, even if no one were to perceive them, they were just as much *there*. It was not knowledge that gave them their signifying function, but the very language of things. From the seventeenth century onward, the whole domain of the sign is divided between the certain and the probable: that is to say, there can no longer be an unknown sign, a mute mark. This is not because men are in possession of all the possible signs, but because there can be no sign until there exists a *known* possibility of substitution between two *known* elements. The sign does not wait in silence for the coming of a man capable of recognizing it: it can be constituted only by an act of knowing. (Foucault 1970: 59)

This cognitive dimension of the sign should be seen in the light of *conditions* limiting its interpretation.[15] These conditions can be reduced to three types:

(A) A metacondition applying to signs: any set of signs receives, by stipulation, a semantic determination.
(B) Conditions affecting the intention of the speaker: the speaker must be sincere and clear. As a matter of fact, a rational instrument for communicating ideas presupposes a rational user.
(C) Conditions affecting the efficiency of the use of language.

These conditions can be stated as discursive maxims:

(C 1) Use ordinary language!
(C 2) Avoid contradictions!
(C 3) Make your information as complete as possible!

These conditions all confirm the *fundamental nature* of our instrument of communication, viz. its rationality. Human language is a system of arbitrary signs, but its elaboration within society implies a rational analysis of reality. This rational analysis is constantly reactualized in the use of signs, not only at the level of expression, but also on the receptive side: a sign is perceived as a sign when the idea of the sign 'excites' the idea of the object represented.

The seventeenth-century doctrine of the clarity of French is inter-woven with this view of the relationship between language and thought. It is important to note that the reasoning is basically valid: to show that the French language is based on reason, one has to 'make clear' that the transparency of its rational nature penetrates the two constitutive levels of discourse, viz. that of *signs* and their *combinations*. The strategy of the seventeenth-century defenders of French clarity consists then in throwing light on the qualities of the French vocabulary and of French word order. This strategy is the one advocated by grammarians, rhetoricians and language observers,[16] such as the abbé Tallemant, who felt that French 'is endowed with such a clarity and neatness that when it is used for translating purposes it has the effect of a real commentary', Father Lamy, and Louis Le Laboureur, who in 1669 wrote in his 'Advantages of the French Language over the Latin' (*Avantages de la langue françoise sur la langue latine*): 'In all our utterances we follow exactly the order of thinking which is the order of nature. . . . Usage and custom cannot be imposed on us where reason can almost be felt and touched' (1669: 173). This argument was the main weapon in the famous *Querelle des Anciens et des Modernes*: why should Latin be preferred to French, if the latter proved to be the most faithful expression of reason? The basic presupposition in all this is that reason, or the chain of reason, has a natural order, common to all men. Here Le Laboureur shows himself a loyal Cartesian, who believes in the essential identity of human reason. This entails a radical distinction between thought and speech: the former is, by nature, uniform, whereas the latter is flexible and varies from one language to another. Le Laboureur follows a consequent line of reasoning when he concludes that the Romans – who have the 'same logic' as the French (1699: 67) – spoke differently from how they

118

thought. In other words, the Romans thought exactly as the French do, but they chose to speak differently, 'against' the order of thinking, much to their own inconvenience: 'La phrase des Latins, entortillée et guindée comme elle est, embarrassait bien souvent leur esprit' (1699: 149).

Le Laboureur's glorification of French nourished Father Bouhours's appraisal of the French language (*Entretiens d'Ariste et d'Eugenie*, 1671; *Doutes sur la langue françoise*, 1674),[17] inspired Desmarets de Saint-Sorlin's attack on the 'chaotic' Latin language (*Défense de la poésie et de la langue françoise*, 1675), and culminated in Charpentier's *On the Excellence of the French Language* (*De l'excellence de la langue françoise*, 1683). Charpentier bases his argumentation on the theory of word order. The refrain is still the same: French has natural simplicity, when compared with Latin and Greek and with other vernaculars. Eschewing inversions, the French language expresses, in the most transparent and direct way, the thoughts of the speaker. This makes French a language most suited for the expression of thoughts *and* feelings: there is no loss of communicative relevance in a discursive sequence which respects the order of nature.

The first period in the theoretical elaboration of 'the clarity of French' is marked by linguistic *naïveté* and short-sightedness: French is superficially compared with a few other languages, and there are no traces of a penetrating investigation of the linguistic structure of these idioms, let alone of the total range of their syntactic possibilities. A second pervasive characteristic is the stylistic slant of the myth creators: most of them are 'language purists' with a strong interest in rhetoric and poetics. This leaves us with two undefined standards of *clarity*, almost invariably appealed to: natural word order (as opposed to 'figurative speech') and precision of the vocabulary. The former concept receives its most explicit definition – still hardly illuminating – in the Port-Royal *Grammar*: 'natural word order' is the order we find 'when all the parts of the sentence are simply expressed, and there is never a word deficient or redundant, but all agreeable to the natural expression of our thoughts' (chapter 'Of the figures of construction'). As to lexical precision, one looks in vain for a comparative investigation which would prove the superiority of French in this respect. Could this be a case of ideological myopia in dealing with the mother tongue?[18]

It is interesting to note that in the eighteenth century the picture changes, although the 'clarity of French' retains vigour. A radical change in the theoretical context was brought about by the rise of a new type of study, viz. that of synonymy. This trend, inaugurated by Jean-François de Pons (*Dissertation sur les langues en général et sur la langue françoise en particulier*, 1716) and by the abbé Girard (*Synonymes françois, leurs significations et le choix qu'il en faut faire pour parler avec justesse*, 1736) is based on a philosophical analysis of a language's lexicon:[19] its aim is to show that there is no complete redundancy in the vocabulary, in other words that there are no perfect synonyms. In Girard's words, 'the similarity between words consists only in the main idea they express, but which each of them specifies in its own way, by adding an idea which gives it a proper and individual character' (Girard 1736: preface). This new trend of synonymy, illustrated by figures no less than Beauzée, Roubaud and Condillac,[20] had one major effect: that of separating the analysis of lexical items in terms of clarity and precision from the much less sophisticated approach of languages as being in conformity with or opposed to the order of nature. The newly created descriptive discipline of synonymy did not, however, loosen all its ties with the attempts to 'evaluate' languages.

What then about the other pillar in the theory of the clarity of French, viz. word order? This criterion was also affected by a number of theoretical changes. The first of these was the fact that word order was no longer seen as an arbitrary phenomenon, but was recognized as a typological option. The abbé Girard was the first to devise a linguistic typology (in his *Vrais Principes de la Langue françoise*, 1747), dividing languages into three types: analogical, transpositive and mixed. His typology[21] is based on the absence or presence of articles, and on word order. Some twenty years later, Beauzée divides languages into those that follow the 'analytical order' and those that do not follow it. Languages following the analytical order express directly, without introducing a positional or 'constructional' change, the consecutive order between the ideas constituting a 'complete' thought. This analytical order lies in fact at the basis of all languages,[22] but in many languages it is reversed on the level of speech. The analytical order can be studied or observed at the level of the sentence (subject – verb – object) and at the level of its (immediate) constituents (article + noun; noun + preposition + noun; auxiliary + infinitive; etc.). The analytical order is the 'invariable prototype' of the observable types of languages, whether these respect it faithfully (as do the 'analogical languages') or deviate from it on the level of discourse (as do the 'transpositive languages'). This view was of course perfectly compatible with the contrastive teaching of classical languages (especially Latin) by means of 'interlinear' translation,[23] allowing the teacher to bring back the Latin sentence to an underlying 'analytical' expression, from which the deviating attested construction could be considered. The criterion of analytical word order was both typologically and descriptively useful. Typologically it was useful for the distinction between languages with a rather strict word order fitting in a SVO pattern, and languages with a more free word order (irrespectively of their basic pattern, SVO or SOV). Descriptively the criterion was useful for the classification of sentence types within one language. Du Marsais, for instance, recognized the coexistence of different 'constructions' (linear ordering types) within one language. His theory provides room for three types of constructions: 'natural or simple', 'figurative' (deviating from the typical order of straightforward enunciation) and 'usual' (this type of construction in fact subsumes the two preceding ones).[24]

It is interesting to note that grammarians such as Beauzée or Du Marsais, who had first- or secondhand experience with a variety of languages, did not use this well-pondered theory of syntactic ordering for the purpose of praising the clarity of French. Their familiarity with various languages and their sensitivity to syntactic variation within one language were certainly instrumental in this, but one should not forget the fact that around 1750 the clarity of French was no longer a sacrosanct notion. The theory had received a serious blow through the discussion on inversions, which was started by Charles Batteux (see Ricken 1978: 111–17). In his 'Letters on the French construction compared with the Latin' ('Lettres sur la phrase françoise comparée avec la phrase latine', 1748), Batteux points out that the clarity of French may be only in the eye of the (myopic) beholder: 'I wonder . . . whether the Latins did not find their language natural, simple and clear. Our language seems to us the clearest of all languages; but this is not surprising: it is the one we know best; it was born with us and we with it. It is like a natural part of us.'[25] What is then 'natural', speaking linguistically? Batteux appeals to a new criterion, viz. 'the order of things' (l'ordre des choses), which refers to the relationship between man and reality. According to the type of relation, we have to distinguish a 'natural' or 'practical' order (reflecting directly our contact with the outer world), and a 'speculative' or 'metaphysical' order (which expresses a distant, more abstract and reflexive view of reality). In adopting the natural order we speak first of qualities or of objects of a particular activity, so that adjectives precede nouns and objects precede verbs, as is the case in Latin (rotundus est sol, 'round is the sun';

panem praebe mihi, 'bread, give (it) to me'). Using the speculative order we start by the logical subject and we put the direct object after the verb. Taking the criterion of the order of things, then, as a yardstick, Batteux concludes that French basically follows the speculative order: its normal order is not a natural one (except in passive constructions perhaps, where the patient is turned into the subject of the sentence).

Batteux's work fits within the discussion, around 1750, of language origins,[26] and of the primitive signs and types of sentences. Condillac in his *Essai sur l'origine des connoissances humaines* ('Essay on the origin of human knowledge', 1746) had posited a primitive *langage d'action*, a stimulus-dependent symbolization by expressive sounds and gestures; this *langage d'action* then developed, through life in society, and through the development of intellectual capacities (especially the faculty of abstraction), into a language system composed of arbitrary (or conventional) signs. Condillac was hardly explicit about the transition from the *langage d'action* to stimulus-free language system(s), nor did he deal extensively with the problem of linear order and inversion. A much more precious testimony is Diderot's *Lettre sur les sourds et muets* ('Letter on the deaf-mutes', 1751),[27] which raises the fundamental problem of linguistic articulation: how is an indivisible sense-datum articulated into a string of symbols? Diderot gives no satisfactory answer to this problem, but his 'hypothetical investigation' brings to light the highly conventionalized word order of French, which is not a matter of nature, but one of *tradition*. Diderot is right in pointing out that the sign-language of deaf-mutes – which is more natural, since it simulates the context of linguistic ontogenesis – does not have SVO order.

This did not seem a convincing counter-argument for those ready to believe that French was synonymous with 'clarity'. The second half of the eighteenth century saw a rapidly increasing expansion of French as a cultural *lingua franca*, especially in Germany at the Prussian Court of Frederick II. Attention was given to the prestige of civilized languages; their literature and their scientific use were regarded as a more trustful testimony than speculations about the language of primitive man and data from an artificial and hardly 'illustrated' sign-language. The prestige of the French language, illustrated by a brilliant literature (the seventeenth-century dramatists; Montesquieu; Voltaire; Diderot; Rousseau and so on), and by an impressive scientific prose (as laid down in the *Encyclopédie*), explains why it was possible to stick to the old myth, and to ignore the linguistically grounded counter-arguments. In 1784 Antoine de Rivarol's *Discourse on the Universal Character of the French Language (Discours sur l'universalité de la langue française)* was published as one of the two prize-winning essays in a contest held by the Berlin Academy of Sciences and Literature.[28] Rivarol's essay was a strikingly worded but unoriginal and linguistically very poor attempt to answer these questions. His answer to the Berlin prize topic focused on the properties of the French language, and boiled down to the reaffirmation of the clarity of French, more specifically of its word order. Rivarol's essay reads like a programmatic *salon* lecture, which one has to endure without thinking about it:

> What distinguishes our language from the ancient and the modern ones is the order and construction of the sentence. This order must always be direct and necessarily clear. The French language puts the subject of the sentence first, then the verb, which is the action, and finally the object of this action: that is the logic natural to all men; that is what constitutes common sense. Now this order so favourable and so necessary to reasoning, is almost always contrary to sensations, which put at the beginning the object which first affects us. This is why all the nations that abandon the direct order have used ways of speaking which are more or less forceful, depending on whether their sensations or the harmony between words required it. Inversion has prevailed all around, since man is more strongly governed by passion than by reason. The French language, by a unique privilege, is the only one to have remained faithful to direct (word) order, as if this language were pure reason. And no matter how one tries to conceal this order, by the most diversified movements and stylistic resources, it must always be there. In vain do passions excite us and invite us to follow the order of the sensations: French syntax is incorruptible. Whence that admirable clarity, the eternal foundation of our language: what is not clear is not French.[29]

4 SUNDOWN: CLAIR-OBSCUR

None of the bold statements made by Rivarol is supported by examples, let alone by an in-depth analysis of French language data. Moreover, there is the striking contradiction between the universal claims and the absence of any comparison with other languages. To sum up, there is no methodological foundation to the *Discours*: Rivarol nowhere defines what he understands by 'direct order' or by 'natural(ness)'. This fact did not pass unnoticed. In 1785 the *Discours* was reviewed by two authors who were to play an important role during the period of the French Revolution, viz. François-Urbain Domergue and Dominique Garat.[30] Domergue, the 'patriotic grammarian',[31] attacked Rivarol's use of the term 'clarity' referring to linear expression. In Domergue's view there is direct order when there is a one-to-one correspondence between the order of words and the order of experience (including sensation and thought):

> One sees that the author [Rivarol] views the clarity of our language as consisting in direct order. . . . But let me first ask, what is direct order? It is certainly not the successive ordering of the subject of the proposition, of the verb and the object; but it is the arranging of the ideas in the order in which the mind presents them. When I see a snake . . . and when it is the first thing my eyes bring before the mind, I follow the direct order, whatever language I speak, when the word 'snake' comes first in the sentence. When I cry out in Latin *serpentem fuge* 'a snake, run away [from it]', or in French *un serpent! Fuyez!*, I am equally faithful to the direct order, and woe betide the chilly and absurd language that would require us to say: *Monsieur, prenez garde, voilà un serpent qui s'approche*, 'Sir, please pay attention, there is a snake approaching!' This is, however, the way the author has Frenchmen speak, this is what he calls direct word order.[32]

According to Domergue, Rivarol – like most of the authors writing on the same topic – made the mistake of confusing direct order with grammatical sequencing. It should be noted that direct order, implying that each word has the same place as the corresponding idea has in the mental construct, is rarely found in a consistent way throughout languages. Garat's criticism is a complementary one in that it points out that clarity is not an inherent, static property, but an *effect*, not linked with a particular syntactic construction, but with the unambiguous use of words and syntactic patterns. 'Well defined and well organized ideas, expressed by the appropriate word or by the word that confers the correct representation, will be clear in all languages; and in all languages one will be obscure if one uses vague ideas, wrong constructions, inappropriate words and false representations.'[33]

After the French Revolution the myth of the clarity of French made its reappearance. It was – and this is no surprise – never defended by philologists or general linguists,[34] but was the favourite topic of historians, literary scholars and generalists. Among the advocates of French clarity in the nineteenth century we find authors such as Allou (1828), Desmarais (1837), Bouillier (1854) and Eliade (1898). One would look in vain for well-founded argumentation: the clarity of French is basically justified by the brilliant representatives of French culture and thought – philosophers and writers of the seventeenth, eighteenth and nineteenth centuries. The 'pillars' of this clarity are the classical ones: word order, lexical precision, and stylistic transparency. But there is no linguistic analysis to support these claims.

This is basically the situation of the last fifty years.[35] In spite of its high degree of homonymy, of its morpho-syntactic anomalies, of its liability to ambiguity and vagueness[36] – which are also fully exploited by French authors – French is still praised for its clarity. Among the 'cult priests' one rarely finds linguists.[37] A few grammarians – especially those who are concerned with the 'purity of language'[38] – sometimes appeal to it, but the faithful servants are almost invariably drawn from the ranks of literary scholars, vulgarizers, and popular historians.[39] And there are some twentieth-century Rivarols who are able to write, while showing complete lack of linguistic background, on the unique clarity of French:

> I take exactness and clarity to be the first qualities of our language . . . to the point that I doubt whether there has ever been, since the Greek, a language more transparent to thought. . . . When used appropriately, the French language throws light on the most difficult things, and this is one of the reasons for its long domination in Europe. . . . It carries farther than any other language the requirement and the capacity for clarity.
>
> (Duron 1963: 27, 83)[40]

We enter here a field where ideology and scientific approach go separate ways, and where there is no possibility of a dialogue between them. Linguists have reached a consensus on the mythical status[41] of the clarity of French. But their counter-arguments, impressive as they may be, are not taken into account, and will never be, by the adepts of *clarté*. What is not 'clear' to the observer sceptical with regard to both ideology and science is whether these adepts are too enlightened, or too blinded. . . .

But now it is night. And shall we wake, or sleep?

NOTES

This chapter is dedicated to Talbot Taylor, Jr, born 16 April 1989: Welcome to life!

This chapter has a historical slant, its purpose being to show how the discussion concerning the 'clarity of French' has developed throughout the past five centuries, and how it has been tied up with ideological issues. For the methodological problem of what criteria should be used to decide on the 'clarity status' of a language, and for a critical application to French, see Swiggers 1988a.

1 See his letter (of 1803) to the Departmental Prefect of the Po region, La Villa di Villastellone, in which Denina pleads for the use of French – which was better known than Italian in Piedmont – as a cultural language. Denina outlines a programme for the diffusion of French in schools, churches and theatres. In the same year he wrote a pamphlet, *Dell'uso della lingua francesa*, which deals with the same topic. Here Denina supports his case by linguistic arguments. viz. the similarities between Piedmontese and the Gallo-Romance dialects. On Denina's views, see Marazzini's studies (1983, 1984, 1985).

2 Original French text (Marazzini 1985: 18–19): 'Il fallut distinguer les noms par des articles, les personnes des verbes par des pronoms, et arranger les mots en sorte qu'on pût saisir la phrase et le sens. C'est pour cela qu'on s'est accoutumé à placer le sujet ou le nominatif avant le verbe, et c'est là, si je ne me trompe, la véritable cause de cet ordre analytique de construction dont la langue françoise se glorifie.'

3 The term *génie*, applied to language, is interesting from the point of view of the history of ideas. Whereas in the seventeenth century the term applies to the idiosyncratic properties of a language (see, e.g., the notion of *génie* in the *Grammaire générale et raisonnée*), in the eighteenth century the word receives a typological load, referring to the *plan d'idées* or the cognitive (mental) structure on which a language is built (as in Girard's *Vrais principes de la langue françoise*, Condillac's *Essai sur l'origine des connoissances humaines*, and James Harris's *Hermes*; cf. Joly 1977). This shift is also attested for *génie* in its 'psychological' application: as noted by Matoré and Greimas (1957), *génie* in its seventeenth-century use refers in general to one specific mental or affective faculty, whereas in the eighteenth century the term refers to a mental organization as an original and autonomous entity.

4 Original text: 'Il est vrai que *vivoit* et *régnoit* ne sont pas des verbes actifs précédés de leurs accusatifs. Mais il n'est pas rare que même le verbe actif soit précédé de son accusatif, moyennant un pronom ajouté par une espèce de pléonasme: *cet homme je l'ai vu*. Dans ces cas ce pléonasme met plus de clarté et de précision dans la phrase. Mais cela ne prouve point que le françois, par son propre génie, soit plus précis que l'italien, mais que les écrivains ont un peu plus soigné leur style. La Mothe le disoit clairement en parlant à l'académie françoise . . .'

5 Denina saw 'naturalness' on the diachronic level, viz. in the splitting of a

language into dialects, and in the link between geographical distance and linguistic (dis)similarity, thus anticipating some insights of the 'neolinguists' (e.g., Bartoli and Bertoni 1928) and of present-day dialectometrics (see Goebl 1982, 1984).

6 See his remarks on language evolution (in Marazzini 1985: 52–3).

7 See the modern edition by Hausmann (1980). For an analysis of Meigret's conceptions placed in the context of the history of sixteenth-century French grammar, see Chevalier (1968: 211–43) and Kibbee (1979: 184–247).

8 Meigret's statement is in line with the prevalent medieval view (based on Aristotle's theory) of a sentence as expressing a movement (see Rosier 1983: 145–50; Swiggers 1988b).

9 For practical reasons I am not using here Meigret's orthography.

10 Meigret uses the expression 'dresser le bâtiment de notre langue', comparing a particular language to a construction. See also his definition of language: 'Le langage, l'oraison, le parler ou propos est un bâtiment de vocables ou paroles ordonnées de sorte qu'elles rendent un sens convenable et parfait' (Language, discourse, speech or talk is a build-up of sound stretches or words arranged in such a way that they convey a fitting and perfect meaning).

11 Original (quoted after the modernized transcription in Hausmann 1980: 140–1): 'De vrai, si nous considérons bien le style de la langue latine et celui de la nôtre, nous les trouverons contraires en ce que communément nous faisons la fin de clause ou d'un discours, de ce que les Latins font leur commencement: et si nous considérons bien l'ordre de la nature, nous trouverons que le style français s'y range beaucoup mieux que le latin. Car les Latins préposent communément le supposé au verbe, lui donnant ensuite le surposé: par ce moyen, le passif, qui par l'ordre de nature dût être le dernier en clause, est le premier en prolation: et le surposé le dernier, qui par raison dût être le premier: d'autant que l'agent est par raison précédant l'action et passion comme duquel est le commencement du mouvement. Le Latin, de vrai, dira pour parler élégamment *Gallos vicit Caesar*: qui sonnerait en gardant le même ordre *les Gaulois a vaincu César*: pour *César a vaincu les Gaulois*. Les Latins, outreplus, préposent les causes aux effets: là où nous aurons le plus souvent les faits en premier lieu, puis nous venons aux causes: et combien qu'elles soient avant que les effets: ils sont toutefois premiers au sens de l'homme. A cette cause, il a été nécessaire à l'homme d'avoir la connaissance des oeuvres et effets de nature, avant que d'en rechercher les causes: ni ne serait la disputation raisonnable de la cause de la mort de quelque homme que premièrement nous ne fussions certains du fait. Je ne veux pas pourtant blâmer la façon des Latins, ni qu'aucun doive sortir hors de la grâce et propriété de leur style en parlant ou écrivant latin: mais aussi ne trouvé-je pas raisonnable qu'on doive s'y asservir et laisser une beaucoup plus facile et aisée manière de dresser le bâtiment de notre langue, suivant l'ordre que nature tient en ses oeuvres et que l'usage de parler a voulu suivre.'

12 Garnier notes that French word order is the natural one, in that French puts (the expression of) substance before (the expression of) the accidents.

13 These signs were introduced during the sixteenth century; for a survey of the use of diacritical signs by sixteenth-century printers, see Catach 1968.

14 On the linguistic relevance of the Port-Royal *Grammar* and *Logic*, see Donzé 1967; Dominicy 1984; and Swiggers 1989a, b.

15 For a more elaborate discussion of these conditions, see Swiggers 1987a.

16 For extensive quotations from the writings of Tallemant, Bouhours, Lamy, and Le Laboureur, see Lefèvre 1974: 229–32.

17 Le Laboureur bases his argument on an observation by Géraud de Cordemoy in his *Discours physique de la parole* (1668): Cordemoy noted that to be called 'perfect', a language must follow the order of nature, naming first objects (and their qualities), then actions and the objects of these.

According to Bouhours, French has a natural elegance, in combining the faithful expression of the order of nature with beauty and simplicity. Whereas other languages attain harmony only by inverting the 'natural order', French achieves this in a direct way.

18 See Cellard's (1971–2: 14) apt remark: 'toute langue est par définition la plus claire, et même la seule claire, pour tous ceux dont elle est la langue maternelle' (Any language is by definition the most clear and in fact the only clear one, for those who speak it as their mother tongue). See also Bally 1952: 34.

19 On the philosophical assumptions underlying the synonymy trend, see Auroux 1986.

20 On the trend of synonymy in the eighteenth century, see Martens 1887; Quemada 1967; Gauger 1973; and Swiggers 1986.

21 On Girard's typology, see Monreal-Wickert (1977: 54–6) and Swiggers (1982: 41–6).

22 See the article '*Langue*' in the *Encyclopédie méthodique: Grammaire et littérature*, vol. 2, 1784: 'Je donne à cette succession le nom d'*Ordre analytique*, parce qu'elle est tout à la fois le résultat de l'analyse de la pensée, & le fondement de l'analyse du discours, en quelque *langue* qu'il soit énoncé. . . . Voilà ce qui se trouve universellement dans l'esprit de toutes les *Langues*' [I call this sequence 'Analytical order', because it is both the result of the analysis of thought, and the foundation of the analysis of discourse, in whatever language it may be uttered. . . . This is what can be found universally in the 'spirit' of all languages].

23 On the practice of interlinear translation, see Kelly 1969: 144–9.

24 For a discussion of Du Marsais's views, see Swiggers 1984: 124–33.

25 Original: 'Je me demande . . . si les Latins ne trouvaient pas leur langue, naturelle, simple, claire. Notre langue nous paraît la plus claire de toutes les langues; cela n'est pas étonnant: c'est celle que nous savons le mieux; elle est née avec nous et nous avec elle; elle est comme un membre de nous-mêmes'.

26 On this discussion, see Aarsleff 1982: 146–209, 278–92.

27 On the important rôle of Diderot's text in eighteenth-century philosophy of language, see Aarsleff 1988: LIII–LIX.

28 On the background of the contest, see Baldensperger 1907.

29 Original (quoted after the edition in Hervier 1929: 88, 95): 'Ce qui distingue notre langue des anciennes et des modernes, c'est l'ordre et la construction de la phrase. Cet ordre doit toujours être direct et nécessaire-

ment clair. Le français nomme d'abord le sujet de la phrase, ensuite le verbe, qui est l'action, et enfin l'objet de cette action: voilà la logique naturelle à tous les hommes; voilà ce qui constitue le sens commun. Or, cet ordre si favorable, si nécessaire au raisonnement, est presque toujours contraire aux sensations, qui nomment le premier objet qui frappe le premier. C'est pourquoi tous les peuples, abandonnant l'ordre direct, ont eu recours aux tournures plus ou moins hardies, selon que leurs sensations ou l'harmonie des mots l'exigeaient; l'inversion a prévalu sur la terre, parce que l'homme est plus impérieusement gouverné par les passions que par la raison. Le français, par un privilège unique, est seul resté fidèle à l'ordre direct, comme s'il était toute raison; et on a beau, par les mouvements les plus variés et toutes les ressources du style, déguiser cet ordre, il faut toujours qu'il existe; et c'est en vain que les passions nous bouleversent et nous sollicitent de suivre l'ordre des sensations: la syntaxe française est incorruptible. C'est de là que résulte cette admirable clarté, base éternelle de notre langue; ce qui n'est pas clair n'est pas français.'

30 On Domergue's and Garat's criticism of Rivarol's views, see Ricken (1978: 161–9) and Hagège (1985: 165–70).

31 On Domergue's linguistic conceptions, see Busse (1985, 1986b) and Christiaens (1986).

32 Original (*Journal de la langue française*, 1785: 886–7): 'On voit que l'auteur fait consister la clarté de notre langue dans l'ordre direct, et la solidité de son empire dans sa clarté. Mais d'abord, qu'est-ce que l'ordre direct? Ce n'est certainement pas l'arrangement successif du sujet de la proposition, du verbe et de l'objet; mais l'arrangement des idées dans l'ordre où l'esprit les présente. Or lorsque je vois un serpent . . . le serpent étant la première chose que mes yeux portent à mon esprit, je suis l'ordre direct, en quelque langue que je parle, si le mot *serpent* commence ma proposition. Que je crie en latin, *serpentem fuge*, ou en français *un serpent! Fuyez!*, je suis également fidèle à l'ordre direct, et malheur à la langue froide et absurde qui voudrait qu'on dît: *Monsieur, prenez garde, voilà un serpent qui s'approche!* C'est pourtant ainsi que l'auteur fait parler un Français, c'est ce qu'il appelle l'ordre direct.'

33 Original (*Mercure de France*, August 1785: 32): 'Des idées bien déterminées, bien ordonnées, rendues ou avec le mot propre ou avec le mot qui fait une image juste, seront claires dans toutes les langues; et dans toutes les langues on sera obscur avec des idées vagues, des phrases mal construites, des mots impropres et de fausses images.'

34 See, e.g., Darmesteter's (1875: 241–6) criticism of the concept of 'clarity'.

35 For a selection of texts, see Bourgaux (1963) and Lefèvre (1974: 252–76).

36 See, e.g., Martinet (1969: 61), who points out that in French there are all possible sources of confusion; see also the analysis in Swiggers (1988a: 626–8).

37 There are however some exceptions, such as Dauzat (1926, 1947), von Wartburg (1946) and Ewert (1958), who stress the lexical precision of French, the neatness of its phonetic system, and its transparent word order.

38 For the ideology underlying the appeal to the 'purity of language', see Bengtsson 1968.

39 See, e.g., Vannier 1923; Vincent 1925; Reynaud 1930; and Martin-Chauffier 1943.
40 Original: 'Je tiens la justesse et la clarté pour les qualités premières de notre langue . . . à ce point que je doute s'il y a jamais eu, depuis les Grecs, langue plus transparente à la pensée. . . . Bien maniée, elle [= la langue française] éclaircit les choses les plus difficiles, et c'est une des raisons de sa longue domination en Europe . . . . Elle porte plus loin que toute autre l'exigence et la capacité de la clarté.'
41 See Kukenheim 1951; Weinrich 1961; and Martinet 1969; as well as the article 'The myth of clarity', in *The Times Literary Supplement*, 4 May 1962.

7

The ideological profile of Afrikaans historical linguistics

Paul T. Roberge

1 PURPOSE AND SCOPE

The emergence of a separate (but cognate) Netherlandic language at the Cape of Good Hope within the first century and a half of European colonization (1652–1806) has been the source of enduring controversy and fascination. Interest in the history of Afrikaans has not been confined to the linguistic sciences. It is something of a cliché that Afrikaners are 'inordinately proud' of the 'survival and development of their once despised "barbarous patois" into a cultural language in the face of prestigious Nederlands and all-embracing English' (Reinecke *et al.* 1975: 322). Vernacular elevation has been a source of pride, myth and ritual celebration. The perception that has emerged over the decades is one of a precious heritage, won at great cost.

The salient linguistic attitudes of Afrikaners are indisputably rooted in their struggle to maintain ethno-racial separation (from English as well as black South Africans). That prevailing cultural precepts can profoundly influence domains of scholarly enquiry is well documented. This is demonstrably the case in at least one other social science in South Africa, viz. ethnology or *volkekunde*, as practised by white Afrikaans-speaking anthropologists (cf. Gordon 1988). Given these facts, it is appropriate to ask whether such attitudes have imparted to Afrikaans historical linguistics a distinctive ideological profile. This chapter investigates this question by critically examining scholarly pronouncements on the history of Afrikaans. Specifically, its focus is on the diachronic study of the language as conducted by white, Afrikaans-speaking linguists.[1]

2 PERCEPTIONS

The consensus outside South Africa is that Afrikaans reflects a semicreolized (creoloid) variety of Dutch that traces its roots to language

131

contact between Europeans, the aboriginal Khoikhoi (Hottentots), and slaves of African and Asian origin.[2] Neither the social context nor the linguistic facts seem to support the hypothesis that Afrikaans is a true creole language. Nevertheless, the structure of Afrikaans has been considerably simplified from Dutch. Although the mechanisms of this transformation are still not fully understood, this simplification could not have occurred within the elapsed time under conditions that reasonable linguists would consider 'ordinary'. Most would agree with Thomason and Kaufman (1988: 255) in their conclusion that 'to argue that Afrikaans arose by a series of perfectly ordinary internally motivated changes from Dutch flies in the face of everything we know about ordinary rates of . . . change'.[3]

It is a rather hackneyed formula of creolistics that the debate on the origins of Afrikaans has not been conducted solely on scientific grounds.[4] The observation may be well-worn, but it reflects a basic reality. Afrikaans linguistics emerged within the context of struggle for the recognition of Afrikaans in all domains. The Afrikaner Broederbond and National Party gave this language struggle (*taalstryd*) a nationalist direction by incorporating it into the larger drive toward political dominance. Valkhoff (1971: 462) saw fit to include the following caveat in his critical bibliography in volume 7 of *Current Trends in Linguistics*:

> When we study the rise of Afrikaans linguistics, we have to do this against the background of a struggle for self-assertion of the Afrikaner people, of which the defense of their Afrikaans language was an integral part. . . . When we read the studies of the Afrikaner scholars, particularly the early ones, we must bear in mind that they are as much advocates of a despised language as practical grammarians and language teachers, and only in the last resort linguistic scientists.

Not surprisingly, the creolization model has not generally been well received in white South Africa.[5] Barnouw (1934: 20) remarked: 'Afrikaners do not like to have it said that the modification of Dutch which they speak is a creole language, the result of a cross between the speech of the early settlers and the prattle [*sic*] of their black slaves.' Such a view is felt to put a stigma 'on the race of the Voortrekkers and on their language'. Reinecke (1937: 567) was more circumspect, explaining the rejection of Hesseling's model 'partly on genuine linguistic grounds, partly out of pride'. It is one thing to attempt to be impartial in considering various approaches to the origin problem from a particular conceptual framework. It is quite another to dismiss a position out of hand because it is not consonant with a particular parochial perspective. Not a few have accused Afrikaner scholars of the latter since Reinecke compiled his material.

Valkhoff (1966: 5–7; 1971: 463–5) noted three broad trends within Afrikaans linguistics. First, Afrikaner scholars have imputed their ideal of racial purity into history and linguistics (1971: 463, 464, 467). Accordingly, the creolization model is abhorrent to most Afrikaner scholars, who want to 'see their language white and pure like their race' (Valkhoff 1971: 467). They are further apt to confine themselves to the study of the language as spoken by whites. Finally, they have applied the idea of apartheid to the history of Afrikaans in so far as they deal with the Dutch of Europeans, Khoikhoi and slaves (and their descendants) as separate phenomena. Valkhoff labelled these tendencies (respectively) *diachronic purism*, *albocentrism*, and *compartimentage*.

Reinecke *et al.* (1975: 322f.) note that the origin question is still an emotional one with many Afrikaners,

> the more so in recent years when the ideal of apartheid has made it harder to face the documented facts of cultural and sexual miscegenation in the simpler milieu of early Cape society. . . . Not the creole like simplification of Afrikaans is offensive but the word *creole* with its smack of color.

Markey (1982: 169) characterizes our topic as 'one of the best known and more frequently debated *ethnolinguistic* [my emphasis] controversies', and describes mainstream Afrikaner views as representing 'the politically-tinged party line of white supremacy'. Makhudu attributes the recalcitrance of the origin question in part to 'the penchant to employ racist, politically motivated argumentation about Afrikaans by many White Afrikaner academics' (1984: 2). Eurocentric theories about Afrikaans are 'emotionally satisfying' because of 'their underpinnings of racial and linguistic purism. Miscegenation, creoles, and mixed languages are taboo subjects in South Africa' (ibid.: 16). To read his discussion of prior research (Makhudu 1984: ch. 2), the uninformed reader might gain the impression of a struggle between children of darkness and children of light. Mühlhäusler (1986: 7) notes that the idea of intense racial mixture in the early years of Dutch colonization is 'understandably unpopular with the large group of white pro-apartheid speakers of Afrikaans, who prefer to regard their language as a continuation of white dialects of Dutch (e.g. Raidt 1983)'.[6] Most recently, Thomason and Kaufman (1988: 251) have written that 'controversy about the development of Afrikaans has been sharper than for any other putative creole, largely (apparently) for political reasons'.

Advocacy of a particular developmental model has to a great (though not unlimited) extent fallen along ethnic lines.[7] Given the prevailing linguistic attitudes (see above) and the fact that Afrikaner linguists have generally taken strong exception to the creolization model, it is very easy to suspect that a racist ideology underlies a significant portion of their scholarship. For individual academics, this is obviously true; their writings do little to contradict this suspicion. For the rest, however, this is much too superficial an explanation. Afrikaner linguistic scholarship boasts some truly distinguished writings.

Unlike ethnology, which impinges more directly upon the legitimation of the power structure, an all-powerful professoriate at South African universities has not simply dictated the parameters of discussion concerning the evolution of Afrikaans. Were such in fact the case, then we should expect linguistic pronouncements to be relatively uniform, incontestable and standardized. Their evaluation would require little more than a genealogy of the discipline and a determination of the effectiveness of the actual modes of thought control (assuming that you cannot always get people to accept ideas by intimidation or regulating their career path). In principle, at least, the issues are open to public debate. Linguistic pride, racism, transference of apartheid, and white hegemony alone do not account for the extent to which creolization models have received such a poor reception in Afrikaner linguistic scholarship. Still, it is fair to say that a more or less consistent ideology has in fact been constitutive for Afrikaans historical linguistics. Having identified this ideology (section 2) and the symbolic universe from which it derives (section 3), I go on to describe its implementation (section 4) and continuation (section 5).

3 FUNDAMENTAL POSTULATES OF AFRIKANER HISTORICAL LINGUISTICS

The major source for my conceptual framework is Moodie 1975. *Religion*, according to Moodie (1975: 295), is a set of symbols (words, objects, ritual actions) that assist an individual or group in meeting the ultimate problems of human identity and destiny. *Civil religion*, as Moodie defines it (1975: 296), denotes the religious dimension of the state. As such, it is associated with the exercise of power and the 'constant regeneration of the social order'. Political sovereignty finds a context in ultimate meaning and transcendent justification. *Social metaphysics* or *social philosophy* defines the unit of social analysis (family, nation, social class, even mankind as a whole) and the vesting of political power (in an individual, an ethnic group, a majority of individuals, and so on); cf. Moodie 1975: 298. The term *ideology* Moodie restricts to prescriptive articulations derived from civil religion and social philosophy. Ideology transforms them into 'directives or a program for political action' (1975: 298).

Moodie's definition of the term *ideology* would be entirely appropriate for applied linguistic endeavours such as language policy and planning.[8] It becomes less appropriate as we turn away from the narrowly political context of such applications to evaluate the conduct of scholarly enquiry. *Ideology* I take to mean instead a set of articulations that derive from a system of beliefs and symbols embedded in popular consciousness, reinforced by civil ritual, and codified in the social order.

Four fundamental postulates have characterized the writings of white Afrikaans-speaking linguists concerning the history of their language and constitute an ideology in this sense.

(1) Afrikaans is to be seen as a direct and linear descendant of Dutch. The transformation of nonstandard Netherlandic dialects at the Cape of Good Hope was a process in which preponderantly internal factors governed the succession of changes. The transmission of language from one generation of colonists to the next was 'bent' somewhat, to be sure, on account of dialectal heterogeneity among the Dutch and the arrival of French and German settlers. In the main, however, language transmission among Europeans was continuous and unbroken.

(2) The catalyst or accelerating factor in this transformation was contained within the European community.

(3) The Afrikaans of the 'coloureds' reflects historically a somewhat more radical break in language transmission. Next to the changing but fully developed linguistic system of Europeans, the Netherlandic speech community at the old Cape saw emerging systems among the indigenes and slaves. Imperfect code-switching on the part of the latter gradually gave way first to continuing improvement in performance in achieving communication with the Europeans and then to the native acquisition of Cape Dutch by succeeding generations.

(4) Influences from the non-European contact languages (viz. Khoikhoi, Creole Portuguese and Malay) are supposed to have been confined chiefly to lexis and single features along the grammatical

periphery. Black varieties of Dutch, which find their origin in naive (that is, untutored) second-language learning, gradually became viable as a primary language. However, there was no fusion with the European community. Breach of the ethological barriers was one-sided in so far as there was no mirror image of black varieties among the Europeans beyond the acceptance of individual linguistic features. As such, black varieties are to be seen as separate developments and warrant separate investigation.

These fundamental postulates and the parameters of enquiry they define do not issue solely from empirical findings and model systems that are internal to the discipline. They derive in no small measure from the sociology of the field as it emerged in South Africa. To overlook civil religion and social philosophy in evaluating this ideology is to overlook the most important factors.

4 HISTORICAL DETERMINANTS

Afrikaner group consciousness and solidarity find their origin in the 1870s as a reaction to the British imperial factor. Prior to that, Afrikaners merely existed as a community with their own areas of residence and vernacular. The concepts 'South Africa' and 'Afrikaner *volk*' had no coherent political significance.[9] Afrikaans-speaking whites in the Cape Colony were isolated in the rural districts and had virtually no sense of identity. Binding elements were lacking; there was a discernible drift toward Anglicization and assimilation into the English stream. With the exception of the Cape Malay, the 'coloureds' did not possess any significant group consciousness, either.

The status of their Cape Dutch vernacular was similarly indeterminate. From as early as 1685, the source material contains copious allusions to the 'vulgar', 'corrupt', 'bastardized' form of Dutch spoken by the descendants of European colonists, indigenes and slaves. This Cape variety was perceived – within the colony as well as without – as linguistically differentiated from the Netherlandic varieties of the continent. It was nevertheless regarded as merely an extraterritorial variety of Dutch until the early part of the present century, albeit with one very important qualification. Educated colonists tended to regard the Cape Dutch vernacular as the language of 'Hottentots' ('coloureds') as well as that of the lowest classes of whites.

The First (1875–98) and Second (1903–19) Language Movements sought explicitly to alter these linguistic attitudes and perceptions.

Realization of the immediate goal of acquiring for Afrikaans linguistic functions previously reserved for English or Dutch – as also the ultimate dream of a united South Africa under Afrikaner rule – required consciousness-raising along two broad parameters.[10]

Potentially the more galvanizing parameter of consciousness-raising is civil religious in nature. In the Afrikaner civil religion there is a divine agent – an active sovereign God – who has elected the Afrikaner people for a special destiny. He has bestowed upon this elect a nation, with its distinct language and culture, and its own history. The civil faith itself flourished in the 1920s and especially the 1930s; the promise of triumph implicit in the civil faith was realized with the electoral victory of the National Party in 1948.[11]

During the late nineteenth century the writings of the Patriot movement evince occasional civil religious comment on Afrikaans. Typical of its propaganda are calls for 'true Afrikaners' to turn to the language of their hearts, to recognize the mother tongue that God has bestowed upon them. The diversity of peoples and languages is the will of God, who has revealed Himself to individual races in their own languages. Isomorphism between language and people is in the divine order of things. The civil religious theme that is discernible in Patriot writings is more one of divine ordinance than election. Gradually, however, there emerged a sense that vernacular elevation was part of a grand enterprise, the scope of which was far broader than the expansion of functional domains. Upon recognition of Afrikaans in lieu of Dutch as an official language of South Africa (1925), the poet C. J. Langenhoven hailed the realization of this promise as 'miraculous' (*wonderlik*) and 'from the Lord' (cited from P. J. Nienaber 1959: 3).

A second parameter involved the promulgation of a social philosophy stressing the interdependence of cultural and human relationships. Language along with race, history, fatherland, religion and culture are the defining characteristics of a people. Language reflects a people's character; no nationality could exist without a language.

One aspect of the social philosophical parameter is the separateness of Afrikaans from its Dutch parent. Both language movements rejected out of hand conservative arguments for the greater literary worth of Dutch and the importance of Dutch culture. Afrikaners could no longer consider themselves Hollanders. In numerous apologia (*pleidooie*) advocates sought to inculcate an awareness of Afrikaans as a language in its own right and to convince the people of its parity with mainstream European languages at comparable stages of development. D. F. Malan's famous address 'Het is ons Ernst' ('We are in earnest') (13

August 1908) represents the genre particularly well. One hears, he said, that Afrikaans can never become a written language (*schrijftaal*); that it is merely a dialect, a corrupt patois (*een bedorven patois*). The fact that Afrikaans can be called a 'dialect' proves nothing. Egyptian, Latin, Greek, German and French all began as dialects. Yet they have all achieved greatness. He then proceeded to deliver an oration on the notions 'language' and 'dialect', describing the former as constitutive of a separate, independent people (*volk*). Dialects exist within the domain of a *volk*.[12]

> The word dialect is entirely relative. Whether a language should be called a dialect or not depends entirely on whether it is spoken by a People (*volk*) or a section of a People. When it is spoken by a single, independent (*zelfstandig*) People, it has every right to be called a language and not a dialect. Dialect and province, People and language go together.
>
> (cited from Nienaber and Heyl n.d.: 101)

Afrikaner social philosophy has always been exclusive in character, and its second aspect is more overtly racist. According to the civil religion, God has preserved the identity of His people. He did not allow them to become Anglicized or bastardized with the indigenous tribes. On the social philosophical level, language and nationality are inseparable. The scope of this exclusivity not only set Afrikaners apart from the other white language group, but extended perforce to the other Afrikaans-speaking people of South Africa; namely, the 'coloureds'. Race provided an ethological barrier to common cause during the language struggle with those who shared a common linguistic heritage. Given that the Afrikaans language was to be understood as the exponent of the white nation, Afrikaners would have to disassociate their form of the language more explicitly from that of their Afrikaans-speaking 'coloured' brethren. Considerations of space do not permit a full discussion. Suffice it to say that the available evidence gives every indication of such a conscious attempt (Roberge 1988).

It might be tempting to conclude from all this that the scholarly pronouncements of Afrikaner historical linguists issue directly from the tenets of civil religion and social philosophy. Although one can differentiate between civil religion and social philosophy, the difference is in practice purely analytical. Moodie (1975: 299) observes that they tend to 'be mingled in a single symbolic universe'. Identification of this universe does not inform us of the mechanisms by which symbols have been projected onto a body of knowledge.

5 FORMATION AND IMPLEMENTATION

With the Afrikaans language approaching something of an apotheosis in the early years of the present century, it is easy to understand why Hesseling's views aroused the ire of many Afrikaners. In the popular mind creole languages were construed essentially as debasements of mainstream languages in the mouths of halfcastes. The notion 'creole' not only implied cohabitation between the races – the repugnance of which to Afrikanerdom has been ubiquitously noted (see Jordaan 1974: 462–5, and section 1 above) – but also intellectual inferiority and cultural impoverishment.[13]

These points were not lost on Hesseling himself, who took pains to differentiate the genesis of a language from its subsequent elaboration. In an obscure little gem (1912) bearing the title 'Is het Afrikaans een beschaafde taal?' ('Is Afrikaans an educated language?'), he stressed the adequacy of Afrikaans for every kind of discourse. He saw no reason why a language could not rise above humble origins. The purity of a language lies not in its genealogy but in its ability to pair meanings with texts. Lest there be any misunderstanding on these points, Hesseling proffered the following analogy:

> Naturally I do not claim that all varieties of Afrikaans are 'educated' [*beschaafd*]. I would then be making the same kind of argument as its opponents, albeit in the opposite direction. What an uneducated Kaffir [*sic*] or Hottentot says – his thoughts being limited to a small circle of daily needs – cannot be called 'educated'. Indeed, it is just as foolish to put forward the language of such an individual against Afrikaans as it is to cite the simple phrases [*zinnetjes*] of a negro who sails on an English or Dutch ship as a stoker in order to prove that Dutch or English are barbaric languages.
>
> (1912: 3)

The subtext contained in the image of a man of colour performing the most menial work imaginable cannot have been lost on anyone.

The prevailing ideology in Afrikaans historical linguistics, as codified in the fundamental postulates, traces its intellectual roots to the historical and comparative paradigm that dominated Europe during the nineteenth and early twentieth centuries. Accordingly, new languages evolve from a single parent by means of incremental change. 'Mixed' languages were considered epiphenomena. To Afrikaner intellectuals with a vested interest in promoting the mother tongue, the idea of a language in the process of elaboration being developmentally different from mainstream European languages defied comprehension. There appears to have been widespread insecurity flowing from the perception that highly inflected languages are developmentally more advanced. In his little primer for English speakers, Langenhoven (1926: 19–20) reassured his readership that 'the structure of Afrikaans is even simpler than that of English – the second simplest [Afrikaans being the first] and most rational speech of civilized men'; and further: 'Afrikaans is a pure language with very little foreign adulteration, so that the words are related *inter se* and the memory associates them into groups.' One philologist sought to justify certain simplifications in Afrikaans with parallel phenomena in vulgar Latin:

> Even Classical Latin had shed its endings (*legonti* had become *legont*), and the process was continued in the transition to Romance – *donatus* becomes French *donné* as Nederlands *gegeven* becomes Afrikaans *gegee*; and we find in late Latin only one oblique case: instead of *pater, patrem, patris, patri, patre* we have only *pater, patre*; so instead of the archaic Nederlands *des vaders, den vader*, Afrikaans simply uses prepositions with the single article *die*.
>
> (Haarhoff 1934: 37f.)

Clearly, it was felt to be important that Afrikaans was in acceptable company as concerns the stripping of inflections.

Within the symbolic universe described in section 3, the Afrikaans language is the hallmark of Afrikanerdom. Postma (1912) put forward the idea that the birth of Afrikaans coincided with the birth of the Afrikaner nation. Boshoff (1921) offered a more robust demonstration of historicity in the form of a Netherlandic tradition (*erfgoed*) integrating autochthonous developments (*eiegoed*) and borrowings (*leengoed*). But he clearly proceeded from the premise that Afrikaans is *the* language of South Africa and that Afrikaners could look forward to a future in which *their* language would be dominant (see especially his closing remarks, pp. 427–30).

If the *volk* is the necessary unit of social analysis, it follows *mutatis mutandis* that its form of the language will be the primary object of linguistic-analysis. The latter being the case, one might not care to look outside the European community to find the accelerating factor underlying the transformation of Dutch into Afrikaans. Nowhere are these postulates more obvious than in the 'spontaneous development' model initially adumbrated by Kruisinga (1906), with whom the Afrikaner linguists Boshoff (1921: 78), Bosman (1916, 1923) and J.J. Smith were in substantial agreement. The absence of prescriptive norms in this colonial backwater and the rapid assimilation of European immigrants of varying linguistic backgrounds greatly accelerated tendencies toward change inherent in Dutch grammar. For its part, the Afrikaans of the 'coloureds' reflects an 'adaptation' (Boshoff 1921: 72) or 'broken' variety (Bosman 1923: 42–3) that their forebears had adduced (imperfectly) from their European masters (cf. also van Rijn 1914: 25ff., Barnouw 1934: 29). Bosman conceded that individual Afrikaans features are attributable to the influence of non-native speakers on the Dutch target language, but only in so far as they are not the result of spontaneous development. One could attribute the origin of single features to the contact languages (cf. le Roux 1923, for example), but the influence of Khoikhoi and slave varieties on the language of the whites was presumed to be marginal in the aggregate (Bosman 1923: 117–20).

It seems superfluous to add that the Afrikaans of the 'coloureds' seemed hardly worth bothering about for so long. Rademeyer's dissertation (1938) stood for years as the only monographic treatment of black varieties of Afrikaans. Rationalization, if any were needed, could be found in the fact that the two communities share neither a common ethno-racial descent nor cultural heritage.

6 CHANGES AND CONTINUITIES

To the generation of Afrikaners born after the Second World War, the traditional symbols do not hold as much relevance. The Afrikaans language is now well established and under no immediate threat. In the present conduct of diachronic enquiry the old ethnocentrisms no longer lurk just below the surface. The field is not impervious to developments in linguistic science overseas, and it has reached an international level. In fact the perceptions cited in section 1 hardly do justice to the very high standards of scholarship that certain South African philologists have set (see p. 142 and note 15). Nevertheless, both trajectories – the Afrikaner symbolic universe and the historical and comparative paradigm – have left their imprint. The fundamental postulates define not an orthodoxy but rather serve as a kind of plausibility metric for the integration of views and facts.

The most significant research on the history of Afrikaans has been conducted within a narrowly philological framework. G. S. Nienaber – one of the most important figures of the older generation – compiled the first (and so far the only) more or less complete history of the language (1949, 1952).[14] He does not neglect the varieties of the Khoikhoi and slaves, even while separating them from the Dutch of Europeans. His treatment of Hesseling is critical but on balance objective. Far more detailed and systematic investigations have issued from what den Besten (1986, 1987a) has called the 'South African philological school', the leading figures of which are J. du Plessis Scholtz (1939, [2]1965, 1963, 1965, 1970, 1972, 1980) and his pupil Edith H. Raidt (1968, 1976a, 1983, 1984, for example).[15]

The philologists have not concerned themselves with the formation of an explanatory model. Instead, they have concentrated on the history of specific linguistic phenomena. This is not to suggest that the South African philological school is theory-neutral, which it surely is not. One can infer a developmental model that assumes evolutive change within a contact situation. Accordingly, Afrikaans evolved from Dutch by a series of internally motivated changes effected through the generalization of Netherlandic dialectisms (or change in progress). The accelerating factor was the large number of non-native speakers using the Dutch target in a multilingual society. There is far greater allowance for mixing and discontinuity of transmission, but this is spread more or less equally among several groups (Germans, French, Khoikhoi and slaves).

Philological investigation establishes that Afrikaans reduplication (*staan-staan* 'stand around', *vyf-vyf* 'by fives', *amper-amper* 'almost, just about') and the object particle *vir* (*ons ken vir hom baie goed* 'we know him very well') are indisputably the legacy of (respectively) Malay and Creole Portuguese (Raidt 1976b, 1981). As before, one can have vigorous debate about the provenance of specific features. Individual cruxes are now open to re-examination. Ponelis (1987: 6) has quite recently suggested that the replacement of the Dutch relative pronouns *die* (common gender) and *dat* (neuter) with *wat* in Afrikaans may have been abetted by invariant *que* in Portuguese. Raidt (1983: 189f.) is entirely opposed to Nienaber's hypothesis (received sympathetically by Combrink 1978: 83f.) that the Afrikaans 'double' negation (*nie . . . nie*) is a hybridization attributable to the Khoikhoi (Nienaber 1965).[16] Waher (1988) believes (correctly, in my opinion) that the Afrikaans pattern is etymologically opaque and that a comparative examination of negation in contact situations is indicated. Nevertheless, the philologists insist on a sharp distinction between creolization and language interference, both of which can result in simplification and reduction of forms – especially in morphology (cf. Raidt 1977). By roughly 1800, linguistic change in progress, abetted by interference on the part of various groups, had resulted in a more or less stable vernacular among the Europeans. Imperfect approximation of the Dutch superstrate resulted in 'broken' varieties among Africans and slaves but not outright creolization.

It is plainly obvious that the emergence of a new code is as much a social fact as it is a purely linguistic one. In the history of the discipline, we find varying degrees of concern with the social context in which linguistic developments took place. Earlier generations of scholars broadened their view to include not only demonstrable facts but a wide range of assumptions about the speakers and their extralinguistic behaviour. The philologists, by contrast, have restricted their view to exclude as much of this as possible.

> The study of the history of Afrikaans was for a long time held firm in the grip of multifarious origin theories. In large measure these theories were aprioristically conceived, and they were kept afloat through arguments – pro *and* contra – based on social data.
>
> (Scholtz 1963: 274)

Origin theories (*ontstaansteorieë*) – whether creolist or spontaneist – are therefore antiquarian and not especially insightful (cf. Raidt 1976c: 163n.; Scholtz 1980: 29–30; Roodt and Venter 1984: 225–7; Conradie 1986: 83–7).

Obviously, an understanding of the evolution of Afrikaans will require any number of investigations that are not particularly tied to the social setting. One of Scholtz's great achievements was to introduce a very high standard of rigour precisely by disallowing nonlinguistic evidence (cf. Raidt 1980, Roodt and Venter 1984). One proceeds inductively from a thorough investigation of the documentary evidence to a comparison of Afrikaans features with what we know of seventeenth-century Dutch and what we can impute to that period on the basis of modern Netherlandic dialects. Because not all of the features that define Afrikaans are traceable to that region, one looks to dialectal substrata.[17] Only in the last resort does one look to the substrate contact languages.[18] For the philologists, there is actually little choice about the primary object of investigation. Linguistic data from the formative periods attesting to the usage of Khoikhoi and slaves is relatively sparse. When we consider further the fact that Afrikaans does not have the appearance of a true creole (cf. den Besten 1986: 187), it is easy to understand why the traditional *Stammbaum* notion of linear and continuous development coupled to a rudimentary conception of naive second language acquisition (not all that dissimilar in spirit from Bosman's 'foreigners' Dutch' theory) has served adequately.

The variationist approach places more emphasis on dialect levelling and remains well within the framework of the fundamental postulates. Convergence of pre-existing Netherlandic variants was the 'driver' in the evolution of Afrikaans. Van Rensburg (1983, 1984, 1985, for example) equates early Afrikaans with non-standard varieties of Dutch already spoken on the continent and in the Dutch colonies (see 1984: 514). With allowance for secondary influences from standard Dutch (*vernederlandsing*) in the early part of this century, the language of rural speakers who established themselves along the eastern frontier and the standard Afrikaans of today can be considered more or less 'the same'.[19] Thus, no explanation of the 'origin' of Afrikaans is necessary. Non-standard Afrikaans (of the 'coloureds') represents varieties that evolved in the western Cape and along the Orange River from interlanguage forms of non-standard Dutch (cf. van Rensburg 1985). These varieties, too, are the topic of intensive research by variationists (see especially van Rensburg 1984) but are treated as discrete entities historically.

The actual mechanisms for perpetuating the fundamental postulates are rather different from other disciplines in which a small group dictates the terms of discussion, even while being just as effective and constraining. The philologists and variationists have effectively captured the entire spectrum of plausible opinion on the evolution of Afrikaans. They have conducted meticulous and thorough investigation of the various corpora, but only within the framework of the implicit assumptions that underlie that spectrum. Outside participation in the discussion has been limited, due to the political realities and the fact that most of the scholarly literature is written in Afrikaans and not easily obtainable overseas[20] (not to use the mother tongue is evidently still considered unpatriotic). The effect is that it is much harder to penetrate to the fundamental postulates and to notice how constraining they are.

To stress the common heritage between the Afrikaans of whites and 'coloureds' is considered a radical view and places one outside the discussion altogether.[21] To insist that linguistic and social facts surrounding the formation of a Cape Dutch vernacular ought to be studied together might be seen as an unacceptable compromise of rigour. People outside of the framework may pursue such lines of enquiry if they wish, but their views do not enter the mainstream. J. L. M. Franken was convinced that Afrikaans descended from a 'broken' form of Dutch that emerged in the seventeenth century as the vernacular of slaves and children of European colonists (1953: 26, 87) and could not have developed by 'normal' means (1953: 95). The Khoikhoi also used a 'broken' variety (1953: 30, 95) of Dutch that apparently shared much in common with that of the slaves. The 'real' Afrikaans is that which has evolved as the spoken language of the 'coloureds'. The language of the Afrikaners represents their adoption of these varieties (not vice-versa), albeit with a pronounced influence from Dutch (1953: 202f.). Now Franken generally contented himself with presenting the archival data concerning miscegenation and the use of Creole Portuguese and Malay and in no sense sought to articulate an explicit model. Yet, the philologists uniformly treat him as merely a transitional figure between the origin theorists (*ontstaansteoretici*) and scientific linguists (Scholtz 1963: 274, 1980: 32; Raidt 1983: 44), an example *par excellence* of *bricolage* (Roodt and Venter 1984: 227f.).[22]

Whereas Afrikaner linguists tend to see Franken in an antiquarian light, they merely dismiss Valkhoff's work as unscientific, speculative, preoccupied with social relations at the expense of 'hard' linguistic analysis, and generally uninformed with regard to seventeenth-century Dutch and the early Cape source materials (Lubbe 1974: 94–8f.; Raidt 1975, 1976c, 1977). The research in Valkhoff 1972 is undeniably slapdash. It is a lamentable fact that his real quarrel was with the spontaneous development model, which by the early 1970s had become entirely obsolete. His refutation (1972: 1–56) of Smith's public lecture (1952) is gratuitous. His principal antagonist H. J. J. M. van der Merwe (e.g., 1966, 1970, 1977) was a particularly easy mark for criticism. The latter's extreme revival of the spontaneist position, in which geographic displacement and influx of new Dutch immigrants upset the equilibrium of Dutch grammar, unleashing a wave of structural readjustments (accelerated drift), was passed over in silence (cf. Raidt 1977: 73).[23]

Afrikaner linguists may be put out, to put it mildly, by the credibility that Valkhoff's work seems to enjoy in the English-speaking world.[24] What is perhaps most damaging about this is that many linguists overseas will continue to see Valkhoff as the standard bearer of the creolist position and will construe his reception as licence to disparage, if not dismiss, outstanding scholarship in a philological or variationist vein. By the same token, the inadequacies in his work provide a convenient excuse for the automatic rejection of creolist views by opponents who are no less indiscriminate about the fuel they use to stoke their fires. If nothing else in his work turns out to be of lasting value his insistence that the genesis of Afrikaans was subject to the continuum principle (that is, that we should speak of more or less 'advanced' forms of Afrikaans) ought to be a serious issue for anybody holding the view that language contact at the old Cape was more than random and unsystematic.

7 CONCLUSION

In the course of this chapter I have argued that two interrelated trajectories in Afrikanerdom shaped the ideological character of Afrikaans historical linguistics: namely, the symbolic universe defined by civil religion and social philosophy and the comparative/historical paradigm. Ideologies are neither static nor universally accepted. They tend to alter over time in response to events and changing conditions. With the realization that the future of Afrikaans is anything but secure (Steyn 1980: ch. 8), it will be no coincidence if the fundamental postulates may have to accommodate some shifts in perspective. Ponelis (1987), for example, stresses that the unity of the Afrikaans speech community transcends political divisions. Using arguments and evidence of a 'sociological' nature, Belcher (1987) focuses on the interdependence rather than discreteness of European, African and Asian determinants during the formative periods. The shift in focus lends support to the premise that the ideological character of Afrikaans historical linguistics has been largely congruent with significant developments in culture. This is not to suggest a causal relationship between individual pronouncements and tenets of civil faith or social philosophy. Rather, developments in the two aspects of culture cannot be regarded as distinct and unrelated but must be seen as different realizations of a single process.

NOTES

My research in South Africa during 1982–3 was supported by a Humanities Fellowship from the Rockefeller Foundation. I am grateful to Rudolf P. Botha and Cecile le Roux (Stellenbosch) for their remarks on an earlier version of this essay, and to Hans den Besten (Amsterdam) for having made a number of his papers available to me. Naturally, I bear sole responsibility for the views presented here and the inadequacies that remain.

1 Reinecke's now classic dissertation (1937: 559–611) contains a thorough discussion of older theories; also Nienaber (1949: 96–141). Though dated and marred by a politicized tone, Valkhoff (1971) still provides some valid historiographical insights. (It may take a specialist to identify them with certainty.) The outstanding bibliography of Reinecke et al. (1975: 322ff.) remains valuable but is in urgent need of updating. Brief summaries of major positions and issues are in Raidt (1983: 41–6), den Besten (1986: 185–9). Chapter 2 of Makhudu (1984) surveys the relevant literature at greater length but should not be approached uncritically.

2 Their descendants – the 'coloureds' in the South African government's system of racial classification – constitute virtually half of the Afrikaans speech community of roughly 4.9 million (figure from Ponelis 1987: 10). I follow February's practice (1981: vii) of placing the term 'coloured' in quotation marks.

3 The most famous proponents of the creolization model are the Dutch linguists D. C. Hesseling (1897, 1899, 1923a, 1923b) and Marius Valkhoff (1966, 1972), the latter having pursued much of his career in South Africa (the anglophone reader will find translations of Hesseling 1897 and 1923b in Markey and Roberge 1979). Den Besten (1978, 1981, 1985, 1986, 1987a) has advanced the most recent formulation of the creolist position; cf. also Makhudu (1984). Elsewhere in the literature one finds considerable incidental discussion of Afrikaans as a creole or some kind of intermundium between creole and noncreole: e.g., Kloss (1978: 151); Shaffer (1978: 56); Markey (1982); Mühlhäusler (1986: 7, 10, 33); Thomason and Kaufman (1987: 251–6). This seems to be the received opinion in non-linguistic scholarship as well, e.g., Jordaan (1974), Ross (1979: 13–17), February (1981: 20–39).

4 Since the appearance of Valkhoff's studies (1966, 1971, 1972), it is widely assumed in the English-speaking world that Afrikaner scholars bear the brunt of exposure on this charge. It is, however, a characterization that fits very well certain pronouncements by non-Afrikaners. As Kloss (1978: 151f.) remarks: 'Solche Thesen werden zuweilen . . . mit starker Affekt-betontheit vorgetragen, die vermuten läßt, daß die Verfasser nicht unvorein-genommen an ihre Aufgaben herangingen, sondern entweder mit dem Wunsch, die stolzen Buren zu verletzen durch den Nachweis, daß sie ihre Sprache eigentlich den Nichtweißen verdanken, oder aber mit dem Wunsch, alle solche Einflüsse von nichtweißer Seite abzustreiten.' Advocacy of the creolization model has in fact been utilized as an expression of dissidence (see Roberge 1988).

5 Notable exceptions are du Toit (1905), who elaborated on Hesseling's views in a doctoral dissertation presented to the University of Ghent, and J. L. M. Franken (1953), who was broadly sympathetic in his early work. J. J. le Roux (1923) conceded some 'Malayo-Portuguese' influence in syntax.

6 Identification of Edith Raidt in this connection is in my opinion quite unfortunate. She is hardly an 'emotional debater', as Makhudu (1984: 11) alleges.

147

7 Two ardent spontaneists – viz. Kruisinga (1906) and Kloeke (1950) – were Dutch, and the latter's dialect geographical approach found endorsement in Europe and North America (Moulton 1952, Mossé 1952, Frings 1953); see most recently Paardekooper (1986) (and den Besten's reply (1987b)). J. L. Pauwels, a Belgian dialectologist, related the Afrikaans 'double' negation and demonstrative pronouns (*hierdie, daardie*) to some (superficially) parallel structures in the modern Flemish dialect of Aarschot (1958, 1959). Wittmann (1928) placed the origin of Afrikaans entirely in the convergence of non-standard Netherlandic varieties represented at the Cape; similarly, Hutterer (1975: 278–87), who makes no mention of the 'coloured' community in his population statistics.

8 Reagan (e.g. 1984, 1985, 1986, 1987) has investigated the ideological dimension of language policy in South African education. Aspects of the prevailing ideology include: use of the mother tongue for as much of a pupil's instruction as is practicable; provision of separate educational facilities for each ethnolinguistic group; elaboration of languages that are below the functional level of English.

9 During the time of Dutch East India Company rule, the term *Afrikaander* distinguished settled colonists of mainly Dutch descent from European-born officials. From the early nineteenth century, however, the terminological use of *Afrikaner* becomes fluid and fraught with difficulties; see du Toit and Giliomee (1983: xxv–xxiv) for discussion; also du Toit (1987).

10 English predominated in the British Cape Colony and Natal. Dutch was the official language of the two Boer republics – the Orange Free State and the South African Republic (Transvaal); it was permitted in the Cape Parliament from 1882. Anglophone readers will find synoptic treatment of the elevation of Afrikaans in Reinecke (1937: 581–96) and Shaffer (1978).

11 See Moodie (1975: ch. 1) for an ideal typical description of the Afrikaner civil faith.

12 It would appear that Malan's vision would not be extended to the confines of Afrikanerdom for some time to come. In 1909 – the year that saw the establishment of an academy dedicated to the maintenance and advancement of Afrikaans (the Suid-Afrikaanse Akademie vir Wetenskap en Kuns), J. F. van Oordt (1909) in his *Manual of Cape Dutch for the use of English Students* declared Afrikaans to be unequivocally 'a dialect of the High Dutch, largely mixed with foreign elements, principally Portuguese and Malay'. In 1939 – some fourteen years after Afrikaans was officially recognized – J. J. le Roux saw a need to devote one of his radio talks to the question: 'Is Afrikaans 'n taal?' ('Is Afrikaans a language?')

13 European dialectology impinges on the historical study of Afrikaans from the late 1930s (e.g. Louw 1948). Rademeyer (1938) is also worth mentioning in this connection.

14 Steyn (1980) is written for a general audience and to my mind belongs as much to cultural history as to linguistics.

15 See Roberge (1986) and den Besten (1987a) for critical overviews of this scholarly tradition. Other scholars whose approach is compatible in method and purport include R. H. Pheiffer, C. J. Conradie, E. Loubser and F. A. Ponelis.

16 On this crux see now den Besten (1985, 1986).

17 Since Kloeke (1950), there has been nearly unanimous agreement that the prevailing dialect of the early Dutch settlers was that of South Holland.

18 To render this methodological principle as 'if it can be Dutch, it's got to be Dutch', as den Besten (1986: 191) does, is a bit of a cheap shot. More deserving is perhaps Kempen (1946), who related associative constructions of the type *pa-hulle* 'father and his people' to Frisian (!).

19 For Louw (1948) and Combrink (1978: 72–7), the exigencies of communicative efficiency required pruning of morphological redundancy. Although the Netherlandic and Low German dialects represented at the Cape were with some charity mutually intelligible, disparities between inflectional systems created noise in the channel.

20 Makhudu (1984: 2) rightly observes that the status of South Africa as an international pariah has discouraged *in situ* investigation of Afrikaans by foreign scholars. See also the remarks in Donaldson (1988: 15).

21 Raidt's introduction (1983) makes no mention of the thorough and annotated bibliography of Reinecke *et al.* (1975: 322ff.), even though the compilers adopt a neutral stance as concerns the degree to which Dutch underwent creolization at the old Cape. I find this a curious omission.

22 Combrink (1978: 86) regards Franken not as a creolist but rather as a 'heteroglossist'; that is, one who sees Afrikaans as the product of contact between Dutch and indigenous languages of Southern Africa. Raidt (1977: 77) is justifiably annoyed by Valkhoff's having identified her with the spontaneists. (Similarly, Combrink places both her and Scholtz alongside Smith and Kloeke as spontaneists.) Other *bricoleurs*, according to Roodt and Venter (1984: 227ff.), are Rademeyer, G. S. Nienaber and Louw.

23 Van der Merwe categorically ruled out any possibility that the 'coloureds' contributed significantly to the shaping of Afrikaans: 'Non-whites, whether as a group or as individuals, did not influence Dutch in such a way that it evolved into Afrikaans. Whatever can be ascribed to our alleged racial prejudice, one thing is very clear: our logical rejection of non-white influence in regard to Afrikaans rests on scientific facts and not on racial prejudice' (1977: 29).

24 E.g. Wood (1984), Thomason and Kaufman (1988: 252).

Part III

POLITICAL LINGUISTICS

8

On freedom of speech

Roy Harris

The intellectual biases built into an academic discipline are most clearly revealed by considering not what range of explanations it makes available for the phenomena falling within its domain but rather what questions pertaining to those phenomena cannot be raised within the theoretical framework it provides. A case in point is linguistics and the question of freedom of speech.

Although modern linguistics has always claimed to have established a science of speech communication, the model of speech communication it has consistently adopted (Saussure 1922: 27–8; Denes and Pinson 1963: 4–7; Katz 1966: 103–4; Chafe 1970: 15; Cairns and Cairns 1976: 17–18) is one which effectively precludes any possibility of raising issues concerning freedom of speech. The reason for this is that the model adopted postulates the legitimacy of three abstractions: (i) it abstracts from the identities of both speaker and hearer, (ii) it abstracts from the social setting of the speech act, and (iii) it abstracts from the content of what is said. By operating these three abstractions, supposedly in the interests of providing a model with maximum generality, linguistics in effect decontextualizes language. Speech is isolated in a theoretical vacuum, in which neither speaker nor hearer is entitled to any linguistic rights, being themselves not persons but anonymous stand-ins.

The orthodox linguist defends this theoretical model by arguing that the question of freedom of speech involves moral and political value judgements, and these have no place in any scientific study of speech. But this is merely to reiterate the segregational abstractions on which modern linguistics is based, not to justify them. On the other hand, it would be one-sided to lay the blame entirely at the door of the linguistic theorist; for philosophers who have dealt with the question of freedom of speech have often likewise dealt with it in a way which simply ignores those aspects which relate to its linguistic basis, and hence indirectly provides support for the linguist's refusal to consider such issues.

A typical example is John Stuart Mill, and it is not coincidental that Mill's treatment of the question remained influential throughout the latter half of the nineteenth century, the formative period of modern linguistics. Even today it remains true that nothing that has been written on freedom of speech surpasses or outdates the pages Mill devoted to that topic in his essay *On Liberty* (Mill 1859). Since 1859 Mill's view of freedom of speech has become widely accepted as part of a common democratic attitude towards authoritarian forms of government, and if called upon to defend it many would simply point to modern political regimes such as those of Russia under Stalin and his successors, Germany under Hitler, or China under the 'Cultural Revolution', as horrendous examples of what may happen to a society which flouts the principles which Mill championed.

For Mill, freedom of speech is the flagship in the fleet of civil liberties, since speech is the external manifestation of our mental judgements, and freedom of judgement cannot be divorced from freedom of speech. The 'region of human liberty', says Mill

> comprises, first, the inward domain of consciousness, demanding liberty of conscience in the most comprehensive sense, liberty of thought and feeling, absolute freedom of opinion and sentiment on all subjects, practical or speculative, scientific, moral, or theological. The liberty of expressing and publishing opinions may seem to fall under a different principle, since it belongs to that part of the conduct of an individual which concerns other people, but, being almost of as much importance as the liberty of thought itself and resting in great part on the same reasons, is practically inseparable from it.

> (Mill 1859: 71)

The 'inseparability' is an important pinion of Mill's argument; for without it he is open to the very objection he mentions; namely, that freedom of speech must not be confused with freedom of thought and is answerable to quite different principles. It is all the more surprising that in *On Liberty* Mill never spells out the nature of this inseparability or marshals evidence in support of it. One might be tempted, however, to construct a case derived from the reasons he adduces in favour of freedom of speech. This case would go as follows. Our judgements are formed on the basis of discussion with others. But if others are not free to express their true opinions, we cannot reliably learn from them what views they hold or why. It follows that discussion would be an unsound basis on which to reach any conclusion or evaluate any issue. In short, a society in which there is no freedom of speech must necessarily be a society in which all judgement is systematically distorted by evasion and prevarication, and in such a society freedom of judgement would be an illusion. (A mental warping of this kind, many would claim, is exactly what happens when freedom of speech is suppressed for long periods by totalitarian regimes.)

The plausibility of attributing to Mill some such line of reasoning as the above reconstruction suggests is lent weight by the importance he evidently attaches to arriving at the truth by weighing conflicting opinions. This is the basis for his refusal to allow that we are ever justified in suppressing a view simply on the ground that it is false. For quite apart from the fact that we may be mistaken in supposing it false, truths can be tested only by setting them against falsehoods.

> Complete liberty of contradicting and disproving our opinion is the very condition which justifies us in assuming its truth for purposes of action; and on no other terms can a being with human faculties have any rational assurance of being right.
>
> (ibid.: 79)

At first sight this appears to leave Mill's position vulnerable to the objection that it sanctions the propagation of lies of all kinds under the indiscriminate umbrella of freedom of speech. Mill's way out of this difficulty is to invoke the caveat that no expression of any view, whether true or false, shall do harm to another person. (The same restriction he applies not only to freedom of speech but to all liberties.) Thus, for example, expressing the view that private property is robbery, although unexceptionable in itself, becomes culpable when it incites a mob to violence.

> No one pretends that action should be as free as opinions. On the contrary, even opinions lose their immunity when the circumstances in which they are expressed are such as to constitute their expression a positive instigation to some mischievous act.
>
> (ibid.: 119)

This is to say, in terms of modern speech act theory, that Mill recognizes that the perlocutionary effects of a speech act are what

155

ultimately determine its admissibility under the license afforded by freedom of speech.

Having granted this, it is difficult to see how Mill can avoid the corollary that the expression of any view, true or false, is likewise culpable if the circumstances in which it is expressed are such as to result in a harmful *failure* to take action. (Thus, for example, an expressed conviction in the power of faith healing would be culpable if it resulted in the death of a person whose life medical treatment could have saved.)

Although the rationale is clear enough, concessions of this order have damaging consequences for Mill's position. For it cannot be simply assumed that the perlocutionary consequences or likely consequences of any given pronouncement are perspicuous. The harmful outcome may have been neither intended nor foreseen at the time when the view in question was expressed. Under what circumstances an expression of the view that private property is robbery constitutes an incitement to violence or illegal acts is not only controversial but controversial in ways which involve invoking the very rights and responsibilities pertinent to freedom of action. What this means is that although the problem of freedom of speech appears to have been resolved, it crops up again at one remove as a problem about freedom of action. Furthermore, what the actual outcome turns out to be in any given case does not help. Whether A had the right to try to persuade B not to fasten the seatbelt does not depend on whether B was injured in the ensuing road accident. What is evident, however, is that once the caveat about 'harmful consequences' is invoked it does become very relevant to take into account who is saying what and to whom. More worrying still is the consideration that it seems impossible in general to calculate the consequences which might, in theory, ensue from any given pronouncement either in the short term or in the long term. So the expression of an opinion is, after all, subject to all the constraints governing a non-verbal act. The king's unguarded remark was no less instrumental in the murder of Thomas à Becket than the actions of the knights who killed him, even if it was a less blatant abuse of the freedom of speech enjoyed by the powerful than the Ayatollah Khomeini's public call for the assassination of Salman Rushdie.

Where does that leave freedom of speech? In much the same limbo, it would seem, as under the aegis of linguistic theory. In other words, just as the linguist's account of speech communication abstracts from the identities of speaker and hearer, the content of what is said, and the social setting of the speech act, so the philosopher's account seems unexceptionable provided similar abstractions are made. But as soon as the speech act is particularized and contextualized the question of freedom – of the rights of the speaker – immediately becomes problematic. Thus the issue which the theoretical linguist passed on to the philosopher has now been passed on by the philosopher too. For it is an evasion to lay down principles whose application to particular cases generates controversies of just the kind which the principles were called upon to settle. The linguistic net and the philosophical net both seem to have let something important slip through.

A clue as to what has slipped through is to be found in the curious final chapter of Rousseau's *Essai sur l'origine des langues*. Rousseau argues: 'There are some tongues favourable to liberty. They are the sonorous, prosodic, harmonious tongues in which discourse can be understood from a great distance.' He goes on to make a variety of rather unconvincing remarks about the relative audibility of different languages, claiming that ancient Greek was far superior in this respect to modern French. Herodotus, he says, recited his history to audiences in the open air and they could hear what he was saying. Any language of low audibility militates against liberty. 'I say that any tongue with which one cannot make oneself understood to the people assembled is a slavish tongue. It is impossible for a people to remain free and speak that tongue.'

Little developed as the sciences of phonetics and acoustics were in his day, it is nevertheless difficult to imagine that Rousseau actually believed in the thesis he superficially appears to be presenting. This final chapter is in fact concerned with the relationship of languages to government, and the audibility thesis is Rousseau's ironically metaphorical way of broaching the question of freedom of speech in eighteenth-century France.

What is remarkable about Rousseau's cavalier treatment of the topic, and greatly in advance of his time, is that he sees that it is a mistake to treat freedom of speech as being merely one of many forms of freedom of individual action. In this his insight was far superior to that of many of his successors, whose thinking on the subject is flawed by precisely that error. Rousseau grasps the fact that the whole question of liberty and language is bound up with the extent to which a linguistic community is also a communicating society. The period at which he was writing falls in the middle of the great trough in Europe between the invention of printing, which in theory made mass communication possible, and the advent of universal literacy, which was its pragmatic prerequisite. Herodotus reciting his history to his assembled fellow citizens is for Rousseau symbolic of the conditions to which communication in a free society aspires. The city-state is from this point of view the ideal linguistic community. All its members can participate in public communication, the possibility of which is nevertheless dependent on their mutual toleration. (Herodotus' audience, as Rousseau points out, had to keep quiet in order to hear.) The antithesis to this ideal is represented for Rousseau by the picture of the French academician mumbling his way through a memorandum, inaudible to the people sitting at the back of the room. Rousseau quotes Duclos to the effect that it would be desirable to study how 'the character, customs and interests of a people influence their language', and facetiously suggests that the audibility of a language declines when authoritarian government replaces government by persuasion.

The mumbling academician can thus be seen (in the context of the special responsibilities assigned to the Académie Française as guardian of the French language) as a biting caricature of what happens to linguistic scholarship in the service of an authoritarian government. The official language it codifies and uses is one which makes it impossible to be heard, a language which is therefore quite useless for public communication. One might naively suppose that the remedy for inaudibility is to raise the voice. But, argues Rousseau, the louder French is shouted the less it is understood:

> Our preachers torment themselves, work themselves into a sweat in the pulpit without anyone knowing anything of what they have said. After exhausting themselves shouting for an hour, they collapse in a chair, half dead. Surely it would not be work that fatigues them so.

Similarly, he claims, if anyone were to harangue the people of Paris in the Place Vendôme they would be none the wiser: 'if he shouted at the top of his voice, people would hear him shouting, but they would not be able to distinguish a word'. These remarkable satiric images of a language which defeats communication instead of facilitating it are perhaps the most striking in European literature before Orwell. They contrast significantly with the Establishment linguistic claims that were made in the eighteenth century concerning the qualities of French, specifically the claim that it was above all the language of *clarté*.

What Rousseau has seen is that although speech is a form of action it does not follow that freedom of speech is reducible to or constitutes one subspecies of freedom of action. In order to be free in the sense in which the human mind is free, the possibility of assent or dissent must exist. And this is a possibility which only language makes available. (Hence the question of intellectual freedom as it arises for most members of the human race cannot arise for individuals or species incapable of language.) That is why the denial of freedom of speech, however temporarily and for whatever reason, is a violation of the humanity of those to whom it is denied. It is through language that we acquire the possibility of persuading others to accept or reject or entertain any of a potentially infinite gamut of beliefs or attitudes or courses of action. This possibility is thus the necessary precondition of all other freedoms which involve an adjustment of the behaviour of members of a community towards one another; and its institutional guarantee in any community is the existence of the community's language.

Thus freedom of speech is basically the right to participate in those communicational activities available in virtue of one's membership of a linguistic community. But this freedom, as Rousseau vividly brings home to us, is a mockery unless what is said can be heard. In other words, if society is organized in such a way (whether through the control of a despotic government, or for any other reason) as to deny effective participation in communication to large sections of the community, then a common language is no longer a guarantee of freedom of speech, and whether the public expression of views by individuals is allowed or suppressed becomes an irrelevance.

Rousseau's 'audibility' thesis was to receive ample confirmation from subsequent events in British politics. At the end of the eighteenth and the beginning of the nineteenth century, a series of petitions to Parliament were denied a hearing on the ground that they were not couched in appropriate language. As Olivia Smith points out in *The Politics of Language 1791–1819*: 'Because both suffrage and ideas about language depended on the question of who was considered to be capable of participating in public life, the two were vitally connected' (Smith 1984: 29–30). The connection between freedom of speech and membership of a linguistic community could hardly be more clearly demonstrated than by a political stance which sets up standards of linguistic propriety as criteria for the right to have one's views heard. The political threat posed by the existence of a common language is countered by denying its commonality, and reserving access to 'proper' language accordingly.

The antithesis of freedom of speech is not censorship but excommunication: the denial of the right to participate. And the ultimate

159

intellectual perversion of politics is to claim that such denials may be justified and sometimes necessary in the interests of the freedom of others, or even of the excommunicated themselves. This is the 'moral' justification for Official Secrets Acts and the like.

That it is also a form of intellectual perversion to which academics are susceptible is unfortunately demonstrated by, for instance, the banning of South African and Namibian archaeologists from the World Archaeological Congress at Southampton University in 1986. The objection, allegedly, was not to the individual scholars banned, nor to their personal views, whether on politics or on archaeology. They were nevertheless denied by fellow academics their right to speak at a professional meeting in their own academic field, in order to register a protest against the political policies followed by the South African and Namibian governments. Thus the innocent are persecuted in order to discomfit the guilty. In the area of freedom of speech, this is the morality of hostage-taking and terrorism. Its adoption by academics is especially repugnant, as Mill would no doubt have been quick to point out, since universities are institutions with a standing commitment to the pursuit of free enquiry. That is why state control of what and how universities teach (on topics relating to religion, race, language and history, for instance) is one of the most serious threats to freedom of speech which western society has had to face in the twentieth century. But universities will hardly be institutions worth saving if they are to be run by academics who gladly use their own freedom of speech in order to deny it to others.

Linguistics, by the same token, will not be an academic discipline worth preserving if it continues to shirk the issue of freedom of speech by perpetuating the convenient theoretical fiction that membership of a (homogeneous) linguistic community automatically confers the same linguistic rights – or none – on all, and attributing any departure from this egalitarian state of affairs to the interference of external, pragmatic factors which are by definition non-linguistic. This is certainly one way of idealizing the problem out of existence, or at least out of linguistics. The difficulty is that it leaves the linguist in no position to construct any plausible account of that particular mode of articulating social behaviour which has traditionally been called 'language'.

Liberty is at bottom a matter of rights and responsibilities. The social exercise of all abilities is conditioned by rights and responsibilities, both individual and collective; for all social behaviour involves transactions between at least one person and another or others. Since

160

language is the social proficiency *par excellence*, it would be absurd to suppose that language was somehow an exception. Yet this is precisely the absurdity inherent in a linguistics which defines speech without reference to such questions, failing to see that their exclusion reduces speech to vocal noise. For it is not clear that it makes sense to say of any social proficiency that it has been acquired and is being competently exercised by persons who simply do not understand the rights and responsibilities involved. That understanding is, by definition, part of the proficiency. Not only is it part of the proficiency, but it is the crucial part which separates the social proficiency from mere technical expertise. That is why a concentration-camp doctor who carries out inhumane experiments on the inmates is, rightly, condemned *qua* doctor, even though the level of medical expertise involved in the experiments may be high.

Granted that societies differ in respect of the rights and responsibilities they recognize as regards various forms of social behaviour, that is no warrant for ignoring the question of rights and responsibilities when attempting to define a form of social behaviour common to different societies. Even less is it a warrant underwriting a relativism which treats freedom of speech as relative to other social practices. On the contrary, to the extent that a society sets up rights and responsibilities which restrict freedom of speech it is not a free society at all, the pursuit of other freedoms being conditional upon freedom of speech. The concept of a society which allowed all other freedom *except* freedom of speech is self-contradictory.

9

What are words worth? Language and ideology in French dictionaries of the revolutionary period

Pieter Desmet, Johan Rooryck and Pierre Swiggers

1 INTRODUCTION

Language and culture have been correlated in various ways, mostly with an eye towards establishing the influence of the one on the other. These endeavours often overlook the fact, which Sapir stressed in 1921, that language and culture are in essence very different phenomena. Whereas language is basically form-oriented (and its proper manifestation is through *form*), culture is a matter of content. 'Culture may be defined as *what* a society does and thinks. Language is a particular *how* of thought' (Sapir 1921: 233). From this it follows that language and culture are intrinsically distinct phenomena, unless one can discover a formal principle within culture:

> If it can be shown that culture has an innate form, a series of contours, quite apart from subject-matter of any description whatsoever, we have a something in culture that may serve as a term of comparison with and possibly a means of relating it to language. But until such purely formal patterns of culture are discovered and laid bare, we shall do well to hold the drifts of language and of culture to be non-comparable and unrelated processes.[1]

> (Sapir 1921: 233–4)

But there is more to language than just form: as is well known from the repeated caveat in comparative grammar, and in some types of structuralist description, language has also a 'contentive' aspect, which is incorporated in the lexicon. While this area of language is less interesting to the descriptive linguist,[2] it opens a vast area of research for those interested in the reflection of culture in language. And here it seems possible to establish significant correlations:

> It goes without saying that the mere content of language is intimately related to culture. A society that has no knowledge of theosophy need have no name for it; aborigines that had never seen or heard of a horse were compelled to invent or borrow a word for the animal when they made his acquaintance. In the sense that the vocabulary of a language more or less faithfully reflects the culture whose purposes it serves it is perfectly true that the history of language and the history of culture move along parallel lines.[3]
>
> (Sapir 1921: 234)

This view is still too narrow, in that it considers culture primarily as 'material culture'. As Sapir wrote in his article 'Culture, genuine and spurious', (1924), there is also a spiritual side to culture, which is embedded in *values*, which allow the individual to assign himself a place within a community.[4]

For the study of these values, language – and more specifically vocabulary – is a most precious guide: this is a common principle of both 'idealist'[5] and 'sociohistorical' approaches.[6] In his trail-blazing essay on method(s) in lexicology, Georges Matoré (1953) stresses the pivotal role of words and, in some cases, groups of related words[7] for the 'inner' study of societies throughout a certain period. As a matter of fact, the word appears to be the link between the psychological and the sociological aspects of societal life. As noted by Matoré, the word carries a semantic charge which has its roots in preverbal behaviour and reaches to the most abstract and rationalized conceptual contents (Matoré 1953: 34–40). From this point of view, words and word choices are never arbitrary: they are motivated by basic needs and interests of a particular society, by specific attitudes towards institutions, events, persons, and by collective or individual associations. Within such a view, a number of lexical items are crucially important: these are the lexical witnesses (*mots-témoins*) and key-words (*mots-clés*). The former term refers to words that function as the material symbol of a psychic datum.[8] In principle, the lexical witness is the symbol of a change in the society, and is therefore a formal or semantic neologism. As an illustration, Matoré mentions the word 'coke': this word, which made its entry in the French lexicon around 1770, is the first sign of the birth of industrial capitalism. Next to these lexical witnesses, which testify to changes in culture and society, there are the key-words: these denote persons, feelings, ideas and so on with which the individuals in a society associate or identify themselves, in an idealized form. As an example one can think of the ideals of 'l'honnête homme' or the 'Victorian sage'.

With respect to the study of history, one basic observation should be made: in our study of past cultures on the basis of lexical witnesses and key terms, it is essential to keep in mind *whose* words we are studying. As a matter of fact, the lexical deposit available to us for the study of older periods should be regarded as a filter, as the selective thesaurus of rather small groups within the society which have been responsible for the transmission of these words. The domain of lexical creation – at least from the point of view of what has come down to us – was a constrained one, not open to everyone. It may therefore be worthwhile to study the lexicon, or at least an essential part of it, of a period when this domain was opened, at least in principle, to all classes. In France this happened with the Revolution, and 1789 marks the beginning of a multifaceted ideological invasion in lexicography.

2 FRENCH DICTIONARIES IN THE REVOLUTIONARY PERIOD (1789–1802)

The period between the Revolution of 1789 and the end of the Consular Republic (1802) is one of prodigious lexicographical activity. In his bibliographical survey Bernard Quemada (1967) lists some 150 titles for these fifteen years, and this list does not include important works such as Gallais's *Extrait d'un dictionnaire inutile* (1790), the anonymous *L'abus des mots* (1792), Rodoni's *Dictionnaire républicain et révolutionnaire* (1794),[9] the anonymous *Synonymes jacobites* (1795), Reinhard's *Le néologiste français* (1796), the anonymous *Wörterbuch der französischen Revolutionssprache* (1799) and Beffroy de Reigny's *Dictionnaire néologique*. Two striking facts should be noted with respect to this intensive production: the scattering of anonymous publications (between 1790 and 1803, there are about thirty-eight lexicographical publications with no author's name),[10] and the pervasive presence of the words 'new'[11] and 'neologism', as can be seen from the following selective list:

1790 (anonymous), *Nouveau dictionnaire à l'usage des municipalités.*
1790 (anonymous), *Nouveau dictionnaire français composé par un aristocrate.*
1792 (A. Buée), *Nouveau dictionnaire des termes de la Révolution.*
1795 (L. Snetlage), *Nouveau dictionnaire français.*

1796 (anonymous), *Neologiste français ou vocabulaire fortatif.*

1796 (C.-F. Reinhard), *Le Néologiste français.*

1799 (Q. Tennesson), *Dictionnaire sur le nouveau droit.*

1800 (J. Le Cousin), *Dictionnaire néologique des hommes et des choses.*

1801 (J.-L. Cormon), *Nouveau vocabulaire ou dictionnaire portatif de la langue française.*

1800–1801 (L. S. Mercier), *Néologie ou Vocabulaire de mots nouveaux.*

1803 (anonymous), *Nouveau dictionnaire d'histoire naturelle.*

Admittedly, not all these works reflect to the same extent the drastic changes that had taken place in French societal life, but before 1789 and after 1804 *nouveau* appears much more sporadically, and *néologie* (and its congeners) almost never on the title page of lexicographical works.

The 'revolutionary' or innovative aspect of the lexicographical production is both a reflection of changes in the society and the expression of a changing view on language. The most important social change is the abolishment of elitism and the progressive spread of institutional functions among the lower classes. This implied the transmission of a new set of symbolic values, and therefore of a new (or renewed) vocabulary to name them. The transmission was not immediate, nor was it uniform: too many obstacles stood in its way. There was first the fact that the lower classes of the French society could hardly speak the 'national language'. This became the major impetus for a language policy aiming at a 'linguistic recycling' of the *citoyens*. To adopt the revolutionary 'newspeak', it was necessary to abandon one's *patois* and learn the national language. 'The unity of the (national) language is an integral part of the Revolution'; 'There must be a linguistic identity'.[12] The 'politicization' of language was advocated by Grégoire,[13] whose investigations on the use of French in the national territory had revealed that only in fifteen departments in central France was the national language spoken, without uniformity, and that some thirty dialects were still very much alive. This state of affairs could only be undone by a programme for the diffusion of the national language; the construction of roads leading from Paris to the provinces and language instruction in school were the pillars on which this programme was based (see Grégoire 1794). But the diffusion of the national language did not go smoothly: while some authors attacked the 'vicious'[14] expressions of dialects and patois, others were convinced that dialects had their own rights and that the imposition of a national language was an act of tyranny. This is clear not only from a number of reactions to Grégoire's questionnaire, but also from the many linguistic[15] and literary publications which give a prominent place to dialects. Moreover, the diffusion of a national language as the main instrument of centralization[16] was not just a matter of spreading new words – for measures (*mètre, gramme, litre*, created between 1791 and 1793), time divisions (months: *germinal, floréal, prairial, messidor, thermidor, fructidor, vendemiaire, brumaire, frimaire, nivôse, pluviôse, ventôse*; ten-day divisions), and of new administrative units and functions (*département, arrondissement, préfet*) – but also, and primarily, a matter of imposing new views. And here the major obstacle was the existence of politically conflicting views.

The political scene in France between 1789 and 1804[17] was very turbulent.[18] After the instalment of the Constituant Assembly in 1789, attempts were made by the bourgeois factions to reach a compromise with the aristocracy. A turning point was the king's attempt to flee the country in 1791, which provoked new tensions between the aristocracy and the revolutionary nation. The Brissotins (later known as Girondins) were the chief instigators of the international war, stimulated by economic problems, which was declared on Europe's *ancien régime* institutions. The international war was a burden to the Girondist bourgeoisie, which proved incapable of setting the situation straight in its own country. Economic crises, social tensions and ideological oppositions within the bourgeoisie led to the insurrection of 10 August 1792. This 'second Revolution' brought about a democratization of the political power, but through the integration of the *sans-culottes* (lower-class craftsmen) it caused new conflicts within the bourgeoisie. The Girondins were overthrown by the Montagnards, a bourgeois faction which had made an alliance with the lower classes, and whose basic programme in Robespierre's words, was to assure 'every member of society of the means of existence'. After the execution of the king in January 1793, and the elimination of the Girondist leaders in the Convention, the revolutionary government imposed strict measures. The Revolution entered a new phase, that of Terror, under Robespierre. This phase is characterized by massive executions of political enemies (the Girondins, the aristocrats, the clergy), by dechristianization, and by a number of military and economic successes. But the revolutionary government was unable to control the popular masses, initially led by the Cordeliers, and it was divided by inner disputes (such as that between the Committee for General Security and the Committee for Public Safety). On 27 July 1794 Robespierre was arrested, and the following day he was guillotined.

From then on, the Revolution went its way to less and less collective dictatorship. The Thermidorian regime could no longer control the national economy, and the popular movement lost its primary force, unity. A new constitution (in 1795) marked the beginning of the First Directory, and reduced equality to juridical or civil equality. The First Directory had a narrow, conservative bourgeois social basis, and met with growing dissatisfaction, due to dizzying inflation and poor harvests. In the meantime, Napoleon's star was rising, and despite a period of relative stability in 1798 and 1799, the second Directory was rather unpopular. The poor economic situation and the military programme paved the way for Bonaparte's *coup d'état* in 1799 and the instalment of the Consular Republic. Bonaparte's successful wars, his monetary reforms, his organization of the state and his diplomatic attitude in religious matters made him popular enough to declare himself emperor in 1804. From then on, the old aristocracy and the upper bourgeois classes regained social preponderance, while being politically harmless. Much of the Revolution of 1789 had been swept away, but what remained was the freedom of enterprise and of profit, so that one can say that the Napoleonic 'tail' of the French Revolution confirmed the instalment of a new economy, which had begun with the abrupt destruction of the feudal structures in 1789.

This historical sketch has no other function than recalling some of the inner tensions that marked the period of the French Revolution. It prepares the way for our analysis of a number of linguistic testimonies from that period. The dictionaries published between 1789 and 1804 reflect variegated, and often opposite views about the ideals of the Revolution, its course, outgrowths, abuses, reorientations; they also reveal an intimate knowledge of the language – and discursive forms – underlying the revolutionary practices and the conflicting ideologies. In recent years the lexicographical works and the public speeches published or delivered in the revolutionary period have attracted the attention of scholars,[19] and work is under way on the specific vocabulary of the Revolution, its reception, and its description by language observers. This chapter is intended as a contribution to this type of research; we will focus on three dictionaries, belonging to the period 1790–6. Apart from practical considerations, our choice is motivated by our concern to compare at least one 'exterior' testimony (Reinhard 1796) with more direct witnesses. As to the latter, we have chosen two works published in the same year (1790) and reflecting different political convictions and aspirations. None of the three works is anonymous.

3 CONFLICTING VIEWS: CHANTREAU, GALLAIS AND REINHARD

It is well known that the period of the French Revolution witnessed several profound transformations of the French lexicon. This is clear from *a posteriori* studies such as Frey's,[20] but it is also evident from observations by contemporary authors. In the preface to his dictionary, Charles-Frédéric Reinhard – who had served for several years in the German embassy in Paris, including the first years of the Revolution – noted the drastic changes in the French vocabulary:

> There is nothing more natural than to see a large nation, which aspires to break its chains and to regenerate itself, forging constantly, in the midst of the general upheaval, new ideas which in their turn require new words to express them. The desire for a new order of things on the one hand, and the hatred of the old order on the other, have banished even the terms that pictured the manners and customs of the previous generation, or referred to the titles and functions of the various divisions of the old administration, and have replaced them with newly created terms. This explains the mass of new and unusual expressions, many of them well chosen, and a few of them grotesque, which hamper, at every moment, the reading of the official documents and other French works of this period. . . . And the present work is the result of remarks and observations, not only on the new language since the beginnings of the Revolution but also on a few neologisms that were already in use a few years before the Revolution.[21]
>
> (Reinhard 1796: *2–*3)

This passage testifies to the lexical innovations which the French language underwent in the years preceding the Revolution and during the first years of the revolutionary period. The revolution carried with it an entire linguistic programme, as is evident from the endeavours of the Société des amateurs de la langue française. This society was founded by the French *grammairien–patriote* François Domergue, who stressed the importance of creating new words and of assigning new meanings to old words. The aim of the society was to diffuse the national language, and to introduce a language policy, which was no longer in the hands of a select group of Academicians, but was a national matter, taken care of by all those interested in the problem, viz. the subscribers to the *Journal de la langue française*, the official organ of the society. In his opening address of October 1791 Domergue outlined a programme for the creation of this 'new national monument', to wit the French language as open to all citizens.[22]

Surely, this was an optimistic view, and an utopian one. The principal idea behind it was the rejection of all words connoting the *ancien régime* institutions, so as to abolish every possible reference to the pre-revolutionary period. The principal strategy underlying or justifying the introduction of new words was to condemn the old words as *abuses*, as evil words. The new order required a new language, the language of liberty, and it rejected the language that had been the vehicle of an unjust and inhumane society. This theme is pervasive throughout all types of revolutionary newspeak (see Barny 1978; Ricken 1982). It prompted Morellet to start in 1793 a chronicle, signed 'Le Définisseur', in the *Mercure de France*, the aim of which was to instruct the nation in the use of the right words, the proper base of moral behaviour. The lexicographer thus has a humanitarian function: he teaches his fellow citizens how to avoid conceptual errors, by using the proper words, and since such errors are at the basis of social conflicts, his work is of primary importance for the society.[23]

But was there only abuse of words in the past? Apparently not. In the *Mercure de France* of 1794 there appeared a series of articles under the title 'Sur l'abus et les différentes variations des idées dans la révolution', the aim of which was to show how the extremist Montagnards had oriented the Revolution towards an uncontrolled massacre, and how they had distorted the ideals of the initial Revolution. These articles, probably written by J.-J. Lenoir-Laroche, appeared between October and December 1794; their attack on the Terror regime is stated in unequivocal terms, and stresses the abuse of words by Robespierre and his followers.

> Words have such an influence on ideas, and ideas on actions, that it would have been a major contribution to the Revolution if the main signs of our ideas in politics could be assigned their true meaning, and if it were possible to clearly *define* before reasoning . . . . It is a remarkable fact that the Revolution, that started by enlightenment . . . was so suddenly turned off its primary course by a handful of scoundrels without knowledge, without principles, without morals, without any other talent than to impress people by a simulated patriotism and some artificial word-play that influenced the masses all the more

when their understanding of the words was poor, the words having been carefully twisted away from their true meaning.[24]

(*Mercure de France* 12, 1794: 161)

The abuse of words, originally the principal means of condemning everything related to the *ancien régime*,[25] was also an efficient means of distracting the minds of the opponents and of the popular masses: in denouncing the old abuse of words, one could turn attention away from the contemporary abuse of words, and from practices which were hardly compatible with the initial aims of the Revolution. Those practices did not pass unnoticed, and there are several texts testifying to the abuse of words by the representatives in the National Assembly. Some counter-revolutionary statements are explicit on this point:

It is unbelievable how much the orators of the National Assembly have abused and are still abusing their young followers with notions and opinions: they have made them believe, according to the circumstances, that it was the constituted organ or the constitutive organ, or the national convention, and by this simple choice of labels, they have led them into confusion about the powers, have made them forget about its origin, and have brought them to commit the crime of *lèse-majesté*, both with respect to its real sovereign the King and with respect to its trumped-up sovereign, the People.[26]

(quoted after Barny 1978)

The most explicit, and most rigorous attack on the abuse of words from the counter-revolutionary side is Jean-François La Harpe's *Du Fanatisme dans la langue révolutionnaire, ou de la persécution suscitée par les barbares du dix-huitième siècle, contre la religion chrétienne et ses ministres*,[27] which was published in 1797 and was sympathetically greeted in the conservative journal *La Quotidienne*.

But the same misgivings were sensed in the revolutionary circles. In 1795, the spokesman of the *Tribun du Peuple*, François-Noël (Gracchus) Babeuf sensed the inherent contradiction between the demands of the right to exist and the proclamation of the right of property. The First Directory hardly corresponded to the real aim of the Revolution, viz. the equality of benefits. Less than a year and a half before his trial and subsequent execution, the propounder of communism based on equal distribution denounced the abuse of words by those who had succeeded in exploiting the Revolution for their own profit (*Tribun du Peuple*, 30 December 1795).

Several shrewd neutral observers also noticed the 'polyphony' of the French lexicon in the revolutionary period. Reinhard, for instance, recognizes a number of coexisting languages, such as the language of the Jacobins and the language of the royalists; he also points out some abuses of words, as in the entry for *Négociantisme*. 'From the word *Négoce* (Trade), *Handel, Handelsgeist, die Klasse der Handelsleute*, the trading spirit, the caste of traders. Word created to create a crime. Negotiantism is worse than aristocratism and royalism, according to the levelers of fortunes, who coveted the wealth of the traders' (Reinhard 1796: 236).[28]

In several of his entries Reinhard stressed the manifold use of words,[29] and vented his indignation about the Terror regime,[30] and about the failure of the Revolution. His short entry *Démagoguinette* is at the same time a denunciation of demagogic practices (see also his articles *Démagogie, Démagogique, Démagogisme, Démagogue* and *Mystificateur*) and a sad state-of-the-art of the Revolution. 'This is what the Constitution of 1789 is called, the daughter of Demagogues, as it were. This promising little girl died in the cradle' (Reinhard 1796: 121).[31] Reinhard's view on the Revolution was bitter, and while his judgement may have been coloured by his high opinion of Louis XVI,[32] it was motivated by the dreary story of the French Revolution:

Liberty. Freyheit. An entity, ideal up to now, to which the French have been stretching out their arms in vain through five years of convulsions. The giant statue of Freedom on the square of the Revolution has been compared to the statue of Moloch, who demanded blood-offerings.

Patriot. A citizen who desires the well-being of his homeland and of his fellow citizens. France, swarming with patriots since the Revolution, has very few corresponding to this definition. For each patriot aiming at the good, the happiness of his homeland, there were a thousand others who only wanted the goods of their fellow citizens. Hence, the title patriot is nowadays very ambiguous without an adjective determining its meaning.

Fourteenth of July. Der 14te Juli (1789). An old word, although it reminds us of a totally new scene in history, where 600,000 French-men, representing 26 million, assembled in the field of the federation, both tall and short, young and old, rich and poor, of both sexes, suddenly became brothers and kissed each other, drunken with liberty and equality, thinking that they had

171

found happiness. This day of elation, of which only memories are left, has been followed by a thousand and one days of mourning, distress, pain, and tears of blood, the end of which is not yet in sight.[33]

(Reinhard 1796: 205, 251, 270)

In short, Reinhard deplores the absence of reason (see the articles *Raison* and *Raison nationale*), the deterioration of the socio-economic situation,[34] the defiguration of the ideals of the Revolution (see the articles *République Française* and *Révolution Française*),[35] and the moral corruption.[36] But Reinhard was able to speak with the hindsight of a few years separating the events of 1789 and the publication of his dictionary; as a German who had witnessed some of the horrid paths the Revolution had taken, he was also able to speak at a certain distance. His distanced outlook found its expression in a carefully executed lexicographical description, which the author intended as a dictionary of words and of facts. The latter aspect is manifest, not only in the examples illustrating the definitions, but also in the systematic inclusion of professional and scientific terms. In addition Reinhard is a talented lexicographer: he is sensitive to stylistic distinctions,[37] to metaphoric shifts (see his articles *Aigrettes électriques*, *Brêche*, *Suppurer*), to the ambiguity of terms,[38] and in general to problems of classification (see his grammatical information on the entries, and his threefold distinction between completely new words, words having taken on a new meaning, and archaic words which have been reused).

To Reinhard's distanced views we can oppose the testimony of two much more time-bound publications, both of 1790, but reflecting diametrically opposed political convictions. In his *Extrait d'un dictionnaire inutile*, the monarchist J.-P. Gallais is strongly critical of the revolutionary ideas. But his criticism is hidden away in the entries of the dictionary, which have a tone very different from the oxymoric dithyramb on the Revolution in the preface. In a few cases Gallais puts the criticism in the mouth of someone else: a member of the Academy (see the article *Droit public*), a man he met in the street (*Journaux*), or a famous lawyer (*Moines*), but in the majority of cases Gallais speaks for himself. And he makes it clear that France is in much worse shape than it was before 1789. In the entry *Patriotisme* we read: 'Never has there been so much aristocracy shown in thinking, so much despotism in behavior, so much tyranny in the most reckless actions, than since we have been free' (Gallais 1790: 235–6).[39]

What has happened, according to Gallais, is a massive linguistic hypnotization, for which the journalists are responsible:

An army of journalists suddenly sprang from the heart of the revolution, like a swarm of venomous or bothersome insects coming out of the heart of the swamps in summer . . . . I would dare say that the true enemies of France and of the revolution are these rowdy writers, who, for a year now, have not stopped sounding the alarm, caressing the people and fawning upon the left side of the Assembly. . . .

But we are being *disenchanted* every day. The principles are the opinions of this or that person; the truth is only the system of a sect or party; the enlightenment is the personal knowledge of the journalist.[40]

(Articles *Journaux* and *Principes*, Gallais 1790: 163–4; 243; see also his article *Talent*).

This is in striking contrast with Chantreau's long article on *Journal* (Chantreau 1790: 85–110), which contains an extensive note on the old and new periodicals. Chantreau praises the revolutionary periodicals, which stimulate critical thinking among all the classes of the society:

JOURNAL: in the *ancien régime* a periodical leaflet, informing about rain and good weather, or giving excerpts from library catalogues, and some letters sent by the subscribers to the editor, which in the pubs were naively taken to be letters. These leaflets informed very accurately about the kind and the number of grimaces of this or that actress in a new play.

But how everything has changed! These leaflets, once the pasture of our unemployed, are now the food for all the classes of citizens. People are eager to have them, they fight for them, they devour them. Our politicians find in them the regeneration of the empire and the ups and downs of the aristocracy. The Muses are silenced, and only the journalist is on the scene, where he has the greatest success. (Chantreau 1790: 85–6; see also the article *Lettre au rédacteur*)[41]

This article is typical of Chantreau's dictionary, which is based on the 'old–new' contrast. Most of the articles in his dictionary tell us how bad it was before, and how splendid everything is now. Now what has changed according to Chantreau? First of all, a number of injustices have disappeared, such as the exploitation of the poor by the clergy[42] or by the aristocracy – the 'bad citizens'[43] – and the king (see the article *Roi des Français*). The Revolution has put an end to political, social and economical abuses,[44] and has done away with the rift between the privileged classes and the exploited masses. There is no longer a third estate,[45] and true liberty reigns:

> LIBERTY: in the *ancien régime* the word had a meaning totally different from its present one, now that it has become the cry of the nation. The word refers to that precious right which nature gives to all men, at least when nature is not counteracted by ministers having their fortresses, and fortresses having their *de Launay*. We have finally achieved the wish of this good nature, which we had never before known so well and which will take us far. We have finally *conquered* this inalienable right to be free . . ..
> A free people is one which lives under the authority of laws, good or convenient, which it has given to itself or through its representatives. (Chantreau 1790: 120–1)[46]

Admittedly, Chantreau wrote these lines when the Revolution could still arouse enthusiasm among its followers,[47] and when the reversal caused by the Revolution was still positively valued. Also, the Revolution had not yet been abused at that time in order to impose a dictatorial regime: it was still possible, in 1790, to be optimistic about the status of *citizen*,[48] to appreciate the role of the revolutionary committees (see the articles *Comité* and *Contre-révolution*). But it was difficult not to see the economic distress or the demagogic practices. Still, Chantreau felt optimistic about matters economic, and saw demagoguery only on the other side:

> MONEY (ARGENT): . . . French-men! Free nation! but you who do not have a penny, may these moments of penury you are going to live in not drive you to despair; they will make you practice virtues you did not have, and which are necessary to a regenerating people . . ..[49]

> DEMAGOGUE: . . . Every time I use the word Demagogue, I take it in the sense referring to a hypocritical aristocrat seeking to smother his brother the democrat by taking him into his arms.[50]
> (Chantreau 1790: 13, 62)

This new era is the era of free words: 'the gift of language will be, as in all free communities, the means leading to all means' (Chantreau 1790: 143, entry *Parole*). And from this new society a number of words are banished, such as *bastille, bourgeois, chanoine, charge, droits seigneuriaux, féodal, monarchisme, ordre du roi, privilège, vassal* and *torture*: a long list of such terms 'which will go out of use' is given in an appendix by Chantreau (1790: 183–95).

We hear a different tone in Gallais's work, which gives a different view of the changeover. We have seen already that the author is very critical of journalists, and he regards revolution as the main objective of demagogues, abusing the poor: 'Always everywhere the popular masses, the instrument of revolutions, served the ambitions of demagogues, and were poor, ignorant, wicked and restless. It is not difficult to incite to a revolution wretches who have nothing, who are always ready to sell themselves and to change masters' (*Démagogue*, Gallais 1790: 86–7).[51] Gallais laughs at the so-called democracy that has been installed (see the articles *Démocrate* and *Peuple*),[52] and is highly sceptical about the 'regeneration' of the nation (see his entries *Législation, Législature, Régénération*). A true advocate of monarchism,[53] Gallais criticizes the National Assembly for its hesitations, its inconsequence, its unfounded decisions, its lack of organization (see the entries *Département, Droit public, Législation, Majorité, Orateurs*). The result is a situation of discomfort and uncertainty: 'The truth, formerly as unchanging as its author, has become as moving as time. Subject to circumstances, it takes all the forms, it follows all the movements that one wishes to imprint upon it. What was true a few months ago is not true anymore' (*Bénéfice*, Gallais 1790: 35).[54]

The new society is one in which people are afraid of being denounced (see *Dénonciation*), in which there is no order (nor *ordres*, distinct social classes), in which the concept of homeland (*Patrie*) has no real content (see *Patriotisme*). Degeneration, then, instead of regeneration, and the economic situation testifies to this: 'Liberty may be a good thing, but in the first place we need bread, and I challenge all the orators of the world, and all the paper-writers of Paris to show me that it is better to be free and die of hunger, than to be fed, clothed and fettered' (*Liberté*, Gallais 1790: 190).[55] In Gallais's eyes, the Revolution was a mistake, since France was made for a monarchist regime (*Monarchie*). His hope – expressed in the last entry – then is that the error will be a temporary one: 'Zealous citizens, zealous fanatics, zealous bastards of all kinds, be aware that errors have their time' (*Zèle*, Gallais 1790: 277).[56]

And things indeed changed, but not in the way Gallais would have wanted it. . . .

4 CONCLUSION

The three dictionaries examined here offer different views of the revolutionary period. Different, because of different experiences, and in the case of Reinhard, a wider experience through time; but different in the first place because of the underlying political persuasions and ideologies particular to each author. These differences result also in different strategies as lexicographers.

Only Reinhard's work is faithful to the scope of a dictionary, viz. to provide information about words for their own sake. Gallais and Chantreau use – and abuse – the lexicographical genre to make public their feelings (or misgivings) about the French Revolution: words are used here as a pretext to speak about realities, and to express value judgements about them. Within this strategy, the dictionary has a basically extralinguistic function: it serves to separate the old and new society by separating the words characteristic of each one. Gallais and Chantreau have given us dictionaries which are not so much selective encyclopaedias of a major political and socio-economic event, but rather alphabetically dispersed commentaries on the referents and the connotations of words. Reinhard's aim is an ideologically more neutral one: his dictionary is intended to help those who want to read (and understand) the 'papiers publics et autres ouvrages Français de cette époque', and is written for all the 'amateurs de la langue Française'. In contradistinction with the 'phatic' orientation of Gallais and Chantreau's works, Reinhard's portable dictionary has a basic 'conative' or public-oriented function. This is clear not only from the German glosses accompanying the entries, but also from the distinction between some kind of lexicographical definition (including a grammatical description) on the one hand and the examples on the other. Nevertheless, Reinhard goes beyond the strictly lexicographical borderlines: his dictionary not only includes 'encyclopaedic' information (see the 'Tableau des quatre vingt-neuf Départemens de la France', Reinhard (1796: 126–9), for example, and the entries containing proper names), but it also contains value judgements, subtly given as afterthoughts on sentences exemplifying the entry (but which could also be read, superficially, as a continuation of the example):

Ça va, ça ira. Das geht, das wird gehen. (All goes well, all will go well) Refrain of the Patriot Song *par excellence*, which has become a familiar expression and the password of the Revolutionaries on different occasions. *Ça va, ça ira*, despite the federalists, the fanatico-royalists who would want to destroy the inalienable rights of mankind. – Nothing goes well at all.

Déprêtriser, se. Sich entpriestern. (To leave the priesthood) –

Many ecclesiastics have left the priesthood in France since the Revolution. Many have repented of it[57].

(Reinhard 1796: 71–2, 131)

Gallais and Chantreau have given us an ideological pamphlet disguised as a dictionary; in a way, their work is their personal dictionary, in which words are treated as *tokens* and as indicators of feelings, convictions and attitudes. Reinhard, the external observer, stands on a higher level: he looks down upon the uses and misuses of words, and marks off his description from the recorded speech. In several cases he uses the strategy of displaced speech:[58] 'dit-on', 'dit un patriote', 'dit un journaliste' ('as one says', 'as a patriot says', 'as a journalist says'). There are however instances where the lexicographer cannot contain himself, and adds a personal comment: 'Avorton démocratique (little democratic runt, lit. democratic miscarriage); this is what Marat was called, the ugliest, the dirtiest, and the most cowardly of all Demagogues' (Reinhard 1796: 39).[59]

Our three witnesses not only share the property of being laden with ideology; they also testify to a common awareness of the power of words. The use and abuse of words is a common theme of eighteenth-century philosophy of language, especially after 1740, and it received a new impetus from the revolutionary and counter-revolutionary practices. It is not surprising that in the revolutionary period Morellet deemed it useful or even necessary to start his series 'Le Définisseur' in the *Mercure de France* and that so many lexicographical works appeared: the power of the word to overthrow had been discovered, and the resulting situation was so disturbing and (economically) gloomy that ideals – present or past – had to be kept alive by words. The beginning of a new era: that of the *idola fori*?

NOTES

1 The passage is followed by a covert criticism of Marrism: 'From this it follows that all attempts to connect particular types of linguistic morphology with certain correlated stages of cultural development are vain' (Sapir 1921: 234).

2 Note the explicit statement by Sapir (1921: 234): 'The linguistic student should never make the mistake of identifying a language with its dictionary'. Bloomfield's separation between grammar and lexicon (Bloomfield 1933: 138) is based on the presence or absence of 'arrangement': the grammar of a language is constituted by the meaningful arrangements of forms (Bloomfield 1933: 163), whereas the lexicon is the *stock* of morphemes (Bloomfield 1933: 162).

3 See also Bloomfield's (1933: 444–60) chapter on cultural borrowing.

4 This term corresponds to Sapir's 'third use' of the term, which stresses the 'spiritual possessions' of the group. 'We may perhaps come nearest the mark by saying that the cultural conception we are now trying to grasp aims to embrace in a single term those general attitudes, views of life, and specific manifestations of civilization that give a particular people its distinctive place in the world. Emphasis is put not so much on what is done and believed by a people as on how what is done and believed functions in the whole life of that people, on what significance it has for them. The very same element of civilization may be a vital strand in the culture of one people, and a well-nigh negligible factor in the culture of another. The present conception of culture is apt to crop up particularly in connection with problems of nationality, with attempts to find embodied in the character and civilization of a given people some peculiar excellence, some distinguishing force, that is strikingly its own. Culture thus becomes nearly synonymous with the 'spirit' or 'genius' of a people, yet not altogether, for whereas these loosely used terms refer rather to a psychological, or pseudo-psychological, background of national civilization, culture includes with this background a series of concrete manifestations which are believed to be peculiarly symptomatic of it. Culture, then, may be briefly defined as civilization in so far as it embodies the national genius' (Sapir [1924] 1949: 311).

5 See especially Karl Vossler's work (e.g., Vossler 1913; 1923: 68–71).

6 See, e.g., Dubois (1962) and Brunot (1927–37).

7 Matoré (1953: 65) goes beyond this in stressing the need of a study of interactions within a particular semantic field.

8 'Le mot-témoin introduit la notion de *valeur*, nous dirions plus volontiers la notion de *poids* dans le vocabulaire. Le mot-témoin est le symbole matériel d'un fait spirituel important; c'est l'élément à la fois expressif et tangible qui concrétise un fait de civilisation' ('The lexical witness brings in the notion of *value*, or as we would rather say the notion of *weight* into the vocabulary. The lexical witness is the material symbol of an important mental fact; it is the expressive and palpable element that concretizes a fact of civilization') (Matoré 1953: 65–6).

9 For a description of this manuscript work, see Schlieben-Lange (1985: 170, 182 and 1987).

10 Compare this with the number of anonymously published dictionaries between 1775 and 1789 and 1804–20: 15 and 20 respectively.

11 The concept of *new* is a complex one: it can apply to various types of innovation, such as the creation of new words, the renewed use of words that had fallen out of use, and the attribution of a new meaning to a term. Some authors, such as Reinhard (1796) and Mercier (1800–1) make this threefold distinction.

12 'L'Unité de l'idiome est une partie intégrante de la Révolution. . . . Il faut identité de langage' ('The unity of the language is an integral part of the Revolution. . . . Identity of language is required') (Grégoire 1794, edition in Gazier 1880: 303).

See also the following passage in an official letter by the representatives of the Corrèze Departement sent to the minister of Justice in 1792: 'la langue française étant la langue universelle de la République, ce serait rendre un mauvais service aux citoyens que de les entretenir dans l'usage d'un baragouin barbare et de ne pas les encourager par tous les moyens à se servir du langage national' ('Since the French language is the universal language of the Republic, it would be of no help to the citizens to converse with them in a barbarous gibberish, and not to encourage them by all means to use the national language') (quoted after de Certeau-Julia-Revel 1975: 162–3 and Droixhe 1978: 342–3).

13 On Grégoire's questionnaire, and the conclusions drawn from it, see de Certeau-Julia-Revel (1975) and Droixhe (1978: 342–3).

14 See, e.g., E. Molard's *Lyonnoisismes ou recueil d'expressions vicieuses utilisées à Lyon*, 1792; new edition *Dictionnaire du mauvais langage, recueil d'expressions vicieuses usitées en France, et à Lyon*, 1797; E. Villa, *Nouveaux gasconnismes corrigés*, Montpellier, 1802; J.-F. Michel, *Dictionnaire des expressions vicieuses*, Nancy, 1807, G. Peignot, *Petit dictionnaire des locutions vicieuses*, Paris, 1807; J.-M. Rolland, *Dictionnaire des expressions vicieuses* (Hautes et Basses-Alpes), Gap, 1810.

15 See, e.g., Gacon Dufour, *Dictionnaire rural raisonné*, Paris, 1808; d'Hautel, *Dictionnaire du bas langage*, Paris, 1808.

16 The French words *centralisation* and *centraliser* are first attested in 1790.

17 It is hard to define the chronological boundaries of the French Revolution; strictly speaking, the French Revolution ended in 1794, when Robespierre and his fellow Jacobins were guillotined and the Thermidor Regime was installed. But most authors include the Thermidor Regime and the first and second Directories (up to 1799) within the Revolution period; often the period is extended so as to include the Consular Republic (up to 1802) and the Empire (up to 1815).

18 On the history of the French Revolution, see Carlyle (1837), de Tocqueville (1856), Pariset (1920–1922), Lefebvre-Soboul (1963), Soboul (1962).

19 On the project of a study of the French social and political vocabulary from 1680 to 1820, see the introductory volume of Reinhard and Schmitt (1985: cf. Swiggers 1987b). See also the studies by Barny (1978), Guilhaumou (1978), Proschwitz (1966), Ricken (1974), Schlieben-Lange (1981) and Tournier (et al. 1969). For a succinct overview, see Gohin (1938). For a selective bibliography, see Gumbrecht-Schlieben-Lange (1981).

20 See Frey (1925); a number of these transformations were already prepared in the period preceding the Revolution (see Gohin 1903). The most extensive survey of the linguistic situation in revolutionary France is still Brunot (1927–37).

21 'Rien de plus naturel, que de voir une grande nation, qui tend à rompre des chaines et à se régénérer, dans l'effervescence du bouleversement général, enfanter à tout instant des idées nouvelles, qui demandent à leur tour des mots neufs, pour les exprimer. Le désir d'un nouvel ordre de choses d'un côté, la haine contre l'ancien de l'autre, ont banni jusqu'à des termes, qui peignaient les moeurs et les usages du ci-devant Français, ou qui caractérisaient les titres et les fonctions des différentes parties de l'ancienne administration', en les remplaçant par d'autres de nouvelle création. De là cette foule d'expressions, neuves, insolites, souvent heureuses, quelquefois grotesques, qui arrêtent, à chaque pas, dans la lecture des

papiers publics et autres ouvrages Français de cette époque. . . . Et l'ouvrage actuel est le fruit de remarques et d'observations, non seulement sur la nouvelle langue, depuis le commencement de la Révolution, mais aussi sur quelques néologismes, qui avaient cours quelques années devant la Révolution.'

22　We quote the crucial passages from this address, after the first volume of the *Journal* (see Ricken 1974: 311–12; cf. Busse 1986a): 'Un dictionnaire vraiment philosophique, qui atteigne notre langue usuelle dans toutes ses parties, manque à notre littérature, à nos besoins journaliers, à notre nouvelle existence politique. Vraiment la nation s'est flattée, pendant plus d'un siècle, de voir élever par l'académie françoise le grand monument pour lequel elle a été instituée; toujours trompée dans sa juste espérance, elle s'est vue réduite à se livrer aux hérésies académiques, comme le vulgaire embrasse les religions fausses, parce que la véritable ne s'est pas révélée à ses yeux. Le jour de la liberté a lui; toutes les erreurs vont s'évanouir, comme les ombres disparoissent devant l'astre qui nous éclaire. Mais des diverses erreurs qui font le malheur de l'homme, la plus funeste peut-être est l'abus des mots, qui nous trompe sur les choses. Persuadé que sans une langue bien faite, il n'est point d'idées saines et que sans idées saines il n'est point de bonheur, j'ai conçu le projet de vous rassembler, pour travailler tous de concert au perfectionnement de notre idiome. La France a reçu de l'Amérique l'exemple de la régéneration des lois; donnons à toutes les nations l'exemple de la régéneration des langues.

Pour bien asseoir le monument national que nous voulons élever, nous devons d'abord nous assurer des bases. La lexique (sic), qui est la science des dictionnaires, nous les fait connoître. Elle exige impérieusement qu'un dictionnaire vraiment philosophique présente, à chaque mot, une classification juste, une étymologie saine, une prosodie exacte, une étymologie lumineuse, une définition logique, des exemples propres aux différentes acceptions; qu'il ouvre les trésors d'une sage néologie, qu'il dévoile les secrets de la logique, de la poésie, de l'éloquence; en un mot qu'il ne laisse rien à désirer de tout ce qui peut contribuer à la perfection de la langue, à l'instruction et au plaisir du lecteur.

Mais comme il est important de ne rien laisser en arrière, comme le succès dépend du soin qu'on prendra de scruter d'un oeil philosophique toutes les parties, pour composer un tout digne des lumières de notre âge, je crois qu'il est nécessaire de former d'abord un comité de lexique, d'où, comme d'un tronc fécond, sortiront tous les autres comités.

Le comité de lexique sera composé d'un nombre indéfini de membres. Tous ceux qui croient pouvoir apporter quelques lumières dans cette partie fondamentale de l'édifice, sont invités à se faire inscrire.

Une vaine modestie ne doit point arrêter les amateurs de la langue françoise. Le désir d'être utile est la seule considération qui doit les déterminer.

Le comité de lexique présentera son travail, à la prochaine assemblée; chaque article sera discuté, et enfin arrêté, à la pluralité des voix. Dès ce moment, nous saurons combien de comités sont nécessaires pour ordonner et préparer les travaux.

S'il m'est permis d'anticiper sur le plan qui vous sera soumis, je crois qu'il y aura sept comités:

Le comité d'étymologie.
Le comité de prononciation et d'orthographe.
Celui de définition, de signification et d'exemples.
Celui de syntaxe.
Le comité de logique et de belles-lettres.
Le comité de néologie.
Le comité de révision.

Tous ces comités, nés du comité de lexique, le rendront inutile.

'Our literature, our daily needs, our new political existence lack a truly philosophical dictionary that attains to our usual language in all its parts. The nation has been priding herself for a century on the fact that the French Academy was raising the important monument it had been created for. Always disenchanted in her just hopes, she was forced to surrender herself to the academic heresies, in the same way as vulgar men embrace false religions because the true one did not appear to them. The day of freedom has dawned; all errors are going to disappear, and shadows disappear before the star that illuminates us. But of all the errors that provoke man's misfortune, the most harmful is perhaps the abuse of words, which deceives us with respect to things. Convinced as I am that without a well constructed language there are no sound ideas, and that without sound ideas no happiness is possible, I have conceived the project of assembling you in order to work together on the perfection of our language. France received from America the example of the regeneration of laws; let us give to all nations the example of the regeneration of languages.

In order to provide a solid basis for the national monument we want to raise, we must first establish the basis. Lexicology, which is the science of dictionaries, makes them known to us. It requires unambiguously that a truly philosophical dictionary present, for every word, a right classification, a sound etymology, an exact prosody, a luminous etymology, a logical definition, examples appropriate to the different meanings; that it open the treasures of a wise neology, that it unveil the secrets of logic, of poetry, of rhetoric; briefly, that it provide everything that may contribute to the perfection of language, to the education and to the pleasure of the reader.

But since it is important not to leave anything behind, since the success of this enterprise depends on the care that will be taken to scrutinize all parts with the philosopher's eye, in order to construct a whole worthy of the enlightenment of our age, I think it is necessary to establish first a lexicology committee, from which, as from a fertile trunk, will spring all the other committees.

The lexicology committee will be composed of an indefinite number of members. All those who think that they can bring some enlightenment into this fundamental part of the edifice are invited to have themselves enrolled.

181

An undue modesty should not withhold lovers of the French language. The desire to be useful is the only consideration that should motivate them. The lexicology committee will present its work in the following assembly; every article will be discussed and eventually decided upon by the plurality of votes. From that moment on, we will know how many committees will be necessary to organize and prepare the undertakings.

If you will allow me to anticipate the plan that will be submitted to you, I think there will be seven committees:

The committee on etymology.
The committee on pronunciation and orthography.
The committee on definition, meaning and examples.
The committee on syntax.
The committee on logic and literature.
The committee on neology.
The committee on revision.

All these committees, born from the lexicology committee, will make the latter useless.'

23 'Pour détromper les hommes de beaucoup d'erreurs, il ne s'agirait le plus souvent que de leur faire attacher aux mots des idées justes et précises, de sorte qu'un bon lexicographe est le meilleur instituteur que pût avoir le genre humain. Cette vérité est surtout sensible pour tous les genres de connaissances qui sont relatives à la morale et à la politique, et qui tiennent de plus près à la prospérité sociale, et au bonheur des individus. Car, les fausses notions en cette matière sont les sources de tous les maux qui affligent l'homme en société' ('In order to disabuse mankind of many errors, it would very often be sufficient to make them link right and precise ideas to words, in such a way that a good lexicographer is the best teacher mankind could have. This truth is especially valid for all knowledge that is related to morals and politics, and that is closely linked to social prosperity and the happiness of the individual. For erroneous notions in this domain are the source of all harm afflicting man in society') (Morellet 1818, vol. 3: 84).

24 'Les mots ont une telle influence sur les idées, et les idées sur les actions, qu'un des plus grands services qu'on eût pu rendre à la révolution, aurait été d'assigner aux principaux signes de nos idées en politique leur véritable signification, et de bien *définir* avant que de raisonner (. . . . C'est une chose bien remarquable que la révolution qui a commencé par les lumières, (. . .) ait été jettée si brusquement hors de ses premieres routes par une poignée de scélérats, sans connoissances, sans principes, sans morale, sans autre talent que celui d'en imposer par un patriotisme simulé, et le jeu artificieux de quelques mots qui exerçaient sur la multitude un empire d'autant plus grand qu'ils étaient moins compris, et qu'on avait eu soin de les détourner de leur véritable acception.'

25 See, for example, the following explicit statement (quoted after Barny 1978): 'L'abus des mots a toujours été un des principaux moyens qu'on a employés pour asservir les peuples . . . . Gardons-nous donc citoyens, de nous laisser abuser par les mots; quand le pouvoir exécutif est venu à bout de nous en imposer sur le sens de certaines expressions, il paraît faire une

chose, et il en fait une autre; et peu à peu il nous chargeait de chaînes en nous parlant de *liberté*. Le mot *aristocrate* n'a pas moins contribué à la révolution que la cocarde. Sa signification est aujourd'hui très étendue; il s'applique à tous ceux qui vivent d'abus, qui regrettent les abus, ou qui veulent créer de nouveaux abus. Les aristocrates ont cherché à nous persuader que ce mot était devenu insignifiant: nous n'avons pas donné dans le piège; et les lumières gagnant de proche en proche dans les retraites de l'aristocratie, ses satellites ont senti qu'ils étaient perdus, s'ils ne trouvaient pas un mot dont le pouvoir magique détruisît la puissance du mot *aristocrate*. Nous ignorons s'il leur en a coûté beaucoup d'efforts; mais nous savons que notre mot de *ralliement* est contrebalancé aujourd'hui par celui d'*incendiaire*, et qu'à l'aide de certaines menaces dont on l'a accompagné, de certaines vexations qui le suivent de près, il glace d'effroi d'excellents citoyens. ('The abuse of words has always been one of the principal means used to enslave nations . . . . Let us thus be careful, citizens, not to be abused by words; when the executive power does not succeed anymore in impressing us with the meaning of certain expressions, it seems to do one thing, and it actually does something else; and slowly it put us in chains while talking of *freedom*. The word *aristocrat* contributed to the revolution no less than the *rosette* (cocarde) did. Its meaning nowadays is very broad; it applies to all those who live off of abuse, who regret abuses, or who want to create new abuses. The aristocrats tried to convince us that the word had become meaningless: we did not fall into the trap; and with the enlightenment slowly gaining the retreats of the aristocracy, its satellites felt that they were lost if they did not find a word the magic power of which would destroy the power of the word *aristocrat*. We do not know whether this has cost them many efforts; but we do know that our word *rallying* (ralliement) is nowadays counterbalanced by the word *arsonist* (incendiaire), and that with the help of certain threats that accompanied it, of certain harassments that follow it closely, it freezes excellent citizens with terror.')

26 'Il est incroyable combien les orateurs de l'Assemblée Nationale ont abusé, et abusent encore de sa jeunesse de notions et d'opinions: ils l'ont persuadée, selon les circonstances, tant qu'elle était corps constitué, tantôt corps constituant, tantôt convention nationale, et ainsi, par un simple choix de dénomination, ils lui ont fait confondre tous les pouvoirs, oublier son origine, et commettre le crime de lèse-majesté, à la fois envers son vrai souverain le Roi, et envers son souverain factice le Peuple.'

27 On de La Harpe's work, see Jovicevich (1973) and Vier (1976).

28 'Du mot *Négoce, Handel, Handelsgeist, die Klasse der Handelsleute*. L'esprit du négoce, la caste des Négocians. Mot créé, pur créer un crime. – Le Négociantisme est pire que l'Aristocratisme et que le Royalisme, disaient les nivelleurs de fortune, qui convoitaient les richesses des négocians.'

29 As in the entry *Démocrate* (Reinhard 1796: 122): 'Un des mots révolution-naires qui a fait la plus grande fortune. Il signifie sujet d'un gouvernement Démocratique, et celui qui par principes ou par mode, est partisan de la *Démocratie*. Chez les uns c'est éloge, chez les autres c'est moquerie et dérision' ('One of the revolutionary words that has had the greatest fortune. It means the subject of a Democratic government, and one who,

by principles or by fashion, is a partisan of *Democracy*. For some it is praise, for others mockery and derision').

30 See, e.g., the article *Peuple de Robespierre* (Reinhard 1796: 255): 'C'est ainsi qu'on a appelé les assassins, les égorgeurs, les buveurs de sang de la Jacobiniere, à la solde de ce Démagogue et qu'il voulait faire passer, pour le peuple Français'. ('This is what the murderers were called, the cut-throats, the blood-drinkers of the Jacobinière, in the pay of that Demagogue who wanted them to be taken for the French people'). See also the articles *Guillotine, Guillotinade, Jacobin, Jacobinière* ('A small tribe in Gaule, which, it is said, lived on human blood, several centuries before the year 2440'; 'Une petite peuplade de la Gaule, qui, dit-on, vivait de sang humain, plusieurs siècles avant l'an 2440'), *Maison de sureté, Populacier, Pouvoir révolutionnaire, Robespierriser, Robespierrisme, Sanguinocratie*, etc.

31 'C'est ainsi qu'on a appelé la Constitution de 1789, comme qui dirait fille des Démagogues. Cette jeune fille, qui donnait de grandes espérances, est morte au berceau.'

32 See the article *Révolution Française* (Reinhard 1796: 292–5).

33 '*Liberté*. F. Freyheit. Un être, jusqu'à présent idéal, vers lequel les Français tendent en vain les bras depuis cinq ans de convulsion. On a comparé la statue colossale de la *Liberté* sur la place de la Révolution, à celle de Moloch, qui demandait des offrandes de sang.'

'*Patriote*. Un citoyen, qui veut le bien de sa patrie et de ses concitoyens. La France qui a fourmillé de *patriotes*, depuis la Révolution, en compte très peu, dans le sens de cette définition. Sur un qui voulait le bien, le bonheur de son pays, il y en avait mille, qui ne voulaient que les biens de leurs compatriotes. Aussi le titre de *patriote* est-il, aujourd'hui, très équivoque, sans un adjectif, qui en détermine la signification.'

'*Quatorze Juillet*. Der 14te Juli (1789). Un mot ancien, mais qui rappelle une scene, absolument neuve dans l'histoire, où 600 000 Français, représentans de 26 millions, rassemblées dans le champ de la fédération, grands et petits, jeunes et vieux, riches et pauvres, des deux sexes devinrent tout à coup frères et s'embrasserent, yvres de liberté et d'égalité, croyant avoir trouvé le bonheur. Cette journée d'allégresse, dont il ne reste que des souvenirs, a été suivie de mille et une journées de deuil, d'angoisses, de douleurs et de larmes de sang, dont on ne prévoit pas encore la fin.'

34 See, e.g. the article *Régime* (Reinhard 1796: 280): 'L'ancien *régime*, le nouveau *régime*, c.à.d. la Monarchie et la République. La différence la plus saillante, entre ces deux *régimes*: sous l'ancien il y avait des carêmes, des jeunes de quelques jours, de quelques semaines, prescrits par le culte dominant, et qu'on observait, tant bien que mal. Sous le nouveau il y a des carêmes, des abstinences civiques de plusieurs mois, de plusieurs saisons, qu'on est forcé d'observer, en dépit des murmures de son estomac' ('The old *regime*, the new *regime*, that is to say the Monarchy and the Republic. The most striking difference between these two *regimes*: under the old *regime* there were fasts for some days, for some weeks, prescribed by the dominant cult, that were observed to the best of one's ability. Under the new *regime*, there are fasts and civic abstinences for several months, for

several seasons, which one is forced to observe, despite the murmurs of one's stomach').

35 'Dans la *Révolution française* le bouleversement est général, rien n'est sacré, rien ne reste à sa place, tout est renversé, écrasé, détruit, pour faire place à un système de liberté, d'égalité et de fraternité, qui ruine et la patrie de ce système et les Etats circonvoisins. Des ambitieux cruels, tour à tour groupés et isolés, se jettent successivement avec fureur, dans l'arêne; des monstres à figure humaine, au nom sacré de la patrie, massacrent, fusillent, guillotinent et noyent dans des flots de sang, tout ce qui s'oppose à leurs barbares projets. Et le feu de cette révolution, qui jette encore des flammes dévorantes à travers les fumées des décombres, menace d'embraser le reste de l'Europe. Les siècles à venir béniront, peut-être, les bienfaits tardifs de la *Révolution*, mais celui-ci et le prochain saigneront, encore longtemps, des playes profondes, portées à l'humanité, par les moyens insolites, violens, destructeurs, employés pour obtenir ces bienfaits' ('In the *French Revolution*, the upheaval is general, nothing is sacred, nothing remains in its place, everything is overturned, crushed, destroyed, to make room for a system of freedom, equality and fraternity, ruining both the homeland of this system and the neighbouring states. Cruel and ambitious people, in turn grouped then isolated, throw themselves furiously into the arena; monsters with human faces, in the sacred name of the homeland, slaughter, shoot, guillotine, and drown in torrents of blood everything that is opposed to their barbarous projects. And the fire of this revolution, that still throws devouring flames through the smoke of the ruins, threatens to inflame the rest of Europe. Future centuries will perhaps bless the belated benefits of the *Revolution*, but this century and the next will bleed for a long time from the deep wounds inflicted upon humanity by the unusual, violent, and destructive means used to obtain these blessings').

36 See, e.g., the articles *Actif, s'Adoniser, Affolé, Agacerie, Aspérité, Baguette, Charme, Dévergondage, Dévirginer, Ehonté, Erotiquement, Etreintes d'amour, Frivolisme, Impure, Maquereller, Physique, Pornographe, Saturé, Traineuses.*

37 He distinguishes between various sociolinguistic and stylistic levels of terms, using qualifications such as *termes familiers, termes vulgaires, termes d'argot, termes nobles, termes plébéiens, termes des bons écrivains,* etc.

38 The ambiguity may be due to a short-range diachronic change of meaning (see the articles *Aristocratie, Département, Despotisme, Diplomatie, Marcher, Pair, Régime*) or to a socially distinct use of terms (see the articles *Démocrate, Ligaments* and *Nationicide*). Finally, some terms may be considered basically ambiguous: see, e.g., the entry *Patriotisme* (Reinhard 1796: 251): 'Mot enchanteur, ensorcelé, qui a fait tourner depuis 6 ans les têtes de tant de millions d'individus; mot, qu'il est presqu'impossible de définir, au juste, malgré la foule d'exemples, que les événemens les plus récens nous offrent de la chose' ('Enchanting, bewitched word that in the past six years has turned the head of so many millions of individuals; a word that it is almost impossible to define precisely, despite the mass of examples that the most recent events give us of it').

39 'Jamais on n'a montré tant d'aristocratie dans la pensée, tant de despotisme dans la conduite, tant de tyrannie dans les actions les plus indifférentes, que depuis que nous sommes libres.'

40 'Une armée de journalistes est sortie tout à coup du sein de la révolution, comme cette foule d'insectes venimeux ou incommodes sortent en été du sein des marais fangeux (. . .). J'oserai dire que les vrais ennemis de la France et de la révolution sont ces écrivains énergumenes, qui, depuis un an, ne cessent de sonner l'alarme, de caresser le peuple et de flagorner le côté gauche de l'Assemblée.'

'Mais on nous *désabuse* chaque jour. Les principes sont les opinions de tel ou tel; la vérité, c'est le système d'une secte ou d'un parti; les lumières, ce sont les connoissances personnelles du journaliste.'

41 'JOURNAL: dans l'ancien régime c'étoit une feuille périodique, qui parloit de la pluie et du beau tems, donnoit des extraits des catalogues de librairie, et quelques lettres de MM. les abonnés à M. le rédacteur, que dans les cafés on prenoit bonnement pour des lettres. Par la voie de ces feuilles on étoit informé très-exactement du genre et du nombre de grimaces que telle ou telle actrice avoit faite dans une pièce nouvelle . . . . Mais que tout est changé! Ces feuilles, autrefois la pâture de nos désoeuvrés, sont à présent l'aliment de toutes les classes de citoyens. On court après, on se les arrache, on les dévore. Nos politiques y lisent la régénération de l'empire et y trouvent les hausses et les baisses de l'aristocratie. Les muses sont réduites au silence, le journaliste seul est en scène où il a le plus grand succès.'

42 See the articles *Abbaye, Abbé, Abbesse, Clergé* (Chantreau 1790: 1–5, 36–8).

43 'Aristocrate: il est synonyme de mauvais citoyen, de pire encore; il désigne un fauteur de complots, un ennemi de la liberté' ('Aristocrat: a synonym of bad citizen, or even worse; refers to an instigator of conspiracies, an enemy of liberty') (Chantreau 1790: 14, see also the articles *Noblesse* and *Vaisselle d'argent*, Chantreau 1790: 132–9, 177–9).

44 'What the free Frenchmen now call *abuse*, we called *right* in the *ancien régime*' ('Ce que les François libres appellent aujourd'hui *abus*, l'ancien régime le nommait *droit*') (*Abus*, Chantreau 1790: 5; see also the article *Droits*, Chantreau 1790: 70–1).

45 See the article *Tiers-Etat* (Chantreau 1790: 174–5): 'Lorsque la nation ou l'état, comme on le voudra dire, étoit composé de trois ordres; le troisième ou dernier étoit le *tiers-état*. Il étoit formé de ce que les deux premiers ordres, le *clergé* et la *noblesse* appeloient les *vilains*, et ces *vilains* c'étoit nous, ces vils enfans que Dieu avoit condamnés à manger le pain à la sueur de leur front, et à payer les violons à *nosseigneurs* toutes les fois que *nosseigneurs* l'ordonneroient ainsi. La volonté de Dieu s'est faite pendant une longue suite de siècles, jusqu'en 1789, époque à laquelle un *oint du Seigneur* a *pris en considération* les vingt-trois millions de vilains qui peuploient son royaume, et a dit: "Je n'aime point cette race parasite de *nosseigneurs* qui reste les bras croisés, tandis que les vilains travaillent. Il n'y aura désormais de *monseigneur* que celui qui sera utile au bien public; plus de distinctions; que *un* soit plus que *vingt-trois* est une absurdité arithmétique dont je ne veux plus entendre parler". Ces paroles ont eu un effet magique, et soudain *nosseigneurs* et *vilains*, *vilains* et *nosseigneurs*, tout a été confondu' ('When the

nation or the state, whichever name one prefers, was composed of three
orders, the third or last was the *tiers-état*. It consisted of those who were
called *villains* by the two first orders, the *clergy* and the *nobility*; and we
were those *villains*, those vile children God had condemned to eat their
bread by the sweat of their brows, and to pay the expenses *to our Lords and
masters (nosseigneurs)* whenever *our Lords and masters* would order us to do
so. The will of God was done for several centuries, until 1789, *when Our
Lord took into account* the twenty-three million villains that inhabited his
kingdom, and said: "I do not like that parasite race of *Lords and masters*
who sit around idly while the villains are working. From now on, the
only *lord and master* will be the one who is useful to the public good; no
distinctions anymore; that *one* be more than *twenty-three* is an arithmetic
absurdity I no longer want to hear of". These words had a magic effect,
and suddenly *Lords and masters* and *villains*, *villains* and *Lords and masters*,
everything was mixed up.'

46 'LIBERTE: dans l'ancien régime ce mot ne signifioit rien de ce qu'il signifie
aujourd'hui qu'il est devenu le cri de la nation; il désigne ce droit précieux
que nature accorde à tous les hommes, quand nature ne trouve point sur
son chemin des ministres qui ont des bastilles, et des bastilles qui ont des
de Launay. Nous venons enfin de remplir le voeu de cette bonne nature que
nous n'avions jamais si bien connue et qui nous menera loin. Nous avons
enfin *conquis* ce droit imprescriptible d'être libres (. . . Un peuple libre
est celui qui vit sous l'autorité des loix, bonnes ou convenables, qu'il s'est
données lui-même ou par ses représentans.'

47 See also the author's preface: 'Cette révolution fameuse qui vous rend
aujourd'hui une des plus célèbres de nos quarante-huit mille municipalités;
cette révolution, MESSIEURS, me ramena sur la bonne route; je fus vivement
frappé de voir notre langue s'enrichir chaque jour d'une foule de mots qui
caractérisent un peuple libre. Je m'écriai: *je suis libre aussi, moi!* Alors l'idée
d'être utile à la nation fut la seule qui s'empara de mes facultés . . . . Ce fut
dans un de ces momens d'enthousiasme que je formai le dessein de
travailler au Dictionnaire que j'ai l'honneur de vous présenter' ('This
famous revolution that made you into one of the best known of our forty-
eight thousand municipalities; this revolution, Sirs, brought me back to
the right track; I was struck to see our language becoming richer every day
with a host of words that characterize a free people. I exclaimed: *I am also
free!* Then the idea of being useful to the nation was the only one that
possessed my powers (. . .). It was in one of these moments of enthusiasm
that I came upon the idea of working on the dictionary that I have the
honour to introduce to you') (Chantreau 1790: 6–7).

48 A moral and civil concept according to Chantreau (1790: 29–30): 'C'est
un membre de la société, qui, non-seulement acquitte les charges civiles,
mais encore est rempli des sentimens qu'inspire l'heureuse liberté dans
laquelle nous vivons.' ('A member of the society who not only fulfils his
civil duties but is also filled with the feelings inspired by the happy
liberty in which we are living'). See also the positive tone of the entries
Citoyen qui brigue l'honneur d'être élu, *Citoyen enrôlé*, *Civisme*, *Milice*, *Patrie* and
Patriote.

49 See also the articles *Caisse* and *Egalité* (Chantreau 1790: 26–8, 71–2).

50 'ARGENT: . . . François! nation libre! mais qui n'avez pas le sou, que ces momens de pénurie, dans lesquels vous allez vivre, ne vous désesperent point; ils vont vous faire pratiquer des vertus que vous n'aviez point, et qui sont nécessaires à un peuple qui se régénère . . . .'

'DEMAGOGUE: . . . Chaque fois que je me sers du mot de Démagogue, je le prends dans le sens où il signifie un aristocrate hypocrite qui cherche à étouffer son frère le *démocrate* en le serrant dans ses bras.'

51 'Dans tous les temps et dans tous les pays, le peuple, qui fut l'instrument des révolutions, et servit l'ambition des démagogues, fut pauvre, ignorant, vil et inquiet. Il n'est pas difficile de conduire à la révolte des malheureux qui n'ont rien, toujours prêts à se vendre et à changer de maîtres.'

52 'Qu'est-ce qui compose le peuple en France? Ce n'est point la noblesse, ce n'est point le clergé, ce ne sont point les riches bourgeois, ce ne sont point les marchands, ce ne sont point les artistes, restent donc les *manoeuvriers*, les *artisans*, les *prolétaires*, qui composent la nation et assurent les fondemens de la constitution. Voilà-t-il pas une constitution bien appuyée?' ('What does the people consist of in France? It is not the nobility, the clergy, the rich middle-class, the merchants, nor the artists. All that is left are the *labourers*, the *craftsmen*, the *proletarians* who make up the nation and ensure the foundations of the constitution. Doesn't this make for a well sustained constitution?') (Gallais 1790: 242).

53 See his articles *Despotisme* and *Monarchie*.

54 'La vérité, jadis immuable comme son auteur est devenue mobile comme le temps. Soumise aux circonstances, elle prend toutes les formes, elle suit tous les mouvements qu'on veut lui imprimer. Ce qui étoit vrai, il y a quelques mois, ne l'est plus aujourd'hui.'

55 'Sans doute, la liberté est un bien, mais avant tout il faut du pain, je défie tous les orateurs du monde et tous les folliculaires de Paris, de me prouver qu'il vaut mieux être libre & mourir de faim, que d'être nourri; vêtu & enchaîné.'

56 'O zélés citoyens, zélés fanatiques, zélés frippons de toute espèce, apprenez que l'erreur n'a qu'un temps.'

57 '*Ça va, ça ira*. Das geht, das wird gehen. Refrain de la Chanson patriotique, par excellence, devenu une expression familière et le mot du guet des Révolutionnaires, en différentes occasions. *Ça va, ça ira*, en dépit des fédéralistes, des fanatico-royalistes, qui voudront anéantir les droits imprescriptibles de l'homme. – Cela ne va guères.'

'*Déprêtriser, se*. Sich entpriestern – Beaucoup d'ecclésiastiques se sont déprêtrisés, en France depuis la Révolution. Beaucoup s'en sont repentis.'

58 As noted above, Gallais also appeals in a few cases to 'a spokesman'.

59 '*Avorton* démocratique; c'est ainsi qu'on a appellé le plus laid, le plus sale et le plus poltron des Démagogues, Marat.'

10

'Reducing' Pacific languages to writings

Peter Mühlhäusler

Men who by force of circumstances were continually at war
and whose central interest in life was head-hunting were not
ideal subjects for a sedentary and seemingly tame pursuit like
vernacular literacy.

(Rule 1977: 388)

1 INTRODUCTION

This chapter explores a number of sociolinguistic problems that have
resulted from the introduction of literacy into the Pacific area where,
prior to the arrival of the Europeans, some 3,000 languages were
spoken. It is of course not possible to consider every single instance of
literacy in a chapter like this. Instead, I have opted to put before you
some rather radical overgeneralizations and observations, hoping
that these will evoke the criticisms I need for pursuing this topic, and
that I have made my prejudices explicit enough for them to constitute
testable hypotheses.

The area I am concerned with comprises the islands of Melanesia,
Micronesia and Polynesia rather than the countries of the Pacific rim.
In this area the number of existing writing systems prior to colonization
was extremely low and possibly restricted to the Rongo Rongo script
of Easter island. No traces of pre-colonial writing systems have
survived. The introduction of vernacular literacy began in the early
nineteenth century and is still continuing in the more outlying areas of
Melanesia. Thus, in 1975 about 200 of the 700-plus languages of
Papua New Guinea had an orthography (cf. Healey 1975: 56ff.). These
languages represented about 80 per cent of the population and even
today literacy for medium-size and small speech communities still has
a long way to go. Next to literacy in the major vernaculars, literacy in
the metropolitan languages is also widespread. Again, its beginnings

can be traced back to the nineteenth century. With near-universal schooling in most of the countries of the area, literacy in one form or another is becoming the norm and purely oral communities are on the way out.

2 SOME THESES

An extensive study of the processes accompanying the introduction of literacy has led me to the following conclusions:

(i) Neither those who introduced nor those who accepted literacy were aware of the consequences of such a step. The economies and dyseconomies that have resulted are best regarded as resulting from invisible-hand processes.

(ii) The most general long-term effect of literacy in the vernacular has been language decline and death.

(iii) Literacy in the metropolitan languages or local pidgins appear to have slowed down the disappearance of local vernaculars. However, in many instances, their demise or decline was not prevented.

(iv) The introduction of literacy has changed many aspects of the lives of the peoples of the Pacific. It seems justified to speak of 'literary revolution' (Parsonson 1967).

(v) The role of literacy in vernacular elevation has been an ambivalent one. In many instances languages were literally 'reduced' to writing.

(vi) The promotion and acceptance of literacy took place in a cargo-cult-like atmosphere: indigenous people expected access to expatriate wealth and status whereas the expatriates hoped for an ample supply of cheap labour or converts.

(vii) The introduction of literacy cannot be separated from other processes affecting the ecology of the Pacific languages.

(viii) With few exceptions literacy did not become a means of recording traditions and 'prehistory' but a medium for encoding experiences triggered off by the advent of colonialism.

(ix) In more than a few instances one of the first uses to which literacy was put was to sign away traditional land to a colonizer.

(x) Even in post-independence societies, insufficient attention is given to the nature and effects of literacy. Planning is urgently needed in this area.

3 SOME CASE HISTORIES

Many of the above statements can be illustrated with examples from
individual languages. Moreover, a consideration of cases can also lead
to further generalizations about the developmental aspects of literacy
– that is, the stages through which it progresses from the initial
imposition/adoption to replacement of vernacular by metropolitan
literacy.

3.1 Maori

The first area affected by the literary revolution in the Pacific was
Polynesia, where writing systems for the major languages (Hawaiian,
Tahitian and Maori) were developed only a few years after European
discovery in the late eighteenth century. The general aspects of this
revolution have been discussed in some detail by Parsonson (1967).
The case of Maori is particularly instructive, since the debate about
Maori literacy is a continuing one (cf. Benton 1981).

New Zealand was first 'discovered' by the Dutch navigator Tasman
in 1642 and explored in greater depth by Captain Cook in 1770, in
which year possession of the colony was taken by Britain. Cook's
visits initiated a transformation which, in the first instance, manifested
itself in the spread of European plants and weapons and later
numerous diseases. Cook was followed by other European explorers
and whalers and by 1814 the first *pakeha* settlers arrived in the Bay of
Islands. They were Church of England missionaries who offered
protection in exchange for European goods and power. Around the
mission station a community of whalers and beachcombers grew up
and intensive trade relations developed between the Maori and
pakeha, the most desired European commodity being firearms. Mission
influence was initially very slow and their eventual success is seen by
some not as the result of their teachings but of the realization that
missions were a way of becoming literate. Parsonson (1967: 44)
writes:

> The Pacific Islanders had long grasped the fact that the real
> difference between their culture and the European was that
> theirs was non-literate, the other *literate*. The key to the new
> world with all its evident power was the written word. Indeed,
> the missionaries had often told them so and every fresh contact
> with the foreigner emphasized the point.
>
> The sheer magic of the written word in primitive eyes needs to

be stressed. Quiros notes how the Taumakoans 'were much astonished at seeing one reading a paper, and taking it in their hands, they looked at it in front and behind'. Henry Williams, speaking of the Maori, mentions how on one occasion he spent some time in reading, writing and drawing: 'This last greatly astonished the natives, to see the effect of a few pencil marks on paper.'

Crosby (1986: 246) offers the following picture of the rapid spread of literacy among the Maori:

> The missionaries, all but a few of them Protestants who viewed literacy as a major virtue, flung themselves at the problem of Maori illiteracy as if it were the boulder to be rolled away from Christ's tomb. They learned the Maori tongue, devised an alphabet for it, and in 1837 published the entire New Testament in Maori. By 1845 there was at least one copy of that publication for every two Maori in the country.
>
> The missionaries offered the Maori a new religion, new skills, new tools, and the magic of the alphabet, but it was the Maori themselves who accepted (no, seized) the opportunities offered. The most effective transmitters of Christianity and literacy were the prisoners taken by the Ngapuhi and allies – the lowest of the low, the slaves – who embraced the new religion with the greatest fervor, and then, as the wars waned and they were freed, returned home bearing the Word with them. When the missionaries penetrated the southern central districts of the North Island, they found the Maori there already clamouring for instruction and books, and often village schools under Maori teachers already in operation.
>
> There were no Maori conversions up to 1825, and only a few – usually of the moribund – between 1825 and 1830. Ten years later, the Anglicans alone claimed 2,000 communicants and thousands more, adult and child, under instruction in Christianity and the basic skills of literacy.

Crosby also comments on the cargo-cult aspects of literacy:

> The Reverend J. Watkins recorded that some Maori believed that the missionaries had a book called *Puka Kakari* that would render the possessor invulnerable to club or bullet. Others had it that the pakeha possessed a book that would restore the dead to life if placed on the chest of the deceased. Watkins found one

of these books at Waikouaite; it turned out to be a publication called *Norie's Epitome*. But we are carping if we make much of Maori superstition. Whatever their confusion about the nature of the new religion and books, the fact remains that they did not succumb to barren cultism or alcoholism or apathy, but took hold of Christianity and literacy with the same enthusiasm with which they had picked up the musket.

(ibid.: 247)

Similarly vigorous illustrations of the spread of literacy are given by Parr (1963). According to Hohepa (1984: 1), by 1856 'some 90% of the Maori population were able to read and write in their own language; in that year, the numbers of white settlers equalled the total Maori population'. With the ever increasing numerical dominance of the *pakehas*, Maori literacy began to decline, the two principal reasons being:

(i) Disenchantment with literacy and the mission school system, combined with growing suspicion of literacy. It was considered by 'some of the Hokianga chiefs that the Europeans taught the Maoris to figure and write only to encourage them to go to England where they would be killed for their land'.

(Parr 1963: 213)

(ii) The growing importance of the state in Maori education reflected in a changeover to English-medium education from the 1850s onward.

As early as 1853 it was considered by the Auckland school inspectors that it was 'doubtless desirable that the English language should be made a vehicle of instruction exclusively, in cases where it is fully understood, and, as far as can usefully be done, in all cases' (quoted from Parr 1963: 231). An increasing number of Maoris shared this view and by 1867 the government had instituted an English-medium education for all races. English had become both the medium and the message and for generations to come Maoris were discouraged and even punished for using their language at school.

The subsequent history of Maori teaching and the recent changes in attitudes and policies are documented in detail by Benton (1981: 15ff.). Of the many points raised by this author only a few can be mentioned here:

(i) There are no signs whatsoever of a return to a Maori-only literacy; bilingualism and biculturalism in Maori and English

193

(with the latter being the dominant language) represents as much recognition as Maori is likely to gain.

(ii) Maori is the weak language in a diglossic situation dominated by English and a growing number of Maoris speak English only and/or encourage their children to do so.

(iii) The language of the media favoured by the Maori population, namely video, television and printed materials (in that order), is almost exclusively English.

With regard to the last observation, Benton notes that the lack of Maori literature is often used as an argument against formal teaching of this language. He goes on to comment on the familiar issue of 'oral literature':

> Some writers have tried to counter the 'no literature' argument by classifying the rich diversity of orally transmitted material to which Maori-speakers still have access as 'oral literature'. Mr Karetu remarks, for example, that 'the language is rich in oral literature and the fact that it is mainly oral does not make it less than literature'. The main point of this assertion, that what has been transmitted by the spoken word is no less worthy of study than that which has been written down, is in the case of Maori, most certainly true. But labelling what has not yet been written 'literature' is likely to confuse the real issue. This is undoubtedly a case where an application of the Confucian principle of the 'rectification of names' is badly needed. The word 'literature' in normal English has until very recently referred exclusively to written materials. The extension of the term to other kinds of verbal compositions (an aberration perpetrated originally perhaps by certain anthropologists appreciative of the value of oral tradition) does violence to the Latin root of the word – *litteratura* meaning 'alphabet writing', and used in the modern sense of 'that which is written' by Cicero – as well as to the conventional English meaning which was taken directly from Cicero's usage.
>
> Those who claim that Maori has no literature clearly mean that there is nothing of any worth *written down* in the language – so to redefine 'literature' as anything worth reading *or* hearing is to evade rather than to refute the argument.

(ibid.: 26ff.)

What Benton fails to see is the fundamental difference between the pre-contact oral society and the English-dominated literate society.

The role of traditional oratory and other forms of oral expression is changed once and for all by the introduction of literacy, and once written down this oral heritage may provide museum exhibits and objects of scholarly study rather than a living tradition. As Benton observes: 'The future of Maori as a living language is far from assured, although there is now no doubt that it would be greatly honoured as a dead one' (ibid.: 44). The story of Maori literacy is mirrored by the other two large Polynesian languages, Hawaiian and Tahitian. In Hawaii, missionary efforts in promoting vernacular literacy had achieved virtually universal literacy in Hawaiian by 1850. In 1853 the first English-language schools for Hawaiians were set up and by 1892 English had replaced Hawaiian as the language of instruction and literacy, a situation which was made official policy of the Republic of Hawaii in 1896. The vast majority of Hawaiians today are monolingual English speakers and Hawaiian is likely to become the first Polynesian language to become extinct in 'historical' times.

Lavondes (1971: 1100ff.) gives a similar account for Tahitian. By 1829 the majority of Tahitians were literate in their language. However, as early as 1860 the transition of literacy in French had been made, though literacy in Tahitian continues to be of some importance as a result of mission policies to teach religious subjects in the vernacular.

The principal lesson to be learnt from the Polynesian languages is that vernacular literacy typically is transitional literacy; a transition often promoted by the existence of writing systems that incorporate orthographic conventions of the metropolitan languages. One also sees the strong link between literacy and cultural transition: vernacular literacy is typically associated with missionization, whilst metropolitan literacy reflects attempts by colonial and post-colonial governments to bring about social and economic change.

Whilst the developments in Polynesia are now past history, very similar processes can still be observed with the smaller languages of Melanesia. This is the topic of the next section of my paper.

3.2 Literacy in Papua New Guinea

Literacy for the Melanesian and Papuan languages of Papua New Guinea would seem to be different from Polynesian literacy because:

(i) The languages concerned have fewer speakers and are more localized.

(ii) Intermediate between the local vernaculars and the metropolitan language of English we have two widely used and highly developed pidgin languages: Tok Pisin and Hiri Motu.

(iii) Literacy in the majority of instances began rather later and thus had the opportunity to draw on the experience of Polynesia.

One of the earliest local languages that was reduced to writing was Tolai (Kuanua), spoken in the Gazelle Peninsula and surrounding areas of New Britain and New Ireland. This language was used in its written forms by Methodist and Catholic missions as well as the German government. As was the case with other languages used by competing mission societies, orthographic standards which were developed differed sufficiently to make it difficult to read publications of the competing mission.

Early literacy in Tolai concentrated almost entirely on non-indigenous issues – transactions with the German colonial administration and religious instruction. Mosel (1982: 162–3) reports:

> The churches take the credit for having made the people literate. The Imperial judge Schnee reports that at the turn of the century 'to some extent actual written correspondence could be carried on' (Schnee 1904: 102) and published a collection of letters he had received from tribal chiefs (Schnee 1901: 239ff.). To what extent writing was practised for private purposes is unknown, but a small collection of letters written to Rev. H. Fellmann suggests that at least some people were able to write and practised it not only in their dealings with officials. Natives also wrote articles for the Church papers *Nilai Ra Dovot* (Methodist) and *Talaigu* (Catholic), but one can hardly speak of indigenous creative writing in these cases, as the articles followed the pattern of European Christian literature. The only book that has been written by a native in Tolai seems to be the autobiography by Hosea Linge, which was translated into English and published in Australia in 1932. It does not seem to have been printed in Tolai, since Threlfall (1975: 134) certainly would have mentioned it. Thus the only literature offered to the people was Christian literature. It is hard to believe that there were no attempts to have people commit their traditional oral literature to writing. If the Catholic missionaries (Meier 1909, Kleintitschen 1924) had not published the old myths in Germany for anthropological reasons, they would be completely lost today. In 1976 and 1978 I tried to collect old stories, but it was almost impossible to find people who could remember any.

The extent to which Tolai speakers became literate in Tolai is not known. However, what seems to have happened is very much what happened in Polynesia. After an initial peak in Tolai literacy, government education policies subsequently advocated the exclusive use of English and literacy skills in Tolai began to decline. The growth of Tok Pisin literacy, though on a modest scale among the Tolai, further undermined literacy in Tolai. Mosel (1982: 164) observes:

> The writing skills of young Tolai people in their native language are on the decline. Thus, for instance, some of my informants did not know whether to write subject markers and tense-aspect markers separately or in one word, or separated them at the wrong point, e.g. *diala* or *dia la* instead of *diat a* 'they will' (such cases are nevertheless interesting for the linguist, as they give some information on the psychological reality of word boundaries).
>
> One can easily imagine what will happen if people lose interest in going to the church services, where they at least have to read passages from the Bible in Tolai, so that they become familiar with its spelling. The writing skills in English of those who have left school after 'standard six' are – naturally – even worse than their writing skills in Tolai. If nothing is done in the very near future, the English based education will result in two kinds of social classes: a privileged class of those who could go to high school and are literate in English and an underprivileged class of illiterates or semi-illiterates. Two things could be done to prevent illiteracy: either reading and writing in Tolai must be reintroduced as a subject in primary schools, or the children must be taught to read and write in Pidgin, so that they become literate in a language they speak.

4 GENERALIZATIONS

Developments as regards literacy in other larger languages have been very similar and, rather than piling case history upon case history, I shall selectively draw attention to some of the dyseconomies that have arisen out of literacy for the languages and their speakers in the following sub-sections.

4.1 The loss of linguistic heterogeneity

There appears to be a direct relationship between the medium selected and the amount of linguistic variability tolerated. Thus, in oral communication a wide range of dialectal variation can be maintained, whereas literacy tends to favour single-standard languages and computers favour a small number of large international languages. The loss of dialectal variation that goes hand in hand with the introduction of literacy is documented 'between the line' of many reports.

Thus, in the case of the Suau dialect continuum (Cooper 1975), the dialect of Suau Island was singled out as the basis for literacy. Cooper writes:

> Within the speech community, SUAU ISLAND speech is generally regarded as being the 'pure' or 'correct' Suau, and all extant mission publications are based on Suau Island speech. STANDARD SUAU or SUAU ISLAND speech shall designate this form of Suau where such precision is necessary. The term SUAU will sometimes be used as a general term for any of the above terms when no ambiguities would result.
>
> (ibid.: 231)

The same process, whereby a formerly egalitarian situation among language varieties is reduced to a non-egalitarian one where one variety is regarded as more correct or better, can also be observed in the case of Kâte, the main mission lingua franca used among speakers of non-Melanesian languages by the Lutheran Mission (cf. Osmers 1981). Of the five principal dialects of Kâte, the Wemo dialect was chosen as the standard variety by the first missionaries in 1892.

Today, the four other main dialects have all but disappeared (cf. McElhanon 1979). An immediate linguistic consequence is that other dialects are no longer available for internal borrowing or as a source for stylistic effects. Such reduction in variability has made Kâte more dependent on other languages such as Tok Pisin and English. There are indications that the use of Kâte as a literary language has diminished considerably in recent years – partly as a consequence of changed government education policies, partly as a consequence of the speakers' realization that literacy in Kâte did not enable them to participate fully in modern Papua New Guinea society. Very much the same has happened with Yabem, the lingua franca chosen by the

Lutheran Church for speakers of Melanesian languages (see Reinecke 1977).

As observed by Ong (1982: 8): 'Writing gives a grapholect power far exceeding that of any purely oral dialect.'

4.2 The encoding of traditional and expatriate concepts

One of the main themes of this paper so far has been that vernacular literacy in the Pacific is transitional – that is, it appears inevitably to lead to literacy in a non-traditional, typically metropolitan language. It is transitional in a second sense as well: the ideas encoded in written form tend not to be traditional ones but new worldly and religious experiences. A typical illustration is found in Rule's (1977: 390) report on the southern and western Highlands:

> Because, in each tribal group, the Mission began its activities in the earliest days of outside contact, the potential students, who had strong motivation for such activities as hunting, gardening, fishing, trading, discussing and fighting, had no motivation except curiosity for learning to read and write. However, as the areas opened up, some of the men went out to work on the coast in towns and plantations, and as the languages were learned and the Christian message preached, some people became Christians. All the missionaries engaged in literacy work are unanimous that the two dominant motives for desiring literacy have been to maintain communication between those at work and those at home in the village, and to read God's Word for themselves in their own language.

Mosel's remarks on Tolai (given above) underline the principle.

In his inaugural lecture for the Chair of Language at the University of Papua New Guinea, Lynch (1979) criticizes the churches for restricting access to information by failing to produce secular materials in any significant quantity. With regard to the Summer Institute of Linguistics, the principal agents of vernacular literacy, Lynch states:

> We are thus left with the impression that in general, church involvement in literacy and in the providing of information has been very restricted. While a good deal of biblical and religious material has been published in many languages of Melanesia, virtually no secular material has been produced by religious organisations. Literates with next to nothing to read soon revert

to illiteracy, so church policy can be seen to be impractical. But I believe that church policy needs to be criticised more strongly than this: I believe that the churches have generally fallen down on the job of providing education, in its widest sense, to Melanesians.

(ibid.: 5)

It is interesting to note Gudschinsky's observation:

Fortunately, the process of reading need be taught only once. When a person has learned *how* to read, he adds new languages and dialects to his reading repertory by extending the inventory of symbols to which he can respond automatically. Time spent teaching someone to read a minority language is not time lost; he will come to the reading – and speaking – of the second language with enormously greater facility if he already knows what reading is, and is prepared to use it as a tool for learning.

(1968: 150)

Rule (1977: 391) also provides evidence that vernacular literacy leads to literacy in other languages:

The first vernacular literacy class in the Kaluli language was conducted in 1971, Norma Briggs has written:

This class was successful if the flow of letters from the coast is any indication! About half of the class has gone to the coast ... To write an intelligent letter is the test in these parts ... no good going to the coast if you can't write home!

On the other hand, Ivy Lindsay from Suki in the Western Province, where the percentage of literates is very high, reports

Our greatest response came following a convention where there was a real movement of the Spirit of God. The people who came into spiritual blessing had the incentive. Scores of them became good readers.

Other motives have been noted in one or more areas. These are: prestige, the handling of one's own affairs or business, a *stepping-stone to English or Pidgin*, the acquisition of 'education and knowledge, when and where it is offering', and a 'new (i.e., added) interest in life' (both these latter from the populous energetic Huli tribe).

4.3 Literacy and religion

In Rule's article we encounter this commendable statement made in support of vernacular literacy: 'It was recognised that for any person, but especially for a linguistically isolated person, his language is the expression of himself, and the most effective communication is vernacular communication' (ibid.: 388). A similarly laudable aim is expressed in Hooly's statement, in his history of SIL in Papua New Guinea:

> What constitutes improvement will depend very much on the philosophical or other bias of the person judging. Therefore, the people concerned need knowledge of the various options open to them, and their implications, so that they can bring sound judgement to bear on their own culture and decide for themselves whether or not they want to change . . . .
>
> To the extent that the people are denied the knowledge they need, to that extent they are open to exploitation in one way or another. To the extent that new information is available in a language and format primarily understandable only to the young people, the social life of the community will be damaged, even by changes which might otherwise be good.
>
> (1966: 2)

I would like to dispute the underlying 'Heinz 57 varieties' assumption that choice in itself is a good thing; more importantly, it appears that the very medium in which the choice is presented virtually predetermines the selection. Goody (1986: 2ff.) argues:

> While much is held in common, the very general differences between the religions of Africa and Eurasia are worth exploring in the light of their association with oral and literate cultures. This is not only a matter of synchronic contrast. The fact that the word is written in one case and not in the other is important, diachronically, to help account for the characteristic diffusing of the so-called world religions (which in Africa's case are Islam, Christianity and Judaism) by conversion and by absorption, a diffusion that was accompanied by the gradual decline, or should one say incorporation or adjustment, of the local religions.
>
> In the West we inevitably take as models, in courses on comparative religion for example, those that have written texts on myth, doctrine and ritual. These are the world religions, sometimes called the ethical religions. I shall suggest that there

201

is an intrinsic connection between the features of these religions which these epithets imply and the literate mode itself, the means by which religious beliefs and behaviour are formulated, communicated and transmitted, at least in part.

If Goody is correct then the traditional local religions would seem to be incompatible with a literate society, and the introduction of literacy thus necessitates the unchoice of such religions. Put differently, once made literate, users of the local vernaculars can choose between a number of new religions (and derived cargo cults) but not between the old religion and the new. Whether deliberate or not, the emphasis of virtually all mission bodies on literacy has provided them with a powerful tool of conversion and religious indoctrination.

4.4 Literacy and truth

Related to what has been said just now is the question of differential practices in oral and literate societies for the establishment of 'truth'. In oral societies this is related to the authority of the speaker, to the fact that a statement is made over and over again or, as in the case of Meriam Mir of the Torres Straits, to grammatical correctness (Cromwell 1982: 26ff.):

> My focus, therefore, is on a particular way of speaking, the way of speaking which is the '*bar kak mir*' of my title. *Bar kak mir* means, literally, 'curves-without talk'. The man who speaks *bar kak* – who speaks 'without curves' – is the man whose words are true. The man who is educated in the ways of dugong, and in the making of spears, will throw his spear only once, for the spear of the educated man flies true and will strike its target. His spear is said to fly *bar kak*. The man who knows good formal language, and who is educated in the making of speech, need speak only once, for his speech is true. It is these few men who are said to command *bar kak mir*.

Ong (1982: 52) reports the absence of certain types of logical truths from oral societies:

> We know that formal logic is the invention of Greek culture after it had interiorized the technology of alphabetic writing, and so made a permanent part of its noetic resources the kind of thinking that alphabetic writing made possible. In the light of this knowledge, Luria's experiments with illiterates' reactions

to formally syllogistic and inferential reasoning is particularly revealing. In brief, his illiterate subjects seemed not to operate with formal deductive procedures at all – which is not the same as to say that they could not think or that their thinking was not governed by logic, but only that they would not fit their thinking into pure logical forms, which they seem to have found uninteresting. Why should they be interesting? Syllogisms relate to thought, but in practical matters no one operates in formally stated syllogisms.

Numerous writers have reported that printed messages are regarded as inherently true by the first few generations of literates. The editor of the Papua New Guinea newspaper Wantok (in Tok Pisin), Mihalic, observes: 'Our readers tend to take as gospel truth whatever is printed' (1977: 1,122ff.). The fact that most printed materials are of a religious nature and that incipient literates are directed towards taking them as true reinforces this. The power of the printed word thus is considerably greater than in older literate societies.

Taken together, the four points discussed here would seem to indicate that vernacular literacy is potentially as powerful an agent of social change and decline of traditional modes of expression and life as literacy in a metropolitan language. Contrary to what has been claimed by the supporters of literacy programmes, literacy has seldom emerged as a response to needs inherent in traditional societies but has in virtually all instances been used by outsiders to achieve certain objectives.

5 CONCLUSIONS

The main conclusion of this paper is that vernacular literacy is neither a 'tame pursuit' nor a neutral medium for recording pre-existing knowledge and experiences, but rather an agent of linguistic, religious and social change. It is best seen as a transitional phenomenon in all but a few large languages: on the one hand it prepares speakers for transition to reading skills in a non-local (typically metropolitan) language (a process often accelerated by modelling spelling conventions for indigenous languages on those of the metropolitan ones): on the other hand literacy accelerates the transition from traditional to modern (westernized) societies. Past advocates of vernacular literacy in the Pacific have tended to overestimate the benefits and underestimate the dyseconomies of this process. Thus:

(i) Fischer's expectation that 'we should expect *a priori* that the development of literacy and an increase in the size of the speech community would favour both the development of a variety of styles in a language and an increase in vocabulary size and other linguistic resources available for stylistic purposes' (1971: 1.134) is falsified by numerous examples from both Polynesia and Melanesia, including the decline of languages such as Hawaiian and Maori and the contraction of lectal variation on Tolai or Kâte.

(ii) I am not aware of any instances of literacy having helped to preserve traditional values. Literacy has not been a medium for expressing the indigenous point of view.

(iii) I remain sceptical of recent attempts to promote literacy in a vernacular as a means of promoting the identity of users of vernaculars (cf. McKay 1982).

(iv) Inasmuch as vernacular literacy leads to literacy in metropolitan languages and non-literacy in the vernacular, the outcome of literacy campaigns is in all likelihood similar to that deplored by Milner:

> What literacy based on education in English or French threatens, is the eventual disappearance of a whole culture under the social and economic impact of changes brought about by acculturation. When this happens, something painfully and patiently learnt from the experience of one's forebears, something which has stood the test of time, something which is valuable and useful, vanishes. Not only that, something unique and irreplaceable disappears in the chain of cultural evolution, an absolute loss for the total heritage of mankind.
>
> What it is that also disappears, is a whole universe of thought and experience, principally born and transmitted by the possession of a different language, of a separate philosophy. It is also poetry and song, music and art. If all that vanishes with the language, mankind must be the poorer for it. If our type of introduced education accelerates this process, are we not destroying their cultural roots, their history and memories? It is of course those very cultures which are transmitted orally that are most directly threatened: it is the frail vessel of a mainly unwritten language which is the essential vehicle of continuity.
>
> (1984: 17)

(v) The views of the principal organization promoting literacy in the Pacific, the Summer Institute of Linguistics, would seem to be particularly questionable. I find it hard to agree with its aims, as expressed by Franklin (1975: 139): 'The goals of SIL centre upon three distinct, but closely related areas: linguistics, literacy and translation. Each of these programmes reflect the dignity of the indigenous people and their languages.' I am led to the conclusion that each of these three activities is likely to lead to the very situation that Franklin (ibid.: 140) would like to avoid: 'if a vernacular is destroyed or allowed to be immersed by a larger cultural group the culture of the smaller group has also efectively been destroyed'. The very process of providing literacy is one of immersion by a larger cultural group.

Thus, if the aim is that of preserving cultures, then the entire enterprise of literacy will have to be rethought. If the aim is to modernize and bring about cultural change then a lot of rethinking will also be necessary. Literacy has in the past promoted numerous invisible-hand processes of culture and language change. If literacy is to benefit the languages of the Pacific, then ways must be found to eliminate the undesirable consequences highlighted in this chapter. Vernacular literacy involves much more than merely devising the optimal orthography for a given language as many linguists would have us believe.

11

Theory of emergence:
towards a historical-materialistic
approach to the history of linguistics
Paul Laurendeau

> How does newness come into the world? How is it born? Of
> what fusions, translations, conjoinings is it made? How does it
> survive, extreme and dangerous as it is?
>   (Salman Rushdie, *The Satanic Verses*, p. 8)

Is it not time to stop viewing linguistics as a solution to the problem of
scientificity in the social sciences?[1] Linguistics is perhaps more of a
problem than a solution. But what sort of problem? We can illustrate
this by a short example. We are back in 1615 in the north-east of the
immense North American continent and here is an anonymous *coureur
de bois* who has decided to leave his infertile French countryside to live
in the forest of Nouvelle-France in order to trade furs. All things
considered, this uneducated man, with no glossary, grammar or even
alphabet to guide him, will in a relatively short while learn the
language of the Indian nations he is trading with.

With what sort of 'theoretical framework' did he operate to obtain
such immediate results in the acquisition of a totally unknown non-
Indo-European language? With what sort of metalanguage did he
grasp the linguistic problems he encountered, a little less than half a
century before the publication of the Port-Royal *Grammaire Générale et
Raisonnée*, a monolingual study of French that a man of his condition
would in any case never have been able – or allowed – to read?
Occurring at a time when linguistics had yet to be conceived, such
historical events lead to the conclusion that there is a very real
problem with the scientific status of this discipline.

The main 'concepts' this *coureur de bois* used to apprehend the
foreign language he was learning would be considered today as
ideological; but the fact is that his praxis brought him to know perfectly
an Indian language which many of today's excellent ethnolinguists do

not know. We are thus approaching the centre of a crucial problem of gnoseology (theory of knowledge).

This simple and concrete fact short-circuits the two main ideologies of gnoseology: *scientism* ('We did *not* know then but we know *now*. Today, we have found the end of knowledge and the end of history' – yet as a matter of fact, the *coureur de bois* did *already* know something); and *agnosticism* ('We will *never* know anyhow. We have found that knowledge and history are an eternal continuum with no step or gap' – whereas as a matter of fact, the *coureur de bois* did *really* know something). It is important to understand the intimate relation between the ideologies of gnoseology and those of history. They cannot be separated. Thus, *scientism* is an anti-historicist position of historical finalism. This means that those who believe in the ultimate power of science also believe that historical reality will not and must not radically change now. And *agnosticism* is a pro-historicist position of historical fatalism. It is the belief that 'things always change' and that 'somebody will always appear with a different idea'. The complexity of reality brings us to reject both of them.

The position proposed here with regard to the question of gnoseology is one of *dialectical materialism* ('By and by we know more, *and* what is to be known has no end'). This position is both anti-scientistic and anti-agnostic. Its consequences are *dialectical*. Historical issues are crucial here also: what we call *knowledge* is both 'true' from the point of view of the historically localized praxis that produces and needs it, and 'false' from the point of view of the system of knowledge resulting from a more highly developed, subsequent historical period. There is a *dialectical fusion and struggle* (a *tension*) of 'ideology' and 'science' in the knowledge of a specific epoch. We mean by *science* a relevant knowledge of a specific reality produced by a praxis confronted with this reality. We mean by *ideology* a reversed consciousness of reality. For example: 'the sun is the centre of the universe' could be called today an *ideological proposition*, although it was not when it was said to people who believed that the earth was the centre of the universe. The *coureur de bois* and the Indian traded together. Their praxis produced a 'scientific' knowledge. It 'worked', and they could talk. And even if they stayed at the level of simple technique, the science of language is totally concerned with the result they obtained. Suppose now that, at a certain time, what they spoke together was a lingua franca, and suppose also that, at that moment, somebody asked them which language they spoke when they traded. It is possible, as specialists of pidgins and creoles put it, that both of them will have believed that he

207

had learned the language of the other. Then the tension (fusion and struggle) between ideology and science appears. They know how to communicate and they try as best they can to explain this knowledge. And even if their explanations about their communicative capacities are wrong, their praxis produces a real 'technical' knowledge. A relevant gnoseology considers such a *tension* between ideology and science in knowledge as the result of historical changes. Also, there is no *a priori* system of representation for gnoseology itself: history reproduces and changes it constantly too.

This brings us to the problem of the history of linguistics. Since linguistics (like any science) is not a disengaged 'free-floating' discipline, there is a close relationship between the dialectical tension of ideology/ science in its content and the historicity of its emergence. As Taylor puts it in Chapter 1, fantastic energy is spent, in contemporary linguistics, in decontextualizing and 'ahistoricizing' the work. This is by no means innocent. My purpose here is to fight this tendency with propositions for *a historical-materialistic approach to the history of linguistics*. Rather than specific results, what I propose is a theoretical and methodological framework that would permit a new approach to problems in the history of the science of language.

There are two main methods of writing the history of an intellectual discipline. The first is *historiography*: the chronological enumeration of intellectual events as if they had a sort of independence from any historicity. The result is the *inversion* of history. The second way is *historicism*: a reaction to the first attitude that puts every intellectual event in direct relation with what could be called its 'anecdotal-historical' context. The result is the *reduction* of history.

It is possible to establish a relation between *historiography* and *scientism*: we are then required to become witnesses to the autonomous so-called 'historical' movement of a 'free-floating' science. It is also possible to establish a relation between *historicism* and *agnosticism*: we then become witnesses to the 'history' of the sordid plots of an institutional discipline that has no real objective knowledge or information to provide.

Consequently, the wealth or heritage of today's historian of linguistics swings between a variety of scientism and a variety of agnosticism. Let's look at some examples.

A case of what I call *historiography* (chronological enumeration of intellectual events as if they had a sort of independence from any historicity) is the following:

[C'est] sur l'enseignement saussurien que purent compter les promoteurs de la phonologie pour étayer leurs théories; la dualité langue/parole avait en effet préparé le terrain ... et, plus encore, l'affirmation 'dans la langue, il n'y a que des différences': toute la phonologie, dont l'élément primaire est la qualité différentielle, s'y trouve en effet en germe.

(It is on Saussurian teaching that the promoters of phonology could rely to establish their theory – the language/speech duality had, in fact, prepared the ground ... and, furthermore, on the affirmation that 'in language, there are only differences': all phonology, in which the primary element is the differential quality, is there in embryo.)

(Leroy 1970: 80–1)

Here, one concept is 'preparing the ground' for the appearance of another: we are in the 'free-floating' world of scientific exchange. When I say that the result of such a presentation is the inversion of history, I mean that the behaviour of social actors appears to be subordinated to the destiny of the ideas they share. The presentation of succeeding linguistic 'schools' is not unlike time-lapse pictures showing the main steps of the eclosion of an intellectual flower.

The opposition historiography/historicism is what we can call a 'theoretical couple'. Theoretical couples are not, in a dialectical analysis of reality, radically opposed. The relation between historiography and historicism is actually more complex: the tension between these two terms leads slowly to a third one. Concretely a discourse like the one quoted above makes, intentionally or not, a partial selection of the reality it describes. But the *dialectical opposite* of what is shown (what is forgotten or hidden or unknown) cannot be completely evacuated. This means that, as in any dialectical reality, we will notice in historiography, as an ideological position of the historian, *the presence of its opposite* (historicism). Actually we also see here the 'promoters of phonology' carefully reading Saussure in search of arguments backing up their new theory. Traces of historical materialism also appear: we somehow manage to understand that the phonologists are in a sense trying to dissimulate the fact that their theory *is emerging from somewhere other than (structuralist) thought.*

In descriptions such as the following we have what I call *historicism*, a reaction to the first attitude which puts every intellectual event in direct relation with what we could call its 'anecdotal-historical' context:

Toute la base formaliste de Saussure, ça ne passait pas pour
Meillet, qui était un réaliste, style IIIe République, alors que
Sechehaye et Bally ont accentué dans le C.L.G. le formalisme de
Saussure [André Martinet, freely quoted by Chevalier and
Encrevé – P.L.]. . . . Jusqu'à sa mort en 1936, Meillet régnait sur
l'Université française pour toute la partie linguistique. Le sort fait
à Guillaume en est un exemple. Il ne serait venu à l'idée de
personne de nommer où que ce soit un linguiste sans l'approbation
de Meillet. Une fois que Meillet avait parlé, on s'écrasait [Jean
Stéfanini, freely quoted by Chevalier and Encrevé – P.L.].
(Although Sechehaye and Bally emphasized Saussure's formalism
in [their edition of] the C[ours de] L[inguistique] G[énérale],
Meillet, a Third Republic realist, found that formalism unacceptable.) Meillet dominated linguistics in French universities
until his death in 1936. Guillaume's fate is an example of that
domination. Nobody would ever have thought of appointing a
linguist without Meillet's approval. Once Meillet had spoken,
everyone followed.

(Chevalier and Encrevé 1984: 61–2)

We are here in the sordid and pragmatic world of gimmick and
institution. The personality of a man in a position of power seems to
be the *nec plus ultra*, explaining what linguistics was and was not in a
specific era. When I say that the result of such a presentation is the
reduction of history, I mean that now the social actors (reduced
generally to 'strong personalities') seem to have a complete control on
the ideas they produce. The historian reproduces here a cartoon-like
world, simplifying social facts to the cartoon character's behaviour.
Here also, we notice in the ideological historian's position the presence of
its opposite – historiography. The 'struggle' between the 'idea' of
formalism and the 'idea' of empiricism or 'realism' is still there,
seemingly 'explained' by the will of the strongest. Finally, traces of
historical-materialism also appear. Some readers might possibly
understand that all this vaudeville is 'in the style of the Third
Republic' – that is, the product of the very peculiar organization of
power at that specific period in the history of a European country.

Historiography, historicism and sometimes a mixture of both seem
to be the main theoretical heritage of today's historian of linguistics.
But it is now time to distance ourselves from this sort of pendular
opposition of two incomplete approaches which do not correctly

apprehend the crucial question of what Crowley (chapter 2) calls external factors, and what I would call *historicity*.

To understand the aims (or duties) of the history of linguistics as we propose them, it is first of all important to explain what we mean by *history* and *science of history*. History is *the development of social structures and struggles as an objective reality, based on the concrete organization of material production*. The science of history is *the science studying the development of social structures and struggles as an objective reality, based on the concrete organization of material production*. The science of history is often mistakenly called 'history' *tout court*. History is the complex reality we produce and at the same time try to study (by the science of history).

According to Marx (*German Ideology*; for quotations and discussion, see Laurendeau 1990: n.2) there is no *history of* politics, law, science, religion and so forth because these realities are (direct or indirect) *emergences* of what we have defined here as history. To understand this important point clearly, we need only to think of tools. Since a thermometer, for instance, is not a living being, would a '*history of the thermometer*'[2] be a serious study without reference to the social system that produces and needs this particular tool and which ameliorates and follows up on the amelioration of *all* technology? Can we seriously speak about an industrial thermometer without speaking about the solution in which it is dipped, of the worker that mixes this solution, of the factory that produces it? What would be the use of a 'Linnean' chronological historiography of thermometers through the ages, or of a complete description of the understandings and misunderstandings of the eminent individuals who shaped thermometers in the course of world evolution? What would be the interest of a 'history' of the thermometer that was not a *historicization* of this tool? We can apply the same argument to more sophisticated institutions and theories – and, of course, to linguistics.

In the theoretical framework proposed here, 'history of linguistics' is nothing but a mistaken, albeit habitual, use of the expression 'history'. Logically, we should say 'historicization of linguistics'. This *historicization* of linguistics, as a subdivision of the *science of history*, is limited to the knowledge of the relations between the ideological and/ or scientific reality of linguistics *and* the objective reality of *history*. This includes many things.

Because knowledge is something rather more sophisticated than a simple tool, we must operate within the framework of a *historical problematic* reflecting the positions presented above about the question of gnoseology. The problematic can be formulated as follows: we have

211

to deal with the problem of an intellectual discipline that has no independence at all from *history* and its ups and downs, and that can bring us *by and by* to a true objective knowledge of reality. The aim of the historian of the science of language is to make this 'by and by' clear – that is, to highlight the complex dialectical relationship between this *dependence* and *independence*.

To summarize, the history of linguistics should be neither historiography nor historicism, but the *historicization* of this intellectual discipline. This implies certain theoretical positions about history. Historical materialism provides the general framework for the *theory of emergence*. This theory sees in every school of linguistics an indirect and relatively autonomous product of concrete socio-historical contexts, and tries to describe the *emergence* of a linguistic school, proceeding backwards from its established results towards the complete mix of its theoretical *and* matrial sources.

All intellectual representation (ideology, theory, science) is, from the historical point of view, an *emergence* erupting from history – from the specific conditions of the praxis of a given society. The phenomenon, as an emergence, appears in an 'already given' context. We can imagine it as the emergence of a liquid or a wave, keeping in mind that this is just a useful representation and not a *reification* of our very complex problem. It takes an expansion, and the intensity and limits of this expansion have to be studied. The wider this expansion, the more the emergence will dissolve and blend with its surroundings (see Cameron in Chapter 4 on the emergence of sociolinguistics and its expansion).

As an emergence, an intellectual phenomenon has also a source or a group of sources which must be found. But the phenomenon remains, even if these sources have dried up, especially if it combines harmoniously with new emergences coming from new sources. These combinations could lead us to believe in the autonomy of the emergences. Also, the main institutional sources of the phenomenon could lead us to believe in their direct historicity.

An emergence is always *in contradiction* with other emergences. An emergence is *always* the collective product of those who make it and of those who accept it. Thus nothing is direct and nothing is simple (Françoise Gadet and Michel Pêcheux make useful preliminary remarks about the phenomenon of emergence: see Laurendeau 1990).

No work has yet been produced in the theory of emergence, but some research is fairly close to its aims. For example, Chervel (1981) describes the emergence of French school grammar (*grammaire scolaire*). The main source of the emergence is the school apparatus. A certain number of *contradictions* are analysed: the contradiction between the speculative grammars of the seventeenth and eighteenth centuries and the teaching of writing (especially orthography) in the nineteenth century: the contradiction between the rigidity of what was taught and the evolution of the French language. The traces of these contradictions in the school grammar take the form of its *eclecticism* (on this theoretical concept, see Laurendeau 1990) and this eclecticism gives us a clue as to the *practical* nature of the emergence. We see it clearly in the description of the activity of the nineteenth-century schoolmaster provided by Chervel.[3] The ideological (that is, reversed) conception of an idealistic, elitist grammar imposed on the people by an oligarchy is replaced by the description of a situation where the collective and gradual praxis of teaching/learning 'French' (that is a certain spelling of French, according to the belief that orthography *is* language) appears as the real objective force that produced the school grammar.

Chervel's method is internal, comparative and diachronic. He works on a corpus of grammars of the nineteenth and twentieth centuries and describes the evolution of a certain number of grammatical categories. The different 'grammars' reveal themselves as successive versions of an incomplete and hesitating description of the reality of language. This historian understands a very important methodological point: a *concrete* analysis in history of linguistics begins by the analysis of the discourse of linguists or grammarians.

The conclusions of Chervel are agnostic and polemic: to him, school grammar is nothing but the ideology of a conformism actualized in the teaching of orthography. With the critical framework we now have, we know in which way this analysis should be completed. It is impossible to say that under the myth of grammar there was absolutely no knowledge at all. This repressive and narrow framework was for decades the only locus of a 'theoretical' reflexion about the French language. A second volume of the history of the school grammar should now be written, describing how, through polemics and social struggles, some sort of knowledge and science managed to preserve itself under the power of the tenants of traditional grammar. But to do so the method of Chervel should probably be modified.

These methodological problems are absolutely crucial and there is no golden rule on this point. I will mention certain methodological elements which the theory of emergence must look for in the actual works of historians of linguistics. Because I consider that the historicization of linguistics will not be done by historians introducing themselves to linguistics but rather by linguists introducing themselves to the science of history, I suggest that the starting point of such an historicization be the *dialectical questioning of linguistics itself* (see Laurendeau 1990). Analysed – in the first stages – from the dialectical viewpoint (Goldmann 1959: 26–44 proposed elements of method for such an analysis; see also Laurendeau 1986b), linguistics appears as the theatre of theoretical or methodological contradictions that will reveal themselves – in the second and third stages – as very complex transpositions of the ideological and material conflicts of the historical period (see, for example, Chervel's conclusions on the *eclecticism* of the school grammar). Another example is the emergence of history as an epistemological factor in a number of nineteenth-century disciplines such as biology, political economy and linguistics. Here, there is a complex relation with the events of this period, especially colonialist conquests and revolutions.

Above all, the approach to the linguistics *text* will be very important (cf. Joseph, Chapter 3). There are two ways of approaching a text. We have the 'first-degree' approach (where the text tends to be taken for itself or for what it speaks about) and the 'second-degree' approach (where it tends to be taken as the reflection of something else or something more than itself or what it speaks about).

In the 'first degree' approach we notice two attitudes. The first one is *either* scholastic *or* polemic. We consider the content of the text as a complete truth (or as something to deal with as if it were the truth) and try to respect it (or to at least show that we respect it), *or* we consider the content of the text as completely false (or as something to deal with as if it were completely false) and try to deny it (or to at least show that we deny it). To this pendular couple is opposed the second attitude: *critique*.

In the 'second-degree' approach we also notice two attitudes. The first one is *either* documentary *or* symbolic. We consider the text as a source of information: not a direct one, as if it were a morning newspaper, but one that is indirect and more or less unintentional (we deal with it as if it were a newspaper of 1850, providing lots of detailed information about how people lived at that time), *or* we consider the text as a system of indirect but more or less intentional coding (the symbols) that can be analysed with reference to specific cultural representations. To this pendular couple is also opposed a second attitude: *hermeneutic*.

The critical attitude is the overtaking of the scholastic/polemic attitude while the hermeneutic attitude is the overtaking of the documentary/symbolic attitude. The old concepts of 'critique' and 'hermeneutic' are, of course, completely reactualized in a dialectical-materialistic way by the theory of emergence. We mean by *critique* a 'first-degree' reading that postulates the tension between science and ideology in every intellectual product, and that looks less for what-is-true-and-what-is-false than for the manifestations of the *struggle* between positions. Conversely, we mean by *hermeneutic* a 'second-degree' reading that does not look for *data* or *symbols* . . . but for *clues* of a socio-historical reality in the text. *The passage from a (dialectical) critique to a (materialistic) hermeneutic is the global method proposed by the theory of emergence.*

The search for contradictions is therefore one of the main purposes of the theory of emergence. Let us not forget that, as a dialectical approach, the theory of emergence does not carry the negative view of contradiction that is the running gag of all discourse wishing to be 'scientific'. As Marxist thought puts it, we should not be surprised, when we search for the essence of things, to encounter more and more contradictions . . . because contradiction *is* the essence of things.

The first type of contradiction the theory of emergence will look for is contradiction within linguistic theory. One can then notice two main facts. First, certain linguistic theories present themselves as ideologically independent and yet are dependent on what I have called an *implicit philosophy* (Laurendeau 1986a: 8–22; Crowley in Chapter 2 discusses the positivist background of synchronic linguistics). Even the complete lack of a theoretical framework is itself an implicit philosophy, and perhaps not the best one (cf. the social theory of Labov as presented by Cameron in Chapter 4). Secondly, certain linguistic theories present themselves as completely subordinated to a philosophical system and yet are strongly original and independent. This is often the case of what I have called *scholastic strategies*: (Laurendeau 1986a: 763) functionalist or generativist on the surface, something quite different in the study itself. The point to keep in mind is that a linguistic theory tends always to negate its heritage and itself. The mechanism of this negation is the key that brings us to the source of the emergence.

At a second level, the set of contradictions to look for could be those between linguistic institutions as reflected by 'theoretical oppositions'. A good example of such an investigation is Coste (1987). In this study, the author describes the recent emergence of the structure of *the teaching of French as a foreign language* (related to the French state apparatus) and the older emergence of *linguistics* (related to the

French university). He also analyses from a sociohistorical point of view the struggle of the defenders of each between 1945 and 1975. This period is considered a moment of strong mutation in the study and teaching of the French language in France. For *French as a foreign language*, Coste speaks of *emergence*, whereas for *university linguistics*, he speaks of 'profound alterations'. A complex contradiction appears between different approaches.

Applied linguistics is interpreted by the author as a zone of contact and transition, as some kind of 'turbulent interface' between the two entities, which are themselves unsettled. Coste explains that this may give rise to attempts to stabilize which can be interpreted as wishes to take control but which are never successful. We are then slowly brought from theoretical to social struggles. *French as a foreign language* and *linguistics* have various internal splits. Always, according to Coste, the group of specialists of French as a foreign language looks a little bit like a fuzzy television set, intermediate and of recent affirmation, like the set of managers. Interests and directions differ widely among sub-groups. Also, in the case of the university linguists, their somewhat less global categorizations (distinguishing, for example, the 'French specialists', the 'foreign-language specialists', the 'Indo-Europeanists', and the 'functionalists') reveal a greater variety in how the relation between linguistics and language teaching is conceived and practised (from BUSCILA 1988: 44–5).

There are various methodological consequences of Coste 1987. The main 'theoretical' contradiction is described here as a set of smaller contradictions, and the global comprehension of this complex system appears as the first step leading to the sociohistorical source of the emergence. Chervel could be quoted as an honest example of what I mean by dialectical critique. Coste is a good example of what I call materialistic hermeneutics.

We began with inner contradictions in a theory, then contradictions between social groups represented by their champions and their theoretical approaches. This brings us to the contradictions between linguistic theory and historical reality, as exemplified by Jucquois (1989) in his study of comparativism.

Jucquois says that the emergence of comparativism cannot occur without the historical possibility for comparison, *but* the theory of comparativism will finally fade out even if these possibilities continue to grow. In order to clarify the understanding of linguistic comparativism, he introduces the necessity for a wide and general investigation of the manifestations of the comparativist attitude and mentality. He notices

216

then that they 'emerged very progressively' in the history of the western world and developed only during modern times. He also considers that the archaeology of comparativism reveals the conditions which have led to its apparition and development. He holds that these conditions are closely linked with the perception and use of language in a specific society, namely in a 'democracy' (*sic* – I would rather say 'an imperialism') and therefore necessarily imply the perception of some irreducible pluralism which is itself related to the very nature of language and of contemporary social reality (from BUSCILA 1988: 49). The last methodological elements I want to mention are then introduced: general intellectual context and its socio-historical ground.

To summarize the methodological framework resulting from the theoretical propositions and the examples of historical studies discussed, I propose the following six steps in the historicization of the emergence of a linguistic 'theory':

(i) Internal dialectical critique I: non-historiographical approach to the main inner theoretical contradictions.

Description of the 'struggles of ideas' as noticed inside the theory, search for contradictions, changes, eclecticism, movements, etc.

(ii) Materialistic hermeneutic I: Non-historicist approach to the theory's immediate external context.

Description of the 'who's who' of this theory. Schools and scholars, bibliographical elements, etc. Hermeneutic of 'trivial' information.

(iii) Internal dialectical critique II: description of the theory's polemic/scholastic and documentary/symbolic dimensions.

Description of what the 'struggle of ideas' in the theory reveals about its relations with other theories. What (who) is it in agreement/opposition with. Who (what) does it consider as bringing good 'cash' documentary information; who (what) does it interpret and how.

(iv) Materialistic hermeneutic II: description of the 'sociointellectual' horizon.

Description of the ideological/scientific horizon of the period when the theory emerged and of its influence on the school that defends the theory.

(v) Internal dialectical critique III: delimitation of the intellectual borders of the emergence.

217

Description of what the theory speaks about, what it hides, what it forgets, what it could never have known, what it introduces and what it speaks about because we 'have to' speak about it. What was before that it does (not) consider. What will come after that it will (not) influence.

(vi) ·Materialistic hermeneutic III: historicization.

On the basis of all these data, description of the possibility/ necessity of the emergence of that very specific theory, according to the sociohistorical means and limits of the epoch considered.

In conclusion, we can say that there are two sorts of history: history of actions, and history of processes. The emergence of a new linguistic theory is always the result of actions *and* processes in a society. We cannot do all of the historical work and, as historians of sciences of language, we are obligated to focus on the emergence, its sources, its scopes, its limits. If we only keep in mind that what we study is only a partial phenomenon, merely a *part of the problem*, we will naturally be brought back to our initial problematic: the dialectical reality of the dependence/independence of linguistics and history. We will then begin to understand that if *history* and *linguistics* are so slow at producing 'results', our work can only be . . . slower.

NOTES

1 This text was presented in December 1988 at the NAAHoLS meeting in Tulane University, New-Orleans. I would like to thank for their precious help Karen Whalen, David Walker and Maurice Blanchard of York University, Ludmila Bovet of Université Laval, George Wolf of Tulane University, and Agnès Lebeau. I would like to give special thanks to Talbot Taylor who criticized this text in a very relevant way and helped me to turn it into something accessible for Anglo-American readers.

2 In 1902, Father A. Tougard, in his preface to Maze (1903), explained that the author of this glossary was working by the year 1899 on an essay titled *Histoire du thermomètre*. According to a passage of a letter quoted in Maze (1903: X–XI) the main purpose of the historian, in the first part of this 'history' of the thermometer, was to refute the arguments of a certain Caverni who pretended that Galileo was the inventor of the thermometer. Maze considered that the real inventor of this tool was the Venetian Doctor Santorio (1561–1636), and to prove it he seems to have done a very sophisticated hermeneutic study of the seventeen volumes of Galileo's works. It is important to notice that, despite achieving a certain 'demythologization' of a historical figure, such research seems more like a lawsuit establishing authorship than a study of history. And it is also important to note that knowledge of the historical emergence of a technical artifact like the thermometer in the Italian Renaissance is not fundamentally changed

if we know that the exact name of its inventor is Santorio instead of Galileo. This was the nineteenth century, but are historians of linguistics doing things very differently today?

3 Chervel describes the activity of the nineteenth-century French school-master as follows:

> La grammaire n'est [au XIXe siècle] pas autre chose, pour le maître, qu'un procédé pédagogique.
>
> Aussi est'il tout prêt à en changer si on lui propose une méthode plus efficace. D'ailleurs, s'il a un peu d'imagination, c'est lui-même qui va introduire des modifications, récrire sa grammaire, pour son usage personnel d'abord, en remplir des cahiers, de son écriture fine et penchée. Tous ses doutes, tous ses tracas, toutes ses trouvailles pédagogiques y prennent leur place. A-t-il un peu d'ambition, brigue-t-il l'école normale ou un poste d'inspecteur: il la publie, et va faire le siège de ses supérieurs hiérarchiques pour obtenir l'inscription de son livre sur la liste des manuels autorisés dans le département.
>
> Évidemment ses mobiles ne sont pas d'ordre spéculatif. Car l'intérêt du maître, c'est d'abord que ses élèves aprennent l'ortho-graphe. En dépend son maintient dans le poste 'lorsqu'il est au service d'une communauté villageoise, ou sa promotion (. . .).
>
> Fondamental est le rôle des élèves dans ce tête-à-tête, ce corps à corps pédagogique par lequel le maître les oblige à assimiler les principes de l'orthographe, et qui aboutit à la lente mise en place de la deuxième grammaire scolaire. Certains l'ont bien vu, tel Vanier, qui présente ainsi sa *Grammaire pratique à l'usage des écoles primaires*: 'Ce petit ouvrage n'est ni le fruit de longues veilles, ni le résultat de profondes méditations; ce sont mes élèves qui me l'ont inspiré . . . '.

(Grammar [in the nineteenth century] was nothing else for the teacher, than a pedagogical procedure.

Thus he was always ready to change his grammar if somebody suggested a more efficient method. And he was even able, if he had a little imagination, to make some alterations and rewrite his grammar, first for personal use, filling notebooks with his fine slating handwriting. All his doubts, all his worries, all of his pedagogical discoveries would be realized there. And if he had a little ambition and wished to apply for the position of professor at the *école normale* or for that of teaching inspector, he would have it published, and harrass his superiors until he succeeded in having his own book listed among the manuals authorized by the department.

His incentives were evidently not of a speculative kind, since the main concern of the teacher was first and foremost that his students learn orthography. On this depended the retention of his position, if he was at the service of a village community, or his promotion . . . .

The role of the students was fundamental in this pedagogical *tête à tête* or struggle in which the teacher had them assimilate the basic principles of orthography and which eventually led to the slow establishment of the new school grammar. Some saw this clearly, such as Vanier, who wrote in the foreword to his *Grammaire pratique à l'usage des écoles primaires*: 'This little book is neither the result of long nights of work, nor the consequence of profound meditations; it was inspired by my students . . .').

(Chervel 1981: 97)

Bibliography

Aarsleff, H. (1967) *The Study of Language in England, 1780–1860*, 2nd edn. 1983, Minneapolis: University of Minnesota Press.

—— (1982) *From Locke to Saussure: Essays on the Study of Language and Intellectual History*, Minneapolis: University of Minnesota Press.

—— (1988) 'Introduction', in Wilhelm von Humboldt, *On Language. The Diversity of Human Language-Structure and its Influence on the Mental Development of Mankind*, trans. P. Heath, Cambridge: Cambridge University Press, pp. vii–lxv.

Allou, C. (1828) *Essai sur l'universalité de la langue française*, Paris: Didot; Mans: Belon.

Auroux, S. (1986) 'La Synonymie et la contrainte de la science: Roubaud 1785', in *Autour de Féraud: La lexicographie en France de 1762 à 1835*, Paris: Ecole Normale Supérieure de Jeunes filles, pp. 73–81.

Bacon, F. (1857) *Novum Organum*, vol. 1, *Works of Francis Bacon*, ed. and trans. J. Spedding and R. Ellis, London: Routledge.

—— (1861) *Of the Proficience and Advancement of Learning*, ed. G. W. Kitchen, London: Bell & Daldy.

Baker, G., and Hacker, P. (1984) *Language, Sense and Nonsense*, Oxford: Blackwell.

Bakhtin, M. (1981) *The Dialogic Imagination*, ed. M. Holquist, trans. C. Emerson and M. Holquist, Austin: University of Texas Press.

Baldensperger, F. (1907) 'Comment le XVIIIe siècle expliquait l'universalité de la langue française', in Baldensperger, *Etudes d'histoire littéraire*, Paris: Hachette, pp. 1–54.

Bally, C. (1952) *Le Langage et la vie*, new edn, Geneva: Droz; Lille: Giard.

Barnouw, A. J. (1934) *Language and Race Problems in South Africa*, The Hague: Nijhoff.

Barny, R. (1978) 'Les Mots et les choses chez les hommes de la Révolution française', *La Pensée* 202: 96–115.

Bartoli, M., and Bertoni, G. (1928) *Breviario di neolinguistica*, Modena: STM.

Batteux, C. (1748) 'Lettres sur la phrase françoise comparée avec la phrase latine', in Batteux, *Cours de belles lettres*, vol. 2, Paris.

Belcher, R. (1987) 'Afrikaans en kommunikasie oor die kleurgrens', in H. du Plessis and L. T. du Plessis (eds) *Afrikaans en taalpolitiek*, Pretoria: HAUM, pp. 16–34.

221

Bembo, P. (1525) *Prose della volgar lingua. Prose e rime*, ed. C. Dionisòtti, 2nd edn 1966, Torino: UTET.

Bengtsson, S. (1968) *La Défense organisée de la langue française*, Uppsala: Acta Universitatis Upsaliensis.

Benton, R. A. (1981) *The Flight of the Amokura*, Wellington: New Zealand Council for Educational Research.

Bloomfield, L. (1914) *An Introduction to the Study of Language*, New York: Holt.

—— (1923) Review of F. de Saussure (1922) *Cours de linguistique générale*, *Modern Language Journal* 8: 317–19. Rep. in C. Hockett (ed.)

—— (1970) *A Leonard Bloomfield Anthology*, Bloomington: Indiana University Press, pp. 106–8.

—— (1926) 'A set of postulates for linguistic analysis', *Language* 2: 153–64. Rep. in C. Hockett (ed.) (1970) *A Leonard Bloomfield Anthology*, Bloomington: Indiana University Press, pp. 128–38.

—— (1927) 'On recent work in general linguistics', *Modern Philology* 25: 211–30. Rep. in C. Hockett (ed.) (1970) *A Leonard Bloomfield Anthology*, Bloomington: Indiana University Press, pp. 173–90.

—— (1933) *Language*, New York: Holt, Rinehart & Winston.

Bodine, A. (1975) 'Androcentrism in prescriptive grammar', *Language in Society* 4: 129–46.

Boshoff, S. P. E. (1921) *Volk en taal van Suid-Afrika*, Pretoria: De Bussy.

Bosman, D. B. (1916) *Afrikaans en Maleis-Portugees*, Groningen: P. Noordhoff.

—— (1923) *Oor die ontstaan van Afrikaans*, Amsterdam: Swets & Zeitlinger.

Bouillier, F. (1854) *Histoire de la philosophie cartésienne*, Paris: Durand; Lyon: Brun.

Bourgaux, L. (1963) *Clarté et prestige de la langue française*, Gembloux: Duculot.

Brown, P., and Levinson, S. (1987) *Politeness*, Cambridge: Cambridge University Press.

Brunot, F. (1927–37) *Histoire de la langue française. Des origines à nos jours.* T. VI, *Le XVIIe siècle*, 4 vols; T. VII, *La Propagation du français en France jusqu'à la fin de l'Ancien Régime*; T. IX, *La Révolution et l'Empire*, 2 vols, Paris: Colin.

BUSCILA (1988) *Bulletin des sciences du langage*, vol. 19, 3. Paris: Association des Sciences du Langage.

Busse, W. (1985) 'François-Urbain Domergue (1744–1810). Kommentierte Bibliographie', *Historiographia linguistica* 12: 165–88.

—— (1986a) ' "La Langue française est un besoin pour tous." A propos du jacobinisme linguistique', in W. Busse and J. Trabant (eds). Benjamins, pp. 343–72.

—— (1986b) 'La Syntaxe à la fin du XVIIIe siècle: La *Grammaire générale analytique* d'Urbain Domergue (an VII)', *Actes du XVIIe Congrès international de linguistique et philologie romanes*, vol. 1, *Linguistique générale et linguistique romane. Histoire de la grammaire*, Aix-en-Provence: Université de Provence, pp. 401–14.

Busse, W., and Trabant, J. (eds) (1986) *Les Idéologues. Sémiotique, théories et politiques linguistiques pendant la Révolution française*, Amsterdam and Philadelphia: Benjamins.

Cairns, H., and Cairns, C. (1976) *Psycholinguistics*, New York: Holt, Rinehart & Winston.

BIBLIOGRAPHY

Cappagli, A., and Pieraccini, A. M. (1985) 'Sugli inediti grammaticali di Claudio Tolomei. I. Formazione e storia del manoscritto senese', *Rivista di letteratura italiana* 3: 387–411.

Carle, R., *et al.* (1982) *Gava* (Festschrift Kähler), Berlin: Reimer.

Carlyle, T. (1837) *The French Revolution*, 3 vols, London: Chapman.

Catach, N. (1968) *L'Orthographe française à l'époque de la Renaissance. Auteurs – Imprimeurs – Ateliers d'imprimerie*, Geneva: Droz.

Cellard, J. (1971–2) 'Français, franglais, Europe'. *Le Monde. Sélection hebdomadaire 1971–1972*, p. 14.

Chafe, W. L. (1970) *Meaning and the Structure of Language*, Chicago: University of Chicago Press.

Chantreau, P.-N. (1790) *Dictionnaire national et anecdotique*, Paris.

Chervel, A. (1981) *Histoire de la grammaire scolaire*, Paris: Payot.

Cheshire, J. (1984) 'The relationship between language and sex in English', in P. Trudgill (ed.) *Applied Sociolinguistics*, London: Academic Press.

Chevalier, J.-C. (1968) *Histoire de la syntaxe. Naissance de la notion de complément dans la grammaire française (1530–1750)*, Geneva: Droz.

Chevalier, J.-C., and Encrevé, P. (1984) 'La création de revues dans les années '60 – Matériaux pour l'histoire récente de la linguistique en France', *Langue française* 63: 57–102.

Chomsky, N. (1962) 'The logical basis of linguistic theory', in *Preprints of Papers from the Ninth International Congress of Linguists*, 27–31 August, Cambridge, Mass., pp. 509–74.

—— (1963) 'Formal properties of grammars', in R. D. Luce, R. R. Bush and E. Galanter (eds) *Handbook of Mathematical Psychology*, New York and London: Wiley, pp. 322–418.

—— (1964a) 'The logical basis of linguistic theory', in H. Lunt (ed.) *Proceedings of the Ninth International Congress of Linguists*, The Hague: Mouton, pp. 914–78.

—— (1964b) 'Current issues in linguistic theory', in J. A. Fodor and J. Katz (eds) *The Structure of Language: Readings in the Philosophy of Language*, Englewood Cliffs, NJ: Prentice-Hall, pp. 211–45.

—— (1964c) *Current Issues in Linguistic Theory*, The Hague and Paris: Mouton.

—— (1965) *Aspects of the Theory of Syntax*, Cambridge, Mass.: MIT Press.

—— (1966) *Cartesian Linguistics: A Chapter in the History of Rationalist Thought*, New York and London: Harper & Row.

—— (1968) *Language and Mind*, 2nd edn 1972, New York: Harcourt Brace Jovanovich.

—— (1979) *Language and Responsibility*, trans. J. Viertel, New York: Pantheon. Orig. publ. as *Dialogues avec Mitsou Ronat*, Paris: Flammarion, 1977.

—— (1980) *Rules and Representations*, New York: Columbia University Press.

—— (1986) *Knowledge of Language: Its Nature, Origin, and Use*, New York: Praeger.

Christiaens, V. (1986) 'Etude sur la "Grammaire françoise simplifiée élémentaire" de F.-U. Domergue', unpublished MA thesis, Louvain.

Cittadini, C. (1601) *Trattato della vera origine, e del processo, e nome della nostra lingua, scritto in vulgar sanese* and *Trattato de gli articoli, e di alcune altre particelle della vulgar lingua*, intro. G. Schlemmer, 1983 facsimile, Hamburg: Buske.

—— (1628) *Le origini della toscana fauella: Riuedute, e riformate da lui stesso*, Siena: E. Gori.

—— (1721) *Degli idiomi toscani. Opere di Celso Cittadini gentiluomo sanese con varie altre del medesimo non più stampate*, ed. G. Gigli, Roma: Antonio de' Rossi.

Clément, L. (1898) *Henri Estienne et son oeuvre française*, Paris: Picard.

Clerk, C. (ed.) (1984) *The Effects of Development on Traditional Pacific Island Cultures*, London: Royal Commonwealth Society.

Combrink, J. (1978) 'Afrikaans: Its origin and development', in L. W. Lanham and K. P. Prinsloo (eds) *Language and Communication Studies in South Africa*, Oxford and Cape Town: Oxford University Press, pp. 69–95.

Conradie, C. J. (1986) *Taalgeskiedenis*, Pretoria and Cape Town: Academica.

Cooper, R. E. (1975) 'Coastal Suau: A preliminary study of internal relationships', in T. E. Dutton (ed.) *Studies in Languages of Central and South-East Papua*, Canberra: Pacific Linguistics C–29, pp. 227–78.

Coseriu, E. (1978) 'Das sogenannte "Vulgärlatein" und die ersten Differenzierungen in der Romania: Eine kurze Einführung in die romanische Sprachwissenschaft', in R. Kontzi (ed.) *Zur Entstehung der romanischen Sprachen*, Darmstadt: Wissenschaftliche Buchgesellschaft.

Coste, D. (1987) 'Institution du français langue étrangère et implications de la linguistique appliquée: Contribution à l'étude des relations entre linguistique et didactique des langues de 1945 à 1975', unpublished thèse d'État, Université de Paris VII.

Cowan, J. M. (1987) 'The whimsical Bloomfield', *Historiographia linguistica* 14: 23–37.

Craik, G. L. (1861) *A Compendious History of English Literature, and of the English Language*, London: Griffin, Bohn, & Co.

Cromwell, L. G. (1982) 'Bar Kak Mir. To talk with no curves', *Anthropological Forum* 5, 1: 24–37.

Crosby, A. W. (1986) *Ecological Imperialism: The Biological Expansion of Europe 900–1900*, Cambridge: Cambridge University Press.

Dannequin, C. (1988) 'Les Enfants baillonnés' ['Gagged children'], *Language and Education* 1: 15–31.

Darmesteter, A. (1875) *Traité de la formation des mots composés dans la langue française comparée aux autres langues romanes et au latin*, Paris: Franck.

Dauzat, A. (1926) *La Langue française, sa vie, son évolution*, Paris: Stock.

—— (1947) *Le Génie de la langue française*, Paris: Payot.

Davies, J. (1855) 'On the races of Lancashire', *Transactions of the Philological Society*, pp. 210–84.

De Certeau, M., Julia, D., and Revel, J. (1975) *Une Politique de la langue. La Révolution française et les patois*, Paris: Gallimard.

De Mauro, T. (1972) Edn of Saussure (1916) *Cours de linguistique générale*, Paris: Payot. Originally published in Italian, 1967. French trans. of De Mauro's notes by L.-J. Calvet.

den Besten, H. (1978) 'Cases of possible syntactic interference in the development of Afrikaans', in P. Muysken (ed.) *Amsterdam Creole Studies II*, Publikaties van het Instituut voor Algemene Taalwetenschap 20, Amsterdam: University of Amsterdam, pp. 5–56.

—— (1981) 'Marking WH-movement in Afrikaans', in P. Muysken (ed.) *Generative Studies on Creole Languages*, Dordrecht: Foris, pp. 141–79.

—— (1985) 'Die doppelte Negation im Afrikaans und ihre Herkunft', in N. Boretzky, W. Enninger and T. H. Stolz (eds) *Akten des I. Essener Kolloquiums über Kreolsprachen und Sprachkontakte vom 26.1.1985 an der Universität Essen*, Bochum: Studienverlag Dr. Brockmeyer, pp. 9–42.

—— (1986) 'Double negation and the genesis of Afrikaans', in P. Muysken and N. Smith (eds) *Universals Versus Substrata in Creole Genesis*, Amsterdam: Benjamins, pp. 185–230.

—— (1987a) Review of E. H. Raidt (1983) *Einführung in Geschichte und Struktur des Afrikaans*, *Journal of Pidgin and Creole Languages* 2: 67–92.

—— (1987b) 'Het Afrikaans: mag het ietsje meer Zuid-Afrika zijn?', *Onze taal* 56, 2/3: 24–5.

Denes, P. B., and Pinson, E. N. (1973) *The Speech Chain*, 2nd edn, Garden City, NY: Anchor

Denina, C. (1785) 'Sur le caractère des langues et particulièrement des modernes', edn in C. Marazzini (ed.) (1985) *Carlo Denina: Storia delle lingue e polemiche linguistiche. Dai saggi berlinesi 1783–1804*, Alessandria: Edizioni dell'Orso, pp. 5–34.

—— (1797) 'Observations sur les dialectes, particulièrement sur ceux d'Italie', edn in C. Marazzini (ed.) (1985) *Carlo Denina: Storia delle lingue e polemiche linguistiche. Dai saggi berlinesi 1783–1804*, Alessandria: Edizioni dell'Orso, pp. 39–63.

—— (1803) 'Lettera al cittadino La Villa, Prefetto del Dipartimento del Po', edn in C. Marazzini (ed.) (1985) *Carlo Denina: Storia delle lingue e polemiche linguistiche. Dai saggi berlinesi 1783–1804* Alessandria: Edizioni dell'Orso, pp. 107–12.

Desmarais, C. (1837) *De la littérature française au dix-neuvième siècle, considérée dans ses rapports avec les progrès de la civilisation et de l'esprit national*, 2nd edn, Paris: Société reproductive des bons livres.

De Tocqueville, A. (1856) *L'Ancien Régime et la Révolution*, Paris: Levy.

Diderot, D. (1751) *Lettre sur les sourds et muets*, critical edn by P. H. Meyer, *Diderot Studies* 7 (1965).

Di Franco Lilli, M. C. (1970) *La biblioteca manoscritta di Celso Cittadini*, Città del Vaticano: Biblioteca Apostolica Vaticana.

Dominicy, M. (1984) *La Naissance de la grammaire moderne. Langage, logique et philosophie à Port-Royal*, Bruxelles: Mardaga.

Donaldson, B. C. (1988) *The Influence of English on Afrikaans*, Pretoria: Serva.

Donaldson, J. W. (1839) *The New Cratylus*, Cambridge: Deighton.

Donzé, R. (1967) *La Grammaire générale et raisonnée de Port-Royal. Contribution à l'histoire des idées grammaticales en France*, Berne: Francke.

D'Ovidio, F. (1893) 'Pei plagiarj del Tolomei', *Rassegna bibliografica della letteratura Italiana* 1: 46–9.

Droixhe, D. (1978) *La linguistique et l'appel de l'histoire*, Geneva: Droz.

Droste, F. G., and Joseph, J. E. (eds) (1990) *Linguistic Theory and Grammatical Description: Nine Current Approaches*, Amsterdam and Philadelphia: Benjamins.

Dubois, J. (1962) *Le Vocabulaire politique et social en France de 1869 à 1872, à travers les oeuvres des écrivains, les revues et les journaux*, Paris: Larousse.

du Plessis, H. and du Plessis, L. T. (eds) (1987) *Afrikaans en taalpolitiek*, Pretoria: HAUM.

Duron, J. (1963) *Langue française, langue humaine*, Paris: Larousse.

du Toit, A. (1987) 'Taal, religie en nasionaliteit, 1824–1886', in H. du Plessis and L. T. du Plessis (eds) *Afrikaans en taalpolitiek*, Pretoria: HAUM, pp. 61–70.

du Toit, A. and Giliomee, H. (1983) *Afrikaner Political Thought: Analysis and Documents*, vol. 1, Berkeley, Los Angeles, and London: University of California Press.

du Toit, P. J. (1905) *Afrikaansche Studies*, Ghent: A. Siffer.

Dutton, T. E. (ed.) (1975) *Studies in Languages of Central and South-East Papua*, Canberra: Pacific Linguistics C–29.

Earle, J. (1901) 'The place of English in education', in *An English Miscellany Presented to Dr. Furnivall*, Oxford: Frowde, pp. 62–7.

Eliade, P. (1898) *De l'influence française sur l'esprit public en Roumanie*, Paris: Leroux.

Ellis, A. J. (1869–89) *On Early English Pronunciation*, London: Asher, Trübner.

Engler, R. (1968–74) *Cours de linguistique générale: Édition critique*, Wiesbaden: Harrassowitz.

Estienne, H. (1579) *Proiect du livre intitulé De la precellence du langage François*, Paris: Patisson.

Ewert, A. (1958) *Of the Precellence of the French Tongue*, Oxford: Clarendon.

Faithfull, R. G. (1962) 'Teorie filologiche nell'Italia del primo Seicento con particolare riferimento alla filologia volgare', *Studi di Filologia Italiana* 20: 147–313.

Fasold, R. (1984) *The Sociolinguistics of Society*, Oxford: Blackwell.

February, V. A. (1981) *Mind Your Colour: The 'Coloured' Stereotype in South African Literature*, London and Boston: Routledge & Kegan Paul.

Ferguson, C. A. (1959) 'Diglossia', *Word* 15: 325–40.

Fischer, J. L. (1971) 'Style contrasts in Pacific languages', in T. Sebeok (ed.) *Current Trends in Linguistics* 8: 1,129–62. The Hague: Mouton.

Fishman, J. (1968) 'The sociology of language', in J. Fishman (ed.) *Readings in the Sociology of Language*, The Hague: Mouton.

—— (1986) Review of R. Fasold, *The Sociolinguistics of Society, Language in Society* 15.

Foucault, M. (1966) *Les Mots et les choses. Une archéologie des sciences humaines*, Paris: Gallimard.

—— (1970) *The Order of Things*, London: Tavistock. Trans. of Foucault 1966.

Franken, J. L. M. (1953) *Taalhistoriese bydraes*, Amsterdam and Cape Town: Balkema.

Franklin, K. J. (1975) 'Vernaculars as bridges to cross cultural understanding', in K. A. McElhanon (ed.), pp. 138–55.

Frey, M. (1925) *Les Transformations du vocabulaire français à l'époque de la Révolution, 1789–1800*, Paris: Presses Universitaires de France.

Frings, T. (1953) 'Ursprung und Entwicklung des Afrikaans', *Beiträge zur Geschichte der deutschen Sprache und Literatur* 75: 157–65.

Gal, S. (1979) *Language Shift*, New York: Academic Press.

Gallais, J. P. (1790) *Extrait d'un dictionnaire inutile. Composé par une société en commandite, & rédigé par un homme seul*, Paris.

Garrioch, D. (1987) 'Verbal insults in eighteenth-century Paris', in P. Burke and R. Porter (eds) *The Social History of Language*, Cambridge: Cambridge University Press.

Gauger, H. M. (1973) *Die Anfänge der Synonymik: Girard (1718) und Roubaud (1785). Ein Beitrag zur Geschichte der lexikalischen Semantik*, Tübingen: Narr.

Girard, G. (1747) *Les Vrais principes de la langue françoise*, new edn with an intro. by P. Swiggers, 1982, Geneva: Droz.

Godel, R. (1957) *Les Sources manuscrites du Cours de linguistique générale de F. de Saussure*, Geneva: Droz; Paris: Minard.

Goebl, H. (1982) *Dialektometrie. Prinzipien und Methoden des Einsatzes der numerischen Taxonomie im Bereich der Dialektgeographie*, Vienna: Verlag der Österreichischen Akademie der Wissenschaften.

—— (1984) *Dialektometrische Studien. Anhand italoromanischer, rätoromanischer und galloromanischer Sprachmaterialien aus AIS und ALF*, 3 vols, Tübingen: Niemeyer.

Gohin, F. (1903) *Les Transformations de la langue française pendant la deuxième moitié du XVIIIe siècle, 1740–1789*, Paris: Belin.

—— (1938) 'La Langue française sous la Révolution', *Revue historique* 182: 104–14.

Goldmann, L. (1959) *Recherches dialectiques*, Paris: Gallimard.

Goody, J. (1986) *The Logic of Writing and the Organization of Society*, Cambridge: Cambridge University Press.

Gordon, A. E. (1983) *Illustrated Introduction to Latin Epigraphy*, Berkeley and Los Angeles: University of California Press.

Gordon, R. (1988) 'Apartheid's anthropologists: The genealogy of Afrikaner anthropology', *American Ethnologist* 15: 535–53.

Graham, G. F. (1869) *A Book about Words*, London: Longman, Green & Co.

Grégoire, H. (1794) 'Rapport sur la nécessité et les moyens d'anéantir les patois et d'universaliser l'usage de la langue française', in A. Gazier (ed.) *Lettres à Grégoire sur les patois de France 1790–1794*, 1880, Paris: Durand & Pedone-Lauriel.

Gudschinsky, S. C. (1968) 'The relationship of language and linguistics to reading', *Kivung* 1, 3: 146–52.

Guest, E. (1882) *A History of English Rhythms*, new edn by W. W. Skeat, London: Bell.

Guilhaumou, J. (1978) 'Idéologie, discours et conjoncture. L'exemple des discours révolutionnaires (1792–1794)', unpublished dissertation, Aix-en-Provence.

Gumbrecht, H. U. and Schlieben-Lange, B. (1981) 'Bibliographie zu Literatur und Sprache in der Französischen Revolution', *Zeitschrift für Literaturwissenschaft und Linguistik* 41: 127–41.

Haarhoff, T. J. and van den Heever, C. M. (1934) *The Achievement of Afrikaans*, Johannesburg: Central News Agency.

Hagège, C. (1985) *L'Homme de paroles. Contribution linguistique aux sciences humaines*, Paris: Fayard.

Hall, R. A. Jr (1942) *The Italian Questione della Lingua: An Interpretative Essay*, Chapel Hill: University of North Carolina Press.

Harris, R. (1980) *The Language Makers*, London: Duckworth.

—— (1981) *The Language Myth*, London: Duckworth.

—— (1983) 'Theoretical ideas', *The Times Literary Supplement*, 14 October.

—— (1987a) *The Language Machine*, London: Duckworth.

—— (1987b) *Reading Saussure: A Critical Commentary on the Cours de linguistique générale*, London: Duckworth.

Harris, R., and Taylor, T. J. (1989) *Landmarks in Linguistic Thought: The Western Tradition from Socrates to Saussure*, London: Routledge.

Harrison, Revd M. (1848) *The Rise, Progress, and Present Structure of the English Language*, London: Longman, Brown, Green, and Longmans.

Hausmann, F.-J. (ed.) (1980) *Louis Meigret: Le traité de la grammaire française (1550). Le Menteur de Lucien. Aux Lecteurs (1548)*, Tübingen: Narr.

Healey, A. (1975) 'Vernacular orthographies in Papua New Guinea', *Kivung* 8, 1: 56–65.

Hesseling, D. C. (1897) 'Het Hollandsch in Zuid-Afrika', *De Gids* 61: 138–62.

—— (1899) *Het Afrikaansch*, Leiden: E. J. Brill.

—— (1912) 'Is het Afrikaans een beschaafde taal?', *Die Brandwag*, 1 July: 3–4.

—— (1923a) *Het Afrikaans*, 2nd edn, Leiden: E. J. Brill.

—— (1923b) 'Het Frans in Noord-Amerika en het Nederlands in Zuid-Afrika', *De Gids* 87: 438–57.

Hockett, C. (ed.) (1970) *A Leonard Bloomfield Anthology*, Bloomington: Indiana University Press.

Hohepa, P. (1984) 'Current issues in promoting Maori language use', *Language Planning Newsletter* 10, 3: 1–4.

Hooley, B. A. (1976) 'Twenty years in Papua New Guinea: SIL', MS, Ukarampa.

Hudson, R. (1980) *Sociolinguistics*, Cambridge: Cambridge University Press.

Hutterer, C. J. (1975) *Die germanischen Sprachen. Ihre Geschichte in Grundzügen*, Budapest: Akadémiai Kiadó.

Jakobson, R. (1969) 'Saussure's unpublished reflections on phonemes', in *Selected Writings, I*, 2nd edn 1971, The Hague and Paris: Mouton, pp. 743–50.

Jespersen, O. (1924) *The Philosophy of Grammar*, London: Allen & Unwin; New York: Holt.

Johnston, R. L. (1979) 'Literary mode in the languages of nonliterary communities', in S. A. Wurm (ed.) *New Guinea and Neighboring Areas. A Sociolinguistic Laboratory*, The Hague and Paris: Mouton, pp. 129–55.

Joly, A. (1977) 'La Linguistique cartésienne: une erreur mémorable', in A. Joly and J. Stéfanini (eds) *La Grammaire générale: Des modistes aux idéologues*, Lille: Presses Universitaires de Lille, pp. 165–99.

Jones, D. (1909) *The Pronunciation of English*, Cambridge: Cambridge University Press.

Jordaan, K. (1974) 'The origins of the Afrikaners and their language, 1652–1720. A study in miscegenation and creole', *Race* 15: 461–95.

Joseph, J. E. (1988) 'Saussure's meeting with Whitney, Berlin, 1879', *Cahiers Ferdinand de Saussure* 42: 205–14.

—— (1989a) 'Demythifying Saussure', *Linguistics* 27: 341–52.

—— (1989b) Review of K. Koerner (1988) *Saussurean Studies/Etudes saussuréennes*, *Language* 65: 595–602.

—— (1989c) Review of J.-L. Chiss and C. Puech, *Fondations de la linguistique*, *Historiographia linguistica*, 16: 184–91.

—— (1989d) 'Bloomfield's Saussureanism', *Cahiers Ferdinand de Saussure*, vol. 43.

Jovicevich, A. (1973) *J.-F. de La Harpe, adepte et renégat des Lumières*, South Orange, NJ: Seton Hall University Press.

Jucquois, G. (1989) 'Recherches sur les fondements du comparatisme', *Actes du 15e colloque de linguistique fonctionnelle*, New Brunswick: Moncton, 251–5.

Katz, J. J. (1966) *The Philosophy of Language*, New York: Harper & Row.

Kelly, L. G. (1969) *Twenty-five Centuries of Language Teaching*, Rowley: Newbury House.

Kempen, W. (1946) 'Samestellinge met "hulle" nie kreools nie?', *Die Huisgenoot*, 15 March: 20–1, 56.

Kibbee, D. A. (1979) 'The establishment of the French grammatical tradition, 1530–1580', unpublished Ph.D. thesis, University of Indiana.

Kington-Oliphant, T. L. (1873) *The Sources of Standard English*, London: Macmillan.

Kloeke, G. G. (1950) *Herkomst en groei van het Afrikaans*, Leiden: Universitaire Pers Leiden.

Kloss, H. (1978) *Die Entwicklung neuer germanischer Kultursprachen seit 1800*, 2nd edn, Düsseldorf: Pädagogischer Verlag Schwann.

Koerner, K. (1988) 'Wilhelm von Humboldt's impact on American linguistics', paper given at Linguistic Society of America Annual Meeting, New Orleans, 27–30 December.

—— (1989) 'Leonard Bloomfield and the *Cours de linguistique générale*', in *Practicing Linguistic Historiography*, Amsterdam and Philadelphia: Benjamins, pp. 435–43.

Kruisinga, E. (1906) 'De oorsprong van het Afrikaans', *Taal en letteren* 16: 417–39.

Kukenheim, L. (1932) *Contributions à l'histoire de la grammaire italienne, espagnole et française à l'époque de la Renaissance*. Amsterdam: Noord-Hollandsche. Rep. 1974, Utrecht: H & S.

—— (1951) *Euphonie – Logique – Clarté. Drie mythen van de Franse spraakkunst*, Leiden: Universitaire Pers Leiden.

Labov, W. (1972) *Language in the Inner City*, Philadelphia: University of Pennsylvania Press.

Langenhoven, C. J. (1926) *A First Guide to Afrikaans*, Cape Town: Nasionale Pers.

Latham, R. G. (1862) *Elements of Comparative Philology*, London: Walton & Maberly.

Laurendeau, P. (1986a) 'Pour une linguistique dialectique: Etude de l'ancrage et de la parataxe énonciative en vernaculaire québécois, unpublished doctoral thesis, Université de Paris VII.

—— (1986b) 'Jespersen et l'imposture des parties du discours', *Histoire, épistémologie, langage*, 8, 1: 141–55.

—— (1990) 'Perspectives matérialistes en histoire de la linguistique', *Cahiers de linguistique sociale*, no. 16, Rouen.

Lavondes, H. (1971) 'French Polynesia', in T. Sebeok (ed.) *Current Trends in Linguistics* 8: 1,110–28, The Hague and Paris: Mouton.

Lees, S. (1986) *Losing Out*, London: Hutchinson.

Lefebvre, G. and Soboul, A. (1963) *La Révolution française*, Paris: Alcan.

Lefèvre, P. (1974) 'L'évolution du concept de la clarté de la langue française', unpublished MA thesis, Liège.

Le Laboureur, L. (1969) *Avantages de la langue françoise sur la langue latine*, Paris.

le Roux, J. J. (1923) *Oor die Afrikaanse sintaksis I*, Amsterdam: Swets & Zeitlinger.

—— (1939) *Praatjies oor ons taal*, Cape Town: Nasionale Pers.

Leroy, M. (1970) *Les grands courants de la linguistique moderne*, 2nd edn, Bruxelles: Editions de l'Université de Bruxelles.

Levy, R. I. (1972) 'Teaching of the Tahitian language in the schools of French Polynesia', *Journal de la société des océanistes* 8.

Locke, J. (1690) *Essay Concerning Human Understanding*, ed. P. Nidditch, 1975, Oxford: Clarendon.

—— (1689) *Letter concerning Toleration*, London.

—— (1689) *Two Treatises of Government*, ed. P. Laslett, 2nd edn 1967, Cambridge: Cambridge University Press.

Louw, S. A. (1948) *Dialekvermenging en taalontwikkeling*, Amsterdam: North Holland.

Lubbe, H. J. (1974) 'Valkhoff en die ontstaan van Afrikaans, veral n.a.v. sy New light on Afrikaans en "Malayo-Portuguese" ', *Tydskrif vir geesteswetenskappe* 14: 89–98.

Lukács, G. (1971) 'Reification and the consciousness of the proletariat', in *History and Class Consciousness*, London: Merlin.

Lynch, J. D. (1979) 'Church, state and language in Melanesia', inaugural lecture, Dept of Language, University of Papua New Guinea.

McElhanon, K. A. (1979) 'Some mission lingue franche and their sociolinguistic role', in S. A. Wurm (ed.) *New Guinea and Neighboring Areas. A Sociolinguistic Laboratory*, The Hague and Paris: Mouton, pp. 277–89.

McKay, G. R. (1982) 'Attitudes of Kunibidji speakers to literacy', *International Journal of the Sociology of Language* 36: 105–14.

Makhudu, D. P. (1984) 'Is Afrikaans a creole language?', unpublished MA thesis, University of Southern Illinois.

Marazzini, C. (1983) 'Carlo Denina linguiste: Aux sources du comparatisme', *Historiographia linguistica* 10: 77–96.

—— (1984) 'Langue primitive et comparatisme dans le système de Carlo Denina', *Histoire, épistémologie, langage* 6: 117–29.

—— (ed.) (1985) *Carlo Denina: Storia delle lingue e polemiche linguistiche. Dai saggi berlinesi 1783–1804*, Alessandria: Edizioni dell'Orso.

Markey, T. L. (1982) 'Afrikaans: Creole or non-creole?', *Zeitschrift für Dialektologie und Linguistik* 49: 169–207.

Markey, T. L., and Roberge, P. T. (eds) (1979) *On the Origin and Formation of Creoles: A Miscellany of Articles by Dirk Christiaan Hesseling*. Ann Arbor, Mich.: Karoma.

Marsh, G. P. (1860) *Lectures on the English Language*, New York: Scribners.

Martens, F. (1887) 'Geschichte der französischen Synonymik, I: Die Anfänge der französischen Synonymik', unpublished dissertation, Greifswald.

Martin-Chauffier, L. (1943) *Ma patrie, la langue française*, Paris: Messages.

Martinet, A. (1969) *Le Français sans fard*, Paris: Presses Universitaires de France.

Mathews, W. (1880) *Words: Their Use and Abuse*, Toronto: Rose-Bedford.

Matthews, P. H. (1986) 'Distributional syntax', in T. Bynon and F. R. Palmer (eds) *Studies in the History of Western Linguistics, in Honour of R. H. Robins*, Cambridge: Cambridge University Press, pp. 245–77.

Matoré, G. (1953) *La Méthode en lexicologie. Domaine français*, Paris: Didier.

Matoré, G., and Greimas, A. (1957) 'La naissance du "génie" au XVIIIe siècle', *Le Français moderne* 25: 256–72.

Maze, C. M. (1903) *Etude sur le langage de la banlieue du Havre*, Paris: E. Dumont. Repr. 1969, Geneva: Slatkine.

Meiklejohn, J. M. D. (1886) *The English Language: Its Grammar, History and Literature*, London: Blackwood.

—— (1891) *The Book of the English Language*, rev. edn, London: Simpkin.

Mercier, L.-S. (1801) *Néologie, ou Vocabulaire des mots nouveaux, à renouveler ou pris dans des acceptations nouvelles*, 2 vols, Paris: Moussard.

Mihalic, F. (1977) 'Interpretation problems from the point of view of a newspaper editor', in S. A. Wurm (ed.) *Language, Culture, Society and the Modern World*, New Guinea Area Languages and Language Study, vol. 3, Canberra: Pacific Linguistics C40, pp. 1,117–28.

Mill, J. S. (1859) *On Liberty*, London; ed. G. Himmelfarb, 1974, Harmondsworth: Penguin.

Miller, C. and Swift, K. (1978) *Words and Women*, Harmondsworth: Penguin.

Milner, G. (1984) 'The new missionaries? Language, education and the Pacific way', in C. Clerk (ed.) *The Effects of Development on Traditional Pacific Island Cultures*, London: Royal Commonwealth Society, pp. 6–72.

Milroy, L. (1980) *Language and Social Networks*, Oxford: Blackwell.

Monreal-Wickert, I. (1977) *Die Sprachforschung der Aufklärung im Spiegel der grossen französischen Enzyklopädie*, Tübingen: Narr.

Moodie, T. D. (1975) *The Rise of Afrikanerdom. Power, Apartheid, and the Afrikaner Civil Religion*, Berkeley: University of California Press.

Morellet, A. (1818) *Mélanges de littérature et de philosophie du XVIIIe siècle*, 4 vols, Paris.

Mosel, U. (1982) 'The influence of the church missions on the development of Tolai', in R. Carle, *et al.* (eds) *Gava* (Festschrift Kähler), Berlin: Reimer, pp. 155–72.

Mossé, F. (1950) Review of G. G. Kloeke, *Herkomst en groei van het Afrikaans*, *Bulletin de la Société de Linguistique de Paris*, 48, 2: 87–8.

Moulton, W. G. (1952) Review of G. G. Kloeke, *Herkomst en groei van het Afrikaans*, *Language* 28: 149–52.

Mühlhäusler, P. (1986) *Pidgin and Creole Linguistics*, Oxford and New York: Blackwell.

Müller, F. M. (1862) *Lectures on the Science of Language*, London: Longman, Green, Longman, & Roberts.

Muysken, P. (ed.) (1978) *Amsterdam Creole Studies II*, Publikaties van het Instituut voor Algemene Taalwetenschap, 20, Amsterdam: University of Amsterdam.

Newmeyer, F. J. (1986a) *Linguistic Theory in America*, 2nd edn, Orlando, FL and London: Academic Press.

—— (1986b) *The Politics of Linguistics*, Chicago: University of Chicago Press.

—— (1989) 'Competence vs. performance; Theoretical vs. applied: The development and interplay of two dichotomies in modern linguistics', paper given at Georgetown Round Table on Languages and Linguistics, pre-session on Developments in Linguistics, 8 March.

Nienaber, G. S. (1949–53) *Oor Afrikaans*, 2 vols, Johannesburg: Afrikaanse Pers.

—— (1965) 'Iets naders oor die ontkenning in Afrikaans', in P. J. Nienaber (ed.) *Taalkundige opstelle*, Pretoria: J. L. van Schaik, pp. 22–38.

Nienaber, P. J. (1959) *Die wonder van Afrikaans*, Johannesburg: SAUK.

Nienaber, P. J., and Heyl, J. A. (eds) (n.d.) *Pleidooie in belang van Afrikaans*, vol. 2, Cape Town, Bloemfontein, and Johannesburg: Nasionale Boekhandel.

Ogden, C. K., and Richards, I. A. (1923) *The Meaning of Meaning*, New York: Harcourt Brace.

Ong, W. J. (1982) *Orality and Literacy*, London: Routledge.

Osmers, D. (1981) 'Language and the Lutheran Church on the Papua New Guinea mainland: an overview and evaluation', Canberra, *Pacific Linguistics* A-61: 71–164 .

Paardekooper, P. C. (1986) 'Het Afrikaans', *Onze taal*, 55, 6: 74–5.

Pariset, G. (1920–2) *La Révolution 1792–1799*, vols 1 and 2 of E. Lavisse (ed.) *Histoire de la France contemporaine*, Paris: Hachette.

Parr, C. S. (1963) 'Maori literacy 1843–1867', *Journal of the Polynesian Society* 72: 211–34.

Parsonson, G. S. (1967) 'The literate revolution in Polynesia', *Journal of Pacific History* 3, 2: 39–58.

Pateman, T. (1980) *Language, Truth and Politics*, Lewes, Sussex: Stroud.

Paul, H. (1888) *Principles of the History of Language*, trans. H. A. Strong, London: Sonnenschein, Lowrey & Co.

Pauwels, J. L. (1958) *Het dialect van Aarschot en omstreken*, Brussels: Belgisch Interuniversitair Centrum voor Neerlandistiek.

—— (1959) 'Afrikaans *hierdie, daardie*', *Leuvense Bijdragen* (Bijblad) 48: 1–3.

Ponelis, F. A. (1987) 'Die eenheid van die Afrikaanse taalgemeenskap', in H. du Plessis and L. T. du Plessis (eds) *Afrikaans en taalpolitiek*, Pretoria: HAUM, pp. 2–15.

Port-Royal (1660) *Grammaire générale et raisonnée*, authors: Antoine Arnauld and Claude Lancelot, Paris: P. Le Petit.

—— (1662) *La Logique ou l'Art de Penser*, critical edn by B. Baron von Freytag-Löringhoff and H. E. Brekle, 2 vols, Stuttgart and Bad Cannstatt: Frommann-Holzboog, 1965–7. Authors: Antoine Arnauld and Pierre Nicole.

Postma, W. (1912) 'Die Afrikaanse taal. Die ontstaan daarvan', *Die Brandwag*, 15 February: 593–6; 1 March: 623–7.

Proschwitz, G. von. (1966) 'Le Vocabulaire politique au XVIIIe siècle avant et après la Révolution. Scission ou continuité?', *Le français moderne* 34: 87–102.

Quemada, B. (1967) *Les Dictionnaires du français moderne 1539–1863. Etude sur leur histoire, leurs types et leurs méthodes*, Paris: Didier.

Quirk, R. *et al.* (1985) *A Comprehensive Grammar of the English Language*, London: Longman.

Rademeyer, J. H. (1938) *Kleurling-Afrikaans*, Amsterdam: Swets & Zeitlinger.

Raidt, E. H. (1968) *Geskiedenis van die byvoeglike verbuiging in Nederlands en Afrikaans*, Cape Town: Nasou.

—— (1975) 'Nuew aktualiteit van 'n ou polemiek', in *Afrikaans – Dit is ons erns*, Pretoria: Suid-Afrikaanse Akademie vir Wetenskap en Kuns, pp. 39–54.

—— (1976a) *Afrikaans en sy Europese verlede*, 2nd edn, Cape Town: Nasou.

—— (1976b) 'Die herkoms van objekskonstruksies met "vir" ', *1875–1975: Studies oor die Afrikaanse taal*, Johannesburg: Perskor, pp. 72–101.

—— (1976c) 'Linguistische und soziologische Faktoren des Sprachwandels

im Afrikaans des 18. Jahrhunderts', in L. Forster and H.-G. Roloff (eds) *Akten des V. Internationalen Germanistenkongresses* 2, 2: 155–64, Bern: H. Lang.
—— (1977) 'Afrikaans and "Malayo-Portuguese": Light and shadow', *African Studies* 36: 70–8.
—— (1980) 'J. du P. Scholtz – taalwetenskaplike', *Standpunte* 147: 2–14.
—— (1981) 'Oor die herkoms van die Afrikaanse reduplikasie', in A. J. Coetzee (ed.) *Hulsels van Kristal: Bundel aangebied aan Ernst van Heerden*, Cape Town: Tafelberg, pp. 178–89.
—— (1983) *Einführung in Geschichte und Struktur des Afrikaans*, Darmstadt: Wissenschaftliche Buchgesellschaft.
—— (1984) 'Interne ontwikkeling van Afrikaans', in T. J. R. Botha (ed.) *Inleiding tot die Afrikaanse taalkunde*, Pretoria and Cape Town: Academica, pp. 52–82.
Reagan, T. G. (1984) 'Language policy, politics, and ideology. The case of South Africa', *Issues in Education* 2: 155–64.
—— (1985) '"Taalideologie" en taalbeplanning', *S. A. tydskrif vir taalkunde* 3/4: 45–79.
—— (1986) '"Language ideology" in the language planning process: Two African case studies', *South African Journal of African Languages* 6, 2: 94–7.
—— (1987) 'Ideology and language policy in education: The case of Afrikaans', in H. du Plessis and L. T. du Plessis (eds) *Afrikaans en taalpolitiek*, Pretoria: HAUM, pp. 132–9.
Reichardt, R., and Schmitt, E. (eds) (1985) *Handbuch politischer-sozialer Grundbegriffe in Frankreich 1680–1820*, Heft 1/2: R. Reichardt and B. Schlieben-Lange, *Die Wörterbücher in der Französischen Revolution*, Munich: Oldenbourg.
Reinecke, J. E. (1937) 'Marginal languages', unpublished Ph.D. dissertation, Yale University.
Reinecke, J. E., Tsuzaki, S. M., DeCamp, D., Hancock, I. F., and Wood, R. E. (1975) *A Bibliography of Pidgin and Creole Languages*, Honolulu: University Press of Hawaii.
Reinhard, C.-F. (1796) *Le Néologiste français*, Nuremberg.
Renck, G. L. (1977) 'Missionary lingue franche: Yabem', in S. A. Wurm (ed.) *Language, Culture, Society and the Modern World*, New Guinea Area Languages and Language Study, vol. 3, Canberra: Pacific Linguistics C40, pp. 847–53.
Reynaud, L. (1930) *Les Français et les Allemands*, Paris: Fayard.
Ricken, U. (1974) 'Zur Sprachdiskussion während der Französischen Revolution', *Beiträge zur romanischen Philologie* 13: 303–18.
—— (1978) *Grammaire et philosophie au siècle des Lumières. Controverses sur l'ordre naturel et la clarté du français*, Lille: Presses Universitaires de Lille.
—— (1982) 'Der Wortmissbrauch als Diskussionsthema der französischen Aufklärung', *Wissenschaftliche Zeitschrift der Universität Halle* 31: 107–17.
Rivarol, A. de (1784) *Discours sur l'universalité de la langue française*, ed. M. Hervier, 1929, Paris: Delagrave.
Roberge, P. T. (1986) 'What's happening in Afrikaans historical linguistics? Remarks on a new introduction', *Zeitschrift für Dialektologie und Linguistik* 53: 194–202.
—— (1988) '"A language is what you can make of it". Remarks on the political meanings of Afrikaans', paper given to the Southeast Conference on Foreign Languages and Literatures, Winter Park, Florida, 25–7 February.

Romaine, S. (1984) 'The status of sociological models and categories in explaining linguistic variation', *Linguistische Berichte* 90: 25–38.

Roodt, D. and Venter, R. (1984) 'Die evolusie van 'n taalhistoriese paradigma in Afrikaans', *Tydskrif vir geesteswetenskappe* 24: 224–36.

Rosier, I. (1983) *La Grammaire spéculative des modistes*, Lille: Presses Universitaires de Lille.

Ross, R. (1983) *Cape of Torments: Slavery and Resistance in South Africa*, London: Routledge & Kegan Paul.

Rousseau, J. J. (1968) *Essai sur l'origine des langues*, ed. C. Porset, Bordeaux: Ducros.

Rule, J. E. (1977) 'Vernacular literacy in the Western and lower Southern Highlands provinces', in S. A. Wurm (ed.) *Language, Culture, Society and the Modern World*, New Guinea Area Languages and Language Study, vol. 3, Canberra: Pacific Linguistics C40, pp. 387–401.

Russell, J. (1982) 'Networks and sociolinguistic variation in an African urban setting', in S. Romaine (ed.) *Sociolinguistic Variation in Speech Communities*, London: Arnold, pp. 125–40.

Sapir, E. (1921) *Language. An Introduction to the Study of Speech*, New York: Harcourt Brace.

—— (1924) 'Culture, genuine and spurious', *American Journal of Sociology* 29: 401–29.

Saussure, F. de (1916) *Cours de linguistique générale*, ed. C. Bally and A. Sechehaye, with the collaboration of A. Riedlinger, Lausanne and Paris: Payot.

—— (1922) *Cours de linguistique générale*, 2nd edn, Lausanne and Paris: Payot.

—— (1964) *Lettres de F. de Saussure à Antoine Meillet*, ed. E. Benveniste, *Cahiers Ferdinand de Saussure* 21: 89–130.

—— (1983) *Course in General Linguistics*, trans. R. Harris, London: Duckworth.

Sbaragli, L. (1939) *Claudio Tolomei, umanista senese del Cinquecento*, Siena: Accademia per le Arti e per le Lettere.

Scaglione, A. (1988) 'Celso Cittadini and the Origins of Romance Philology', paper given at the annual meeting of the American Association for Italian Studies, Brigham Young University, 14–16 April.

Scherer, K. and Giles, M. (1979) *Social Markers in Speech*, New York: Academic Press; Cambridge: Cambridge University Press.

Schlieben-Lange, B. (1981) 'Die Französische Revolution und die Sprache', *Zeitschrift für Literaturwissenschaft und Linguistik* 41: 90–123.

—— (1985) 'Die Wörterbücher in der Französischen Revolution (1789–1804)', in R. Reichardt and E. Schmitt (eds) *Handbuch politischer-sozialer Grundbegriffe in Frankreich 1680–1820*, Munich: Oldenbourg, pp. 149–89.

—— (1986) '"Tu parles le vieux langage . . .". Le "Dictionnaire Républicain et Révolutionnaire" de Rodoni, citoyen de Genève', *LINX* 15: 77–97.

Scholtz, J. du Plessis (1939) *Die Afrikaner en sy taal, 1806–1875*, Cape Town: Nasionale Pers. 2nd edn 1965, Cape Town: Nasou.

—— (1963) *Taalhistoriese opstelle*, Pretoria: J. L. van Schaik.

—— (1965) *Afrikaans uit die vroeë tyd*, Cape Town: Nasou.

—— (1970) 'Internal history of Afrikaans', in D. J. Potgieter *et al.* (eds) *Standard Encyclopaedia of Southern Africa*, 1: 80–113, Cape Town: Nasou.

—— (1972) *Afrikaans-Hollands in die agtiende eeu*, Cape Town: Nasou.

—— (1980) *Wording en ontwikkeling van Afrikaans*, Cape Town: Tafelberg.

Sensi, F. (1892) 'Per la storia della filologia neolatina in Italia. I. Claudio Tolomei e Celso Cittadini', *Archivio glottologico italiano* 12: 441–60.

Shaffer, D. (1978) 'Afrikaans as a case study in vernacular elevation and standardization', *Linguistics* 213: 51–64.

Silverstein, M. (1979) 'Language structure and linguistic ideology', in R. Clyne, W. Hanks and C. Hofbauer (eds) *The Elements: A Parasession on Linguistic Units and Levels*, Chicago: Chicago Linguistic Society, pp. 193–247.

Skeat, W. W. (1873) *Questions for Examination in English Literature*, Cambridge: Cambridge University Press.

—— (1895–8) 'The proverbs of Alfred', *Transactions of the Philological Society*, p. 415.

—— (1912) *English Dialects from the Eighth Century to the Present Day*, Cambridge: Cambridge University Press.

Smith, O. (1984) *The Politics of Language 1791–1819*, Oxford: Clarendon.

Soboul, A. (1962) *Précis d'histoire de la Révolution française*, Paris: Gallimard.

Steyn, J. C. (1980) *Tuiste in eie taal. Die behoud en bestaan van Afrikaans*, Cape Town: Tafelberg.

Swiggers, P. (1982) 'Introduction', G. Girard, *Les Vrais principes de la langue françoise*, repr., Geneva: Droz, pp. 11–73.

—— (1984) *Les Conceptions linguistiques des Encyclopédistes. Etude sur la constitution d'une théorie de la grammaire au siècle des Lumières*, Heidelberg: Groos.

—— (1986) 'Grammaire et lexique au XVIIIe siècle: Réflexions sur la "valeur" des mots', in *Autour de Féraud: La lexicographie en France de 1762 à 1835*, Paris: Ecole Normale Supérieure de Jeunes Filles, pp. 63–71.

—— (1987a) 'La Sémiotique de Port-Royal: du savoir au vouloir(-dire)', *Semiotica* 66: 331–44.

—— (1987b) Review of R. Reichardt and E. Schmitt (eds) *Handbuch politischer-sozialer Grundbegriffe in Frankreich 1680–1820*, *Le français moderne* 55: 239–43.

—— (1988a) 'La Clarté du français: examen historique et méthodologique', *Zeitschrift für Phonetik, Sprachwissenschaft und Kommunikationsforschung* 41: 618–30.

—— (1988b) 'Grammatical categories and human conceptualization: Aristotle and the Modistae', in B. Rudzka-Ostyn (ed.) *Topics in Cognitive Linguistics*, Amsterdam: Benjamins, pp. 621–46.

—— (1989a) 'Port-Royal et le "parallélisme logico-grammatical": Réflexions méthodologiques', in P. Swiggers (ed.) *Moments et mouvements dans l'histoire de la linguistique (Cahiers de l'Institut de linguistique de Louvain-la-Neuve*, vol. 16), pp. 23–36.

—— (1989b) 'La *Grammaire* de Port-Royal et le parallélisme "logico-grammatical"', *Orbis* vol. 33, 29–56.

Tavoni, M. (1982) 'The 15th-Century controversy on the language spoken by the ancient Romans: An inquiry into Italian Humanist concepts of "Latin," "Grammar", and "Vernacular"', *Historiographia linguistica* 9: 237–64.

Thomason, S. G. and Kaufman, T. (1988) *Language Contact, Creolization, and Genetic Linguistics*, Berkeley, Los Angeles and London: University of California Press.

Tooke, J. Horne (1857) *The Diversions of Purley*, ed. R. Taylor, London: William Tegg.

Tournier, M., Arnault, R., Cavaciuti, L., Geffroy, A., and Theuriot, F. (1969) 'Le Vocabulaire de la Révolution. Pour un inventaire systématique des textes', *Annales historiques de la Révolution française* 41: 104–24.

Trabalza, C. (1908) *Storia della grammatica italiana*, Milano: Hoepli. Rep. 1963. Bologna: Forni.

Trench, R. C. (1851) *On the Study of Words*, London: Parker.

—— (1855) *English Past and Present*, 2nd edn, London: Parker.

Trudgill, P. (1978) 'Introduction: Sociolinguistics and sociolinguistics' in P. Trudgill (ed.) *Sociolinguistic Patterns in British English*, London: Edward Arnold, pp. 1–18.

—— (1983) *On Dialect*, Oxford: Blackwell.

Turner, K. (1988) 'Newmeyer's glasnost', *Linguistics and Politics Newsletter*, no. 6.

Valkhoff, M. F. (1966) *Studies in Portuguese and Creole, With Special Reference to South Africa*, Johannesburg: Witwatersrand University Press.

—— (1971) 'Descriptive bibliography of the linguistics of Afrikaans: A survey of major works and authors', in T. Sebeok (ed.) *Current trends in Linguistics*, 9: 455–500. The Hague and Paris: Mouton.

—— (1972) *New Light on Afrikaans and 'Malayo-Portuguese'*, Louvain: Editions Peeters Imprimerie Orientaliste.

van der Merwe, H. J. J. M. (1966) 'Afrikaans 'n basterkind van Hollands-Kreools-Portugese fornikasie aan die Kaap!?', *Tydskrif vir Geesteswetenskappe* 6: 377–94.

—— (1970) *Herkoms, en ontwikkeling van Afrikaans*, Johannesburg: Afrikaanse Pers.

—— (1977) 'Die onststaan van Afrikaans', in H. J.J. M. van der Merwe (ed.) *Afrikaans – sy aard en ontwikkeling*, Pretoria: J. J. van Schaik, pp. 15–66.

Vannier, A. (1923) *La Clarté française*, 7th edn, Paris: Nathan.

Vannini, A. (1920) *Notizie intorno alla vita e all'opera di Celso Cittadini*, Siena: S. Bernardino.

van Oordt, J. F. (1909) *Manual of Cape Dutch for the Use of English Students*, Cape Town and Amsterdam: HAUM.

van Rensburg, M. C. J. (1983) 'Nie-standaardvorme, variasiepatrone en Afrikaans uit die vorige eeu', in G. N. Claassen and M. C. J. van Rensburg (eds) *Taalverskeidenheid: 'n Blik op die spektrum van taalvariasie in Afrikaans*, Pretoria, Cape Town, and Johannesburg: Academica, pp. 134–61.

—— (1984) 'Oranjerivier-Afrikaans', in M. C. J. van Rensburg (ed.) *Die Afrikaans van die Griekwas van die tagtiger jare*. Bloemfontein: University of the Orange Free State.

—— (ed.) (1984) *Die Afrikaans van die Griekwas van die tagtiger jare*, Bloemfontein: University of the Orange Free State, 12: 513–18.

—— (1985) 'Taalverskeidenheid, taalversteuring en Afrikaans', in H. J. Lubbe (ed.) *Fokus op die taalkunde*, Bloemfontein: University of the Orange Free State, pp. 123–66.

van Rijn, C. J. (1914) *Het zeer nauwe verband tussen het Afrikaans en het Nederlands*, Cape Town: T. Maskew Miller.

Vaugelas, C.-F. de (1647) *Remarques sur la langue françoise*, ed. A. Chassang, rev. edn, 1911, 2 vols, Versailles: Cerf; Paris: Baudry.

Verhaar, J. W. M. (1962) 'Speech, language, and inner form (Some linguistic remarks on thought)', *Preprints for the Ninth International Congress of Linguists, 27–31 August, Cambridge, Mass.*, pp. 377–82.

Vier, J. (1976) 'Le Meurtre par les mots. J.-F. de La Harpe: "Du fanatisme dans la langue révolutionnaire"', *Itinéraires, Chroniques et documents* 203: 53–61.

Vincent, C. (1925) *Le péril de la langue française*, Paris: De Gigord.

Vitale, M. (1955) 'Sommario elementare di una storia degli studi linguistici romanzi', in A. Viscardi (ed.) *Preistoria e storia degli studi romanzi*, Milano: Cisalpino, 5–169.

—— (1978) *La questione della lingua*, 2nd edn, Palermo: Palumbo.

Vivaldi, V. (1894–8) *Le controversie intorno alla nostra lingua dal 1500 ai nostri giorni*, 3 vols, Catanzaro: Caliò.

—— (1925) *Storia delle controversie linguistiche in Italia da Dante ai nostri giorni: Da Dante a M. Cesarotti*, Catanzaro: G. Mauro.

von Wartburg, W. (1946) *Evolution et structure de la langue française*, 3rd edn, Bern: Francke.

Vossler, K. (1913) *Frankreichs Kultur im Spiegel seiner Sprachentwicklung*, Heidelberg: Winter.

—— (1923) *Gesammelte Aufsätze zur Sprachphilosophie*, Munich: Hueber.

Waher, H. (1988) 'Eenders of anders?' n Vergelyking tussendie ontkenning in Afrikaans en Afro-Portugees', *S. A. Tydskrif vir Taalkunde* 6: 109–27.

Wartburg, W. von (1946) *Evolution et structure de la langue française*, 3rd edn, Bern: Francke.

Weinrich, H. (1961) 'Die clarté der französischen Sprache und die Klarheit der Franzosen', *Zeitschrift für romanische Philologie* 77: 528–44.

Weiss, A. P. (1925) *A Theoretical Basis of Human Behavior*, Columbus, Ohio: R. G. Adams.

Weiss, R. (1946) 'The Sienese philologists of the *Cinquecento* – A bibliographical introduction', *Italian Studies* 3: 34–49.

Whitney, W. D. (1875) *The Life and Growth of Language*, New York: Appleton.

—— (1877) *The Essentials of English Grammar*, Boston: Ginn & Heath.

Wittmann, J. (1928) 'Die sprachgeschichtliche Entwicklung des Deflexionstypus im Afrikaans', unpublished dissertation, Bonn.

Wolfson, N. and Manes, J. (1980) 'Don't "dear" me!', in S. McConnell-Ginet, N. Borker, and R. Furman (eds) *Women and Language in Literature and Society*, New York: Praeger, pp. 79–92.

Wood, R. E. (1984) Review of *Tijdschrift voor Nederlands en Afrikaans 1*, *The Carrier Pidgin* 12, 1: 6.

Wundt, W. (1900) *Völkerpsychologie, I: Die Sprache*, Leipzig: Englemann.

Wurm, S. A. (ed.) (1977) *Language, Culture, Society and the Modern World*, New Guinea Area Languages and Language Study, vol. 3, Canberra: Pacific Linguistics C40.

—— (ed.) (1979) *New Guinea and Neighboring Areas. A Sociolinguistic Laboratory*, The Hague: Mouton.

Wyld, H. C. (1907) *The Growth of English*, London: Murray.

—— (1927) *A Short History of English*, London: Murray.

Name Index

239

Subject Index

243